American Janus
Southern Warrior Series, Book 1

BY

DOUGLAS W SHOUSE

Cover Art and Illustrations By

Keith Hobgood

Copyright © 2024 by – Douglas W Shouse – All Rights Reserved.

It is not legal to reproduce, duplicate, or transmit any part of this document in either electronic means or printed format. Recording of this publication is strictly prohibited.

To all those whose ancestors fought not for the evils of slavery, but for their homes and a belief in self-determination.

Author's profile

Douglas Shouse is an amateur historian with a special passion for American military history. He has spent more than thirty years as a marketing strategist in corporate brand marketing and marketing agencies where he honed his craft in creative writing. He is a graduate of Wake Forest University with a B.A. in Economics and MBA from WFU's School of Management. He lives in Winston-Salem with his lovely wife, Ruth.

Author's note

This is a work of fiction. While I have included real people and events, others are the product of my imagination. For example, the ill-fated Zinzendorf Hotel was never rebuilt on the site after its destruction by fire in 1892. Additionally, the description and timing of some events have been changed to fit the narrative.

The war history is taken primarily from the Southern Historical Society Papers first published in the late 19th Century and includes histories of most Confederate regiments. I have taken some liberties with this history in the story. For example, the 1st Battalion was actually positioned along the Rappahannock River in early May 1863 during the battle of Chancellorsville instead of joining Stonewall Jackson's flanking maneuver.

The history of the 21st NC Regiment and 1st Battalion Sharpshooters is personal for me. My great-grandfather, Eli Augustus Shouse, enlisted in the 21st NC Regiment in June 1861 and was later re-assigned to the 1st Battalion for the remainder of the war. He was paroled at Appomattox Court House, Va., in April 1865.

"What is past is prologue"

William Shakespeare, *The Tempest*, 1611

Contents

PROLOGUE	1
CHAPTER 1: CHRISTMAS 1899	5
CHAPTER 2: NEW YEAR 1900	34
CHAPTER 3: SPRING 1900	54
CHAPTER 4: LATE SUMMER 1900	71
CHAPTER 5: AUTUMN 1900	86
CHAPTER 6: CHRISTMAS 1900	108
CHAPTER 7: WINTER 1901	117
CHAPTER 8: EARLY SPRING 1901	139
CHAPTER 9: SPRING 1901	168
CHAPTER 10: EARLY SUMMER 1901	185
CHAPTER 11: SUMMER 1901	208
CHAPTER 12: LATE SUMMER 1901	226
CHAPTER 13: EARLY AUTUMN 1901	257
CHAPTER 14: LATE AUTUMN 1901	275
CHAPTER 15: CHRISTMAS 1901	295
EPILOGUE	336

PROLOGUE

December 1899

The grayish-blue cigar smoke slowly curled upward and away from the well-appointed, polished mahogany desk. Outside, the darkening December afternoon brought with it a quick and even rain shower that suddenly turned the cobblestones slick and a bit muddy. Pushing back from the desk with one knee, he closed his eyes and tried to close his mind. But, there it was: the low-grade grinding of banded wheels and twisting tack – more than one hundred wagons trekking the pitted roads. The incessant moans, most low yet some plaintive howls, worked their way into one's very soul. It had never been too far away, but as of late, this insistent companion was most inescapable.

Was it never quiet then? Had it really been more than three decades? Had he changed thoroughly – or had he changed at all?

Checking his silver pocket watch, he rose, straightened slowly, and stepped to the window. The sidewalks were virtually clear of pedestrians, having been driven inside by the rain. A few carriages, their drivers with heads down, made their way up Liberty Street to appointed destinations. Harper Clayton, "Harp" to his family and friends, was about to turn sixty years old but, strangely, felt much younger most days. His large dark brown eyes and even, angular face had always attracted attention. His hair, now somewhat silver, was full. His build was solid enough, although a bit worn by the years and many physical engagements.

In the 35 years following the war, Harper Clayton had achieved success on many levels and failure on a few. Building the respected Clayton-Harmon Esq. law practice with his lifelong friend, Christian Harmon, was a particular source of pride. He believed his work in guiding the Freedmen's Bureau in the piedmont area of North Carolina and into Reconstruction a qualified success. Just how much success, of course, depended on one's political and cultural viewpoint. Yet, respect had been undeniably earned among many factions, both locally and across the state.

His family was where his heart ultimately resided. If there was a legacy to convey, Harp was convinced it lay in the virtues and potential of his large and passionate family. He had married Susan Bostic the year after he returned home from Appomattox with parole in hand. He remembered the little Lutheran church in Bethania overflowing with family and friends. The occasion was bright on that fine early spring day, even in the face of turbulent times and terrifying uncertainty. Yet, Susan had risen above all that. Her grey hazel eyes, soft-as-down skin, and generous smile filled him with a wondrous zeal when she was near, an ardor that had never totally left him in all these years. She had that special, giving quality that made those around her better in both small and not-so-small ways. And Harper loved her deeply for such a benevolent spirit.

Children came as if ordered on some heavenly bill of lading. There was Eli, the eldest, who had come into the world kicking and screaming and seemed to insist on maintaining that dynamic trait from childhood into adolescence and adulthood. Eleanor was the second born, a raven-haired beauty that saw the good in all of God's creations around her. Then there was Jacob. This small and clever lad always seemed to see around the next corner and be patiently waiting for others to catch up. Phillip had followed and just refused to be missed. "Philli's" effervescence and humorous escapades had brought regular light and laughter into the home. Eight years had produced four offspring. Finally, with a long intervening space of time came Cornelia, "Nell," truly an unexpected joy. Harp and Susan were not exactly Abraham and Sarah but felt just as blessed in their middle-aged years with this wonderful child of God with her bright yet silent nature.

By all appearances, Harper Clayton had achieved a great deal. But as the year was coming to a close, he felt a struggle in his soul. He sensed both a reckoning from the past and a euphoria for the coming 20th century — the dark and brutal crucible of his coming of age and the intense draw of what was to come.

Grabbing his leather satchel, overcoat, and black wool scarf, yet forgetting his hat, Harp closed and locked the door to the empty office. The others had already left for home and families, including Christian, who had announced he was done for the week and the law could wait until Monday. Harp knew Christian couldn't wait to get home to "his own girls," wife, Eloise, and four daughters.

Holding the satchel over his head to block at least some of the rain, he walked briskly to the carriage house where Silver would have his simple sulky hitched and ready. "Old Tom" Silver had been loyal to Harper all these years since the Freedmen's Bureau, and they had a common bond. Heck, they were friends, and while around town, he was known as "Old Tom," Harp called him "Silver." In a time when most black folks were known by only a given name, Harp purposely used

Thomas Silver's sir name as a statement of both admiration and respect.

The raw and windy afternoon had Harp shaking the rain from his wet head. He was anxious to get home to Susan as well. "You always know my timing, Silver. Get on home to Sadie and Jeff now. They'll be lookin' for you."

CHAPTER 1: CHRISTMAS 1899

The town of Winston was quickly becoming an economic force in the Carolinas. With its tobacco markets and manufacturing as well as emerging textile mills, the fifty-year-old burg now attracted businesses, entrepreneurs, and seekers of all kinds. Richard Joshua Reynolds had trekked from southern Virginia twenty-plus years earlier to create what was becoming a dominant factor in the tobacco manufacturing business. The demand for RJR's flavorful pipe and chewing tobacco was strong and responsible for driving much growth in the area. New mills were quickly emerging in sync with the burgeoning southern textile industry. From wagon works to tanneries and machine shops, from the new Wachovia Bank to new law firms like Clayton-Harmon and other service companies, Winston had rapidly become the fastest-growing city in the state. By all accounts, the future was indeed bright.

The Christmas season in 1899 reflected this optimism. The black double-arm gas street lamps were wound with cedar garland, and the shop windows on 4th Street displayed each merchant's effort to draw attention to their Christmas offerings. Mother Kiger's dress shop and women's emporium on Trade Street was a holiday destination in itself for locals and farming families in the region. Its big windows, showcasing a family of mechanical dolls in Christmas décor, regularly attracted a crowd of children and grown-ups alike. Bodenhamer's Hardware, not to be outdone, proudly presented what was thought to be the largest electric train display in the state. Its winding bi-level track and tunnels channeled a marvelous locomotive and sixteen-car payload. Wiley's Candy shop was another favorite. Its enormous hard-sugar sleigh was always packed with a wondrous array of colorful treats; Mr. Moon macaroons, spun sugar evergreens, peanut brittle cottages, chocolate drums and horns, and other delicious temptations. And, of course, Father Christmas, with his carved staff and canvas bag, was sure to be seen on the street passing out sugar canes and other tasty morsels to the youngsters crowding around.

Loaded with two bags of her own and several other packages in her arms, Eleanor turned the corner at Liberty and 4th, almost colliding with a swarm of kids playing a running game of tag.

"Whoa, there, lovelies! Please don't bowl me over," she exclaimed while smiling broadly.

Sorry, Missus Moser," one of the urchins panted. "We are seein' who can touch all the lamp posts the fastest!" Eleanor recognized little Wiley Tuttle from Sunday school. He was always on the move as if perpetually wound up with a church key.

"That's ok, Wiley. Saturday is for fun, but do watch for riders and carriages."

She headed toward the Bryson livery stable where Tom should have their Welsh pony, Darlin, already hitched to the phaeton carriage. She thought of Tom and grimaced. Tom and Eleanor had been sweethearts for the longest time. When they married eleven years ago, families and friends thought theirs was a match made in heaven. They just seemed to fit together like well-worn and rounded puzzle pieces.

Early on, Tom Moser's colorful dreams of success and accomplishments were exciting, and Eleanor dreamed along with him. But, now, it had become clear that these dreams were, at best, visions that lay unfulfilled at their feet. Tom had become more manic in his insistence that fame and riches were within reach. He struck a Faustian bargain with bond speculators resulting in a loss of much of their savings. Last year, they had reluctantly taken eight hundred dollars from father to hold the line. This had put a sharp blade into Tom's pride. He had pursued other questionable schemes in start-up milling and other businesses, with losses in nearly every case. The next deal was always to be the one to break through to glory. The crush of these failures had taken a toll on Tom. Once he saw the ripe possibilities of a grand future. Now, his spirit was dulled and angry. He had drawn into himself, more unreachable as time passed.

Eleanor could hear Tom grumbling as she entered the enclosure.

"Damned rogues trying to get rich with these prices. I remember when you could board two fine trotters for a week at what they're wantin' just to keep Darlin overnight. I bet I go to the city stables in the future and don't give these boys anymore of my damned business."

"Now, Tom," Eleanor chided, "everyone has to take care of their family, especially here at Christmastime."

Tom exploded, "That's what I'm tryin' to do, 'cept these thieves are takin' more than their share!"

"Now, just you hush down," she softly spoke. "Here, give this late apple to Darlin, and please help your dear wife with these packages," winking with that special Eleanor sparkle. She knew it was not just the stable's jump in board that was kindling Tom's hair-trigger emotions.

She always knew how to bring Tom around, and her trademark wink and smile were sure to soften him up a bit.

"Hey, Darlin gets an apple, but what about ol' Tom? he japed as he fed the eager pony.

"I didn't forget "ol' Tom," laughed Eleanor. "I have for you, sir, that one and only delicious sugar cake from the Moravian bakery. If you're an extra good boy, I'll give you a piece."

Tom gave Darlin the bit, untethered the lead, and lifted his wife onto the phaeton. Climbing up, he held out his hand and solemnly said, "payment, please." Eleanor reached into the white paper bag and handed him a cake square with matching solemnity. With that, Tom leaned over and kissed her cool pale cheek with gusto. He grabbed the reins and, with a familiar click, started the pony out to the alley and onto Trade Street.

***

And there it stood; a splendid twelve-foot eastern red cedar with more than a dusting of snow presenting bowed branches and standing apart from the mix of pines, hickory, and other hardwoods.

The twins, running hard, shouted in unison, "Father, this is the one!" Noah quickly followed up, "It's just a perfect fit for the big room, Papa."

Eli, catching up and a bit winded, puffed, "Very good, boys. I think you're right." Sky, their rambunctious English shepherd and constant companion to both boys, jumped up to him as if confirming the choice. He chuckled and thought to himself, "Well, this was easy. Last year, we walked the woods for a good hour before they could decide on a tree."

"Ok, let's cut this one. Your Mother and sissies will love it. James, here is the bow saw. You boys get under there and go to work on it!" He stepped back and breathed in the cold, clear December air.

Elias Augustus Clayton, recently turning thirty-three, was feeling prime. At just over six feet tall, he was taller than Harper, as he sometimes reminded his father. His features more closely matched his beautiful mother, with thick black hair, somewhat pale skin, and those strikingly unique grey-hazel crystal eyes. The eldest son of Harper was named after Harp's own father, who had traveled the Great Wagon Road south from Nazareth, Pennsylvania, over seventy years ago in search of fertile farmland and a better future for his family. Eli the younger had recently purchased the family farm from Harper, vowing to maintain the two hundred-plus acres of tobacco and grazing fields. He had decided that business and the law were not suited to his keen desire for open spaces and independence. Accepting the inevitable, Harper had deeded the house and land to Eli with an agreement for the yearly tobacco and cattle sales to be put into escrow at the recently opened Wachovia bank to benefit all the sibling families.

Eli helped the boys hoist the cedar tree onto their slim shoulders, and they proudly carried it through the light snowfields to the welcome sight and smells of the two-story brick, stone, and clapboard farmhouse. He knew Katherine would have something bubbling and tasty underway on the black woodstove.

The two spry tree soldiers ran up the stone steps and burst into the front door, yelling, "Mama, Sissies, we have the best tree ever!" Eli followed, knocking the snow off his boots on the wide-open threshold and smiling broadly.

The two little girls leaped up, forgetting their attempts at cat's cradle, and began jumping around the dripping tree. Emmy, now seven years old, was the spitting image of her mother with soft, round, and fair features and light brown hair and eyes. Anna, only four, was a skinny little waif with a pale countenance, dark brown almost black hair, and icy-grey eyes like her father.

Katherine Clayton stood at the stove with her enormous spoon and greeted the breathless invasion with a whistling voice, "Now it's feelin' like Christmas! You know the corner there is our tradition for the tree, boys." From the two-gallon pot on the woodstove came the savory aroma of beef stew flavored with fall carrots, peppers, potatoes, and of course, shoots of rosemary. Eli was sure that Kat, his pet name for her, had also baked several pans of her delicious skillet bread with crispy, buttery tops.

Whisking Anna up and onto his shoulders, Eli crossed the front room into the open kitchen and kissed his wife on the back of her neck. Katherine instantly drew her head back and shrieked playfully, "Yow that tickles!" With that, she turned and hugged him and the little girl all in one loving squeeze.

Leaning over her, Eli took in the delicious sight and smell of the stew and exclaimed, "Now that's worth our journey in the woods, right boys?" No response. Noah, James, and Emmy had already bolted outdoors to run Sky around the woodshed and hay barn, leaving the cedar tree on its side in the gathering room.

With Christmas day only one week away, Eli and Kat would work together to prepare for the large family to assemble and celebrate the birth of the Christ child, another longstanding Clayton tradition. The homestead was the natural place to gather with all its warm memories and familiarity.

***

He could not get warm. Even dressed under two blankets, Harp continued to shiver with his whole body in a cold sweat. Susan held her slender hands against his flushed face and frowned. This was a surprise because Harp was rarely ill. In fact, he took great pride in his robust constitution.

"I'll be just fine in the morn, though I do love your hands on my face," he said, smiling weakly.

"Well, if only they were healing hands," she said lovingly.

"Oh, they are. Trust me, they are."

With that, Susan whispered, "Now sleep, my darling. I'll be back to check on you in a while with a mug of hot lavender tea."

Within minutes, Harper drifted into a fitful sleep. At once, he was transported to the ice and mud and blood of Fredericksburg, Virginia, in December 1862. Two armies colliding in and around the colonial town on the Rappahannock River had quickly devolved into total war, with civilians fleeing for their lives and Union frontline troops looting the town.

Lieutenant Harp Clayton led the company of seasoned fighters, including Captain Upton, down Charles Street southward out of town to take up defensive positions adjacent the river along the Plank Road.

Company E made up a full third of the 21st North Carolina Regiment. In the 18 months since he, brother Jacob, Lansford Hall, and other Bethania boys had joined up, the 21st had been engaged in a number of significant battles. These included Stonewall Jackson's brilliant Shenandoah Valley campaign, the "Seven Days" battles around Richmond (specifically Gaines Mill and Malvern Hill), Second Manassas, and the bloodletting at Antietam just a few months past. Harper and the others had traveled to Danville, Virginia, in June 1861 to enlist after North Carolina was one of the last southern states to join the Confederacy. He had enlisted as a private, but his ability to inspire and lead the men around him, as well as casualties in the officer ranks, soon resulted in several promotions to his current position.

To Harp, joining up was part duty and part adventure. He did believe that defending his state from invading Yankees was a cause worth fighting for. The cause to defend slavery, however, was not his fight. While he knew several slave-owning families, Harper Clayton came from a line of both

Scottish and German immigrant farmers whose self-sufficiency and independence were prized. He had seen men, women, and even whole families sold on the block. He had seen black men whipped for the slightest cause. The injustice and immorality of it all sickened him and called up the deepest emotions of disgust. He had sworn never to be a part of such degradations. Yet, deep down, he knew that in the South, state sovereignty and slavery were inexorably intertwined, no matter how much he tried to separate the two in his mind.

The regiment quickly dug trenches on the rise called Marye's Heights behind the Plank Road and parallel to the river. The ground was essentially frozen, and it took significant effort, even with the picks and shovels shared within E Company.

"They'll be comin' soon, boys," Harp called out. "Cap'n says to form lines for firin' in twos," meaning sequential lines of fire. Harp was exhausted and electrified all at the same time. It was a strange sense that blocked out the cold and misery of the winter campaign. He looked over to Lans and slowly nodded. "Keep your caps and cartridges close to your body to keep them drier and warmer. That way, they'll be easier to handle and not foul. Thank the Lord they gave us a double issue. I feel we can hold here for a while." They had never fought a winter battle.

Lansford Hall, at twenty years old, was almost two years younger than Harp. He was a small man, just over five and a half feet tall, with a small frame. What he lacked in physical stature, he made up in pure grit and fortitude. Harp remembered the time back home when Lans pulled the tack off the wall and corralled a fiery stallion while others watched in wonder. He and Harp had grown up together and had grown close, especially after Harp's younger brother Jacob had died from wounds at Malvern Hill last June. It was in that disastrous sanguine affair that Lans had stayed on the field with Jacob while the regiment retreated to the tree line, comforting him as he quickly bled out from multiple wounds to his head and body. Lans had changed that day. In fact, they all had. The losses were great, so senseless. Now, there was no romance of war left in them. It was killing, pure and simple.

The December sky was dark and full of storm clouds. By late morning rain with sleet and some snow was falling, quickly turned the new trenches to icy mud and overcoats and uniforms to heavy impediments. Harp walked the length of the company line offering words of encouragement.

Upton motioned for Harp to join him on the small hill above the line. "They're bringing the artillery up now to weaken our defense line, motioning across the river and wide field west of Fredericksburg. Have the company ready, Lieutenant, and expect the assault immediately after the cannonade."

Captain James Upton, Virginia Military Institute Class of "61, had taken command of the company immediately following Antietam in late September. He was the only son of a wealthy tidewater Virginia trader and was no older than Harp. Rather imperious and excitable, Upton used his formal military training to call out even the most insignificant breach of order. The men were wary of his conceit and had not warmed to the captain. Instead, they increasingly looked to Harp for reassurance and direction. This had not gone unnoticed by

Upton, and he continued to berate Harp on minute rules and protocol, especially in front of the company.

The rain and sleet abated, and within minutes, the ranks of Union artillery opened up from Stafford Heights across the river on the entrenched Confederate lines. The previous evening Generals Lee, Longstreet, and Jackson had agreed on this rise, much of it behind the old stone wall adjacent to the Plank Road. At least a half-mile of open fields lay before the position, making it ideal for a defensive stand. The solid and exploding shot of the mass of cannons was a terrible cacophony of man-made thunder and lightning. The crash and ear-pounding assault and massive flashes of light were the most fierce any of the boys and men had endured in the war. It lasted almost an hour, inflicting some casualties from direct hits and shrapnel. However, Company E and most others of the line survived the cannon fire essentially intact. Dense smoke blanketed the open field.

"Reform your lines in twos, boys! Check your cartridges and fix bayonets! Harp yelled, hearing himself as if from a distance.

Within moments the smoke began to drift clear, aided by the cold wind. A mass of spectral blue shapes began to appear in the streams of mist and smoke as the Union infantry formed its line of battle. The sight was as awesome as it was terrifying—tens of thousands of boys in blue spread across the half-mile-long field.

"My God!" muttered Private Josiah Burge from Rockingham. "There's the whole of the state of New York headed straight away."

"Yeah, and I'm gonna take down my share of 'em," replied Lans, his grim face set hard.

"Hold fire until ordered!" shouted Upton while traversing the line. "I want all fire aimed true."

Bugles and drums set the march, and the wave of blue troops moved forward at the quick step. Harp turned to see the cluster of officers on horseback close to the rear. He saw General Jackson with his staff, calm and sure. This gave Harp a boost of reassurance as he grabbed his Enfield rifled musket and climbed down beside Lans, positioned in the middle of the company line. Watching the oncoming closely packed Union regiments as well as Upton for the signal, he felt for Susan's small oval-framed photograph in his breast pocket. Holding the frame inside his coat, Harp said a quick prayer for God to protect and return him to his love.

Confederate artillery on Marye's Heights was having a horrendous effect on the blue lines, but they continued to reform, and on they came. Upton and Harp locked eyes, and when the Yankee line was about one hundred yards away, they nodded in concurrence and cried, "Fire!"

The next hour was madness, a chaos of rifle fire, smoke, and screaming men. The bitter cold was forgotten as Harp took his place in the firing line and submerged into an intense and instinctive action of tearing cartridges, pouring powder and ball, ramming the load, taking dead aim, and firing.

Whole swaths of men disappeared under the withering fire from the trenches. The assault force then took to the ground as the grey sky darkened. The unique and sickening sound of bullets striking flesh, a high-pitched hiss followed by a heavy, dull smack, echoed in Harp's brain. A young private who was notoriously always out of sync with his comrades took a minie ball perfectly in the middle of his forehead. Standing motionless for a moment, the boy was dead before his body fell forward onto the trench.

The defensive line held firm, taking casualties but inflicting far greater on the exposed masses of Union infantry. Incredibly, the Union troops repeatedly tried to breach the stone wall and trenches throughout the late afternoon, even as darkness overtook the field. Marching headlong into the line, the assaulting forces would be cut down, retreat a bit, reform, and come on again; in some cases, ten times or more. The company's ammunition was almost totally spent, with most either depleted or only a handful of rounds left. Requests for resupply went unheeded. Harp wondered how they could hold if the Union infantry made another assault. It was now dark with the wind up from the west across the river. A few stars broke through the thick night sky, and the temperature dropped rapidly. The sounds from the field were encouraging as it became clear that the enemy was pulling back. Left behind were the thousands of dead and wounded with the mournful cries above the wind heard by the Southern soldiers in the defense line. Throughout the night, sharpshooters found their mark as Union troops tried to withdraw with wounded comrades. Dead and wounded were frozen alike during the night.

The pre-dawn was eerily quiet. Harper had tended to the wounded, strengthened his remaining boys, and finally laid back on his bedroll in the early hours of the day. He quickly fell into a deep sleep, a place where he wanted to stay forever.

He felt a hand shaking him awake and, with closed eyes, said, "See to the boys, Lans. See to them." He opened his eyes only to see Susan with a knowing expression on her gentle face.

***

It was a tradition that spanned at least four generations of Clayton men, as far as Tom Moser knew. He had heard Harp talk about his father and grandfather waking him and his brothers in the pre-dawn darkness on Christmas Eves to venture into the cold North Carolina foothills to hunt the whitetail deer. The wall of ten and twelve-point racks and a magnificent sixteen-point trophy was there in the home place as a testimony to the tradition. The party had grown this year. In addition to Harp, Eli, Jacob, Phillip, and himself, there was Tom's son, "Tee," as well as Eli's twins, Noah and James. All three boys were now ten years old, and this season was their rite of passage into the noble family ritual.

Eli had guided the group to a tree line just north of Pilot Mountain facing a meadow that opened to the iconic geologic feature. Leaving Harp, Jacob, and the twins, Eli and Phillip then led the others several more miles to a well-concealed rise overlooking a bend in the Yadkin River. The river had thin ice sheets on its edges where the flow was gentler and even placid in spots around the various rocks and detritus from the early winter rains. Phillip continued upriver, navigating the water's edge while the others settled in to await the appearance of their anticipated quarry.

The Deer Hunt

Back at the meadow, Harp motioned to the open field and whispered, "Boys, this is one of my very favorite places to find mister whitey-tail. They come out early to find the thistle and thorny scrub. Hand me my old musket, and we'll get her ready."

James handed the large rifled musket over to his grandpa, happy to be relieved of the weight. Jacob pulled his repeating Winchester around off his shoulder and smoothly loaded four rounds. He was without question the best shot of all the Claytons, including Harp. While never bringing attention to himself, Jacob reliably brought home game from a hunt. While noticeably smaller than either Eli or Phillip, Jacob could trek day and night while carrying more than his share of provisions and other loads.

"Now, who wants the first shot?" Harp said, smiling at the two boys, wide-eyed and fully alert.

Noah glanced at James, then back to his grandfather, and said, "I guess I'll take the shot."

James quickly nodded in agreement, causing Jacob to chuckle quietly. "So, little man, take my musket, keep it downrange, and rest the barrel on this big log to hold it steady. I have it primed and loaded, ready to go. Let's just see how long before mister whitey-tail comes along."

Noah held the gun against his right shoulder, closing his left eye to sight down the barrel.

"That's right. Just like your Papa and I have shown you, boys," Harp said approvingly.

The first hint of light was breaking through the trees behind them, and within minutes, two, then several more deer ventured into the open meadow about fifty yards from the concealed hunters. Four does, two young bucks, and a full buck began to graze on the rather sparse grasses.

"Ok now. This is a fair presentation," Harp whispered. "Let's go for the big buck. Wait for him to present. That's it. Sight square on his shoulder. Take a breath, slowly breathe out when you're ready, and slowly pull the trigger."

Noah shook involuntarily and blinked rapidly. Again he put his head down to the barrel and tried to calm his body. The buck turned and provided a broadside target. The young boy took deliberate aim and squeezed the trigger.

The blast of the gun immediately rent the peace of the early morning. The tranquil scene erupted with whitetails springing instantly in all directions, including the buck, which Noah had only grazed the neck. In a flash, Jacob brought his Winchester into position. He quickly fired, catching his target in mid-air with a perfect shot through the shoulder and heart of the noble creature. Harp and the others stood frozen for several long seconds absorbing the full sensory impact of the moment.

Eli and Tom heard the distant reports, nodded to one another, and settled back into their lair above the river with young Tee. Eli had a fleeting sense of regret that he would not have witnessed his boys' first efforts to bring down a deer. Putting that thought aside, he said, "Tee, this could be the day you take your first deer."

Tom looked at Tee, who hesitated, "I'm…I'm not sure I'm ready, uncle," the young boy stammered. "I…I haven't practiced like James and Noah, and I'm scared."

"Don't you worry, son," Tom said, putting his arm around the boy. "You can see how Eli and I do it, and you'll be ready to shoot next time." Tom was always protective of his only son, somewhat over-protective by Eli's way of thinking. "Yessir, today you just see how we handle these rifles, and you'll be ready."

"Just takin' that first shot makes a big difference," Eli reassured the boy with a kind but firm voice.

It wasn't long before a cluster of deer stepped through the thick mountain laurel to drink at the river's edge. Two young does pawed the thin crust of ice to get to the water while two adults waited and watched.

Eli thought about Tom and Tee and then whispered, "Tom, take that buck by the big rock when you're ready. It's your shot."

Tom took his rifle to his left shoulder and slowly turned his head to the right and then left, looking down the barrel. Tee, wide-eyed, heard his father exhale and then an ear-splitting explosion, which to the boy was deafening. The big buck jumped sideways and back into the laurel thicket. The other deer vanished before the report died away.

"I think I got it," exclaimed Tom.

"I sure hope so. Let's go see," replied Eli, but he was not sure at all.

The three climbed down the slick bank and crossed where several big river rocks made the crossing possible. Heading through the laurel, they saw slashes of blood on the broad-tipped leaves. They followed the blood trail for several miles but then lost it when it ended at the water's edge.

"Too deep to cross here," said Eli, his mouth set tight with frustration. "We'll have to backtrack to the ford to get across."

Tom complained, "Let's just leave it be and go back to our spot before we lose the day."

Eli, looking at Tee and holding his temper in check, said, "No, we have to find the old boy. He may be suffering, and we can't have that."

It took them most of the morning, but Eli, Tom, and Tee finally came upon the near-lifeless body.

"I told ya I got him," proclaimed Tom.

"That you did, Tom," Eli responded. Pointing to the mid-torso wound, he said quietly, "It was a gut- shot that took him and us on a five-mile death trail. He has suffered, and I'm sorry for it." Pulling his long knife from its sheath, Eli then quickly plunged it into the deer's heart, producing a gasp from Tee.

"It's a shame," said Tom without feeling, "but it was an ambitious shot through the thick laurel."

Eli stood staring at Tom and slowly nodded.

As a milky sun was low in the winter sky, the party reassembled on the familiar spot along the Guilford Road. Harp's group had shot a good size doe and another buck with a balanced ten-point rack. With Jacob taking the lead, he and Harp field-dressed the three deer in less than an hour. The two boys observed, close in, and were astounded as the deer were gutted and internal organs removed. The carcasses were then laid across the travois that Jacob had fashioned from green hickory branches and tied with leather strips from his pack. Eli and company arrived soon after, with Tom's kill stretched across a similar frame. They had not seen any other deer for the rest of the day. James and Noah ran to Tee to hear what adventures he had that day. Tee told them about the river-crossing journey to find the wounded animal.

Harp looked around and asked, "Where is Phillip?"

Eli grinned and said, "Aw, you know him, Pa. He struck out on his lonesome first thing, and we haven't seen him since. I'll bet he trekked clear to Virginia looking for his ghost elk. No doubt we'll hear all about it soon enough!"

With that, the group made their way back to Bethania and Winston, treading carefully in the growing darkness. Eli and Jacob had finished dressing the deer around midnight. They hung all four on the big J-hooks in the icehouse for the processing of the meat in a few days. With some soaking in watered vinegar to remove the blood and curing some of the meat as well, the three bucks and doe would produce steaks, tenderloin, and ground venison for the four families, plus enough for Jacob himself.

"Where the hell is Philli? Eli demanded. I didn't want to worry Pa earlier. We both know he has taken off on his own before and can sure take care of himself in the woods, but it being Christmas and all… it's just strange." Being quite a bit older than his two brothers Eli had always felt protective over them, even as grown men.

"You know how game he is to surprise us," Jacob replied with a weak smile. "Remember last year when, just out of the blue, he said he was joining the fight down in Cuba and then comin' home afterward with Maria and the babe? Boy, I never saw father so astounded in my life. My bet is that we will surely see him tomorrow with some new prize."

***

Christmas morning broke fine and clear. A brilliant sun spiked through the trees and penetrated the glazed glass windows of the big farmhouse. The air was cold and fresh as Eli stepped onto the front porch and stretched his arms toward the sunlight. While a bit stiff and sore in the legs from yesterday's trek, he had slept deeply beside Kat under the thick goose down-filled quilt. Feeling refreshed and alert he descended the stairs and stepped to the woodshed. Gathering up an armload of hardwood, Eli smiled as he remembered the boys excitedly talking over each other as they recounted their first deer hunting experience. He knew they were enthralled with the natural world, just as he had been his whole life. Both boys, exhausted from yesterday's adventure, were still sound asleep. Eli decided he would let them sleep a bit longer.

Kat was already well into her last preparations for the day's feast. She was all business and very good at bringing the many dishes together with various spices, sugar, and flour covering the polished hickory counters. Kat was an orchestra conductor who could create a symphony of sensory delights. The brown sugar and mustard ham were already in the roaster. Hefty side dishes of candied yams sweetened with molasses, sour slaw "chowchow" tinged with vinegar and peppers, green beans with "fatback" – a seasoning staple, black-eyed pea tomato salad, and "sharp corn" with green onions were all in various states of prep. Pickled beets from the root cellar would be added to the feast. Susan would bring her jars of chocolate sauce, chess pies, and a box of her fancy little teacakes containing that special vanilla ingredient. Eleanor, of course, would showcase her hummingbird cake with exotic pineapple and coconut pieces that she seemed to mysteriously locate year after year. While Kat and Susan had tried to get her to reveal her source, Eleanor would always smile and, with a wink, say, "Ladies, you know it's my own particular secret, and that will just have to do."

"This is my very favorite time of day," exclaimed Eli, "early in the morning and just the two of us. And, of course, this spread of deliciousness certainly helps." He put his hand on Kat's shoulder, turning her to him.

"It is lovely, isn't it?" she said. "But, I have to keep after it to be ready for the coming invasion," she laughed while tapping his forehead gently with the big stirring spool. "And dear, please get some heat in the parlor stove and stoke the kitchen fire here so I can finish the ham and cornbread dressing."

"Yes, ma'am," he replied while smartly saluting his kitchen commander.

***

With its steep gabled roof, corner turret, and expansive rounded porch, the 5th Street Queen Anne-style home was a fine example of the Guilded Age architecture popular in the late nineteenth century. Susan, with frequent correspondence with Jacob, had actually worked with local architect firm Simeon-Stone, to build the home five years prior in 1894.

Within a few years, notables such as tobacco kings RJ Reynolds and his brother, Will, had built homes up and down west 5th Street as well. The stretch had taken on the moniker "Millionaire's Row," which never failed to create a laugh from Harper as well as a tug of embarrassment. Harper and Susan, while more financially able than most, were hardly millionaires and didn't want to be seen as such.

Clayton and Silver had agreed on a late morning departure for the several-hour trek to Bethania. The wind had come up making the Salisbury Rainey coach rather brisk, but the winter sun would help warm the ride to Bethania. Silver had placed two thick wool blankets and a canvas bag of hot stones on the padded bench seat to help make the journey more comfortable. He also put the basket of biscuits, honey, and jam in the coach that the cook, Blanche, had prepared along with Susan's pies and other goodies for the Christmas dinner.

Nell took her place in the coach between her mother and father. With that, Silver took his seat up top, untied the reins, and called out to the twin mares, Jenny and Lucy. "Ok now, girls, let's get goin'!" Both horses raised their heads in a snort and started at a lively trot.

"Happy Christmas, Harp!" shouted the couple on east 5th Street as they trotted by.

"And Happy Christmas to you. A fine Christmas day it is," Harp called and waved in return. As they continued north out of town, Harp turned to Nell and said, "Well, are you ready for this crowd of Claytons?"

The thirteen-year-old blushed and replied, "I hope no one asks me to recite any Christmas poetry like Christmas last. I nearly died with Noah and James teasing me."

Susan said, "Nelly, you did a fine job, and everyone was so pleased."

"Certainly not Noah and James," Nell retorted.

Silver popped the lead forcing the mares to pick up the pace and settle into a rhythmic canter heading north on the road to Bethania.

***

Rolling over in the overstuffed featherbed, Jacob inhaled the wonderful smell of fresh coffee coming from the downstairs kitchen. Last year he took two rooms in the smart Vogler boarding house in south Winston to realize quiet and independence. Uninterrupted work on his new set of architectural drawings was what he desired most. Since his graduation from Boston Tech[*] and short tenure at the renowned NYC architectural firm of McKim, Mead & White, Jacob had come home with a vision to design Winston's gilded age structures, both private and public. With such a pedigree, he had little trouble securing a position with the Simeon-Stone firm. His exposure to the latest ideas at McKim had quickly established him as the wunderkind of building design in Winston and, in fact, the state.

Yesterday had been a tonic for Jacob, it being the first time he had been with his father and brothers on a hunt since he had returned home. He relished the escape to the foothills and mountains of his youth. Climbing out of bed, he reflected, "The pace and scale of New York and Boston are inspiring, but this is where I want to be. This is where I belong."

Stripping off his nightshirt, Jacob limped into the adjacent room. He had twisted his knee slightly while tracking the second buck. Vogler had recently installed modern Kohler baths with running hot water in a few of the rooms. He ran the bath with steaming water and settled into the simple luxury. Closing his

---

[*] *MIT today*

eyes, he remembered that this was Christmas Day, and the Claytons would be gathering in the early afternoon. Within the hour, he was dressed, had enjoyed Mrs. Vogler's coffee and breakfast, and was checking the saddle on his purebred Morgan quarter horse.

He called out to Hiram, Vogler's man that oversaw the stables, "Hey Hiram, my boy's been watered and had his oats, right?"

Hiram replied brightly, "Oh yes, sir! He is frisky and ready for the day!"

"Thanks to you, Hiram," Jacob said, handing the man a fifty-cent piece. The little man nodded appreciatively as Jacob quickly mounted the horse, leading him toward First Street.

The trip to Bethania was only an hour or two, and Jacob knew he would arrive before most of the others to the home place. He was anxious to see his mother. Susan and Jacob had always had a special relationship. It seemed each of them was connected to the other in an unspoken, serene bond. It had been that way since he could remember. He loved his father and knew his father loved him, but he and his mother just seemed to be from a common realm. Interestingly, he looked much more like his father, with bright brown eyes and a pale complexion. With his wool hat pulled low and scarf close around his neck, he spurred his horse into a canter and headed north.

***

"And it came to pass in those days, that there went out a decree from Caesar Augustus, that all the world should be taxed," Harper read from

the old King James family bible. It was a long Clayton tradition to read the Christmas story on Christmas Day with the whole family gathered near. Tee, with Nell's guidance, pointed the decorative willow stick toward the carved Joseph and Mary in the Christmas nativity. This ritual had been passed down through the generations of Claytons from as far back as Moravia in the old country. *"And the angel said unto them, Fear not: for, behold, I bring you tidings of great joy, which shall be to all people,"* Harp continued as the young lad abruptly jumped his pointer to the shepherd figures causing Emma and the twins to giggle. Eleanor smiled with contentment, remembering that special Christmas years ago when she and her father had carved 14 additional pieces as well as repaired the aged Mary and Christ child figures from the Germanic krippe. *"And they came with haste and found Mary, Joseph, and the babe lying in a manger,"* Harper said with a note of finality. "Now, that's the Christmas story; God's greatest gift to all of us. Amen!" he added emphatically.

"Amen!" everyone responded in chorus.

Once all had arrived, the family crowded into the large front room, the gathering room as they liked to call it. The wood stove had been fired since early morning and gave the room a very warm and almost surreal, dizzy sensation. The big red cedar standing in the corner was adorned with colorful hand-made and store-bought decorations. Red and green ribbons, yellow tin stars, multi-colored glass balls, and thin strands of silver tinsel all gave the tree an appearance of glittery illumination.

"Now, who's ready for a feast?" Eli proclaimed.

With that, the children scrambled to create a line at the large kitchen workbench where a feast was truly spread before them.

The enormous ham, baked with brown sugar and cinnamon, occupied the center of the table, with the array of sumptuous side dishes crowding the remaining space. Separate, on the side table, were the pies, cakes, and cookies in their own tempting arrangement. It wasn't long before the entire three generations were seated at the generous farmhouse table that Harper had built long ago.

"Well, are you going to tell us about your grand adventure yesterday, Philli?" Eli inquired of his younger brother while spearing a piece of ham with his fork. "We've waited patiently all day, so I believe it's time for the show."

Both Harper and Susan looked at Phillip expectantly.

Phillip had been curiously silent about his experience, which was quite out of character for the usually garrulous and effusive brother. With his open and effervescent personality, he was always quick to laugh and tell a story for everyone's pleasure. Phillip was taller than his brothers, with an athletic build and remarkably fair features. In fact, he was unique in his appearance compared to the other Claytons. Susan thought he looked like the Craters on her mother's side of the family based on depictions she had heard over the years.

Pushing his shirtsleeve up and pulling his collar aside, Phillip revealed white bandages with a hint of red coming through. Pausing for effect while the others revealed their astonishment at the sight, Phillip grinned and then said with uncharacteristic understatement, "It was him or me."

"Who, Uncle Philli?" young James blurted. "Who did this to you?"

"Not who, but what," Phillip replied and smiled. "When I left you yesterday after dawn, I followed the river for a bit," he said, nodding toward Eli and Tom. "I was quick to pick up some big tracks. I believe it was my ghost elk, and I made the five or six miles to the Sauertown Cliffs."

"I knew it!" Eli exclaimed. "You won't rest until you bring that big boy down."

"Well, that will have to wait for another day," Phillip replied. "I was climbin' the cliff trail and ran into a most unwelcome antagonist. About the top, I turned right blind into a rather sizable ol' mountain lion. I expect he was on the ghost's trail just like me. Anyway, before I could raise a barrel, he was on me. I was just able to pull my Jim Bowie. You know, Papa, the one you gave me a few Christmases ago. I was lucky… took him down with one jag to the neck."

"Oh, Philli," Susan exhaled. "Are you hurting? Why do you always have to go on your own?"

"I'm just fine, Mama," he smiled while rolling his sleeve down. "Maria took real good care of me, right sweetheart?" he grinned as his young wife tenderly took his hand. "I even brought the ol' crony back with me."

"Where is he, Uncle Philli?" Where did you put him?" Noah cried.

"Why, he's in my barn right this moment. All of you boys can come to see him tomorrow right before I take him to Taxidermy Bill. He'll look fairly imposing up on my wall."

Harper quickly jumped in to bring the assembly back to order. "That's sure how to enthrall your audience, Phillip," he said. "I have to say I'm with your Mama on this. You need a second out in those hills. You *were* lucky," he said, staring directly at Phillip. Both Eli and Jacob beheld their brother while shaking their heads. The room was quiet, and after a pause, Harp continued, "Now, let's get this table cleared so we can have some of those fine desserts. Then we can open that mountain of presents under the tree."

With that, it seemed everyone collectively exhaled after being held captive by Phillip's epic tale. The scene was a cacophony of benches scraping, platters and plates clacking, and of course, everyone talking at once.

As the afternoon wore on, presents were exchanged and opened, children laughed and ran in the yard, fires were re-stoked, steaming mugs of wassail were savored, and the relations settled into a familiar contentment.

Susan, surveying her large family while resting her head on Harper's shoulder, looked up into his dark eyes and whispered, "We've done good, Harp. We've done real good."

Harper stroked her beautiful silver hair and smiled.

CHAPTER 2: NEW YEAR 1900

Clayton House on 5th Street

And on it came. A day and a night and another day and night it came. It was the greatest winter storm that anyone, even the old-timers, could remember. Fine crystalline snow, big featherlike flakes, and even lashing sleet to sting the face all played a major role in covering everything in sight with a most beautiful yet ominous deep blanket. It was a storm that seemed to stop time. It certainly stopped the town. Tremendous drifts of pure white barred doors and gates and other portals across Winston and piedmont North Carolina. It would become known as the New Century Disturbance.

And disturb it did. All businesses closed for days. Wagons were encased in ice along the roads. Town services were halted. Telegraph lines were disabled, and the few telephone lines around the center of town were also down. Of course, New Year's festivities were abandoned. It was a new century, and it began in a most onerous fashion.

Harper, with snow knee-high, dug the shovel deep around the front gate. The snow was still coming down hard, but he knew he had to make some progress against the onslaught. Silver was doing the same at the carriage house. He even recruited some of the young boys that lived in the Holly Avenue neighborhood to come and earn a small wage. How Silver got the word out was beyond Harper. He was glad nonetheless to see the young lads pitching in, even though there was as much snow ball fighting as shoveling going on. He looked back at the house in time to see Susan in the big front window, anxiously waving him inside. Harper began to trudge back through the snow as Silver struggled around the corner of the rounded porch. "Silver, get those boys over here to clear off the front steps and sidewalk," Harper said, pointing down at the gathering snow.

"Right, Harp. We're tryin' to stay ahead of it," Silver replied with a hint of frustration in his voice.

"I know, I know. Now in a bit, come on into the kitchen and get you some hot cider. Those young cubs, too," Harper said over his shoulder. Feeling weary, he brushed the snow off his pants, stamped his boots clean, and quickly entered the house where Susan was waiting with a steaming cup of apple cider.

"Please don't wear yourself out, Harp. Let the others do the shoveling," she implored.

"I'll be just fine. And hey, Silver is older than I, in case you forget," Harper said with amusement as he shed his wool coat, scarf, and gloves.

"Yes, but he's used to working for a living," she quickly rejoined with a wink.

"You win, but you know I like to get out there myself and get my hands dirty, unlike these other "millionaires" up and down 5th street," he joked. He took the mug of hot cider with both hands from his wife and thought once more how lucky he was.

Harper did keep to the house the rest of the day. He, Susan, and Nell enjoyed a lunch of barley and bean soup with hard bread and pickled herring and beets. Susan had told Blanche and her kitchen helper, Sweetie, to rest and take care of their own needs on this first day of the year. Afterward, Nell ventured down the back steps and gathered a large pot of fresh, fluffy snow. She and her mother then made snow cream flavored with vanilla, sugar, and a touch of cinnamon, as they had numerous times before.

The storm made the daylight grey and flat so Susan lit several gas lamps giving the downstairs a peculiar ethereal appearance with its wavy shadows. At the small round kitchen table, they finished their treat. The New Year's unusual weather had intervened with their normal routine of commitments and general busyness and, thus, created an interesting pause of thought and introspection. Susan said,

"Harp, here we are in the year 1900, a new century, and I just wonder what's to become of things. So much is changing around us. It's quite frightening."

Harper closed his eyes as if in a trance and then blew a long breath. "Don't let it make you fearful, Sudie. These times are full of promise and opportunity. The world is getting smarter, closer, and more hopeful…and little Winston with it. More telephone lines are coming, more electricity to power, and more lighting. Heck, we'll have the electric line to our house this year to enable electric lamps and other machines that do the work. I'm hearing about motorized carriages in Europe are coming our way soon. New machines are doing new things quicker and better. It's a revolution for us to embrace. Why, look at your mechanical sewing machine from Mr. Singer. You and Nell can do in an hour a job that used to take all day. Yes, American ingenuity is on the march, and our lives are the richer for it."

"I do like that sewing machine, Papa," Nell interjected. "And I believe I'm faster than Mama," she proclaimed, which caused them to all laugh together.

"It's just a wonderful time to be alive, my girls," Harper enthused while spreading his arms wide. "And with that, I am going to the study to study a nap on the divan," he declared, smiling broadly.

He pushed the glass-paneled pocket doors open to the book-filled room. This was his place of sanctuary. Floor-to-ceiling bookshelves lined the walls with a menagerie of books, archives, and various exhibits, creating a multi-colored tapestry. In the salon was an old walnut desk that he had bought from Thadeus Wilkins, the Raleigh lawyer he had collaborated with on a Freedmen's case thirty years ago. Two hardback chairs faced the desk, and the Turkish divan was positioned parallel to one of the book-filled walls. Harper grabbed a black folder from the desk and settled into the couch to read.

The folder contained fresh witness testimony from recent meetings of the Winston Tobacco Board of Trade. Retained by the Reynolds brothers to provide counsel on their aggressive acquisitions of local tobacco concerns, Harper had become more deeply engaged in the economic development of the region. While Christian had taken over most of the criminal work in the firm, Harp's role had evolved to advising clients and other constituents on economic and political matters. He quickly became drowsy from his morning exertions in the snow as well as the rather mundane reading. Reclining his head on the divan, he soon was dreaming, carried to the distant past.

***

Galloping down the Frye Road, Harper could smell the strong and bitter aroma of wood smoke on the winter sky long before he was met with the sight of the new Gaines School being wholly consumed by flames…orange and yellow flames reaching one hundred feet into the night sky. He felt the heat as quickly as he saw the devastation. Coming to a stop, he looked around to see the schoolteacher, Miss Ruth and her helper, Opal, holding each other, the intense light reflecting off their shocked and frightened faces.

Dismounting, he shouted above the crackling and collapsing structure, "What has happened here?"

Miss Ruth's lamentation was clear as she cried, "that bunch of white boys said we shouldn't have *"this damn school"* and they were going to see to it!"

"What white boys? Who are they?" Harper responded angrily.

"Levi Kiger, that Morris boy and those other brutes that follow them around," Miss Ruth nervously responded. Harper grimaced as he thought about these known mischief-makers.

The Gaines School, built in 1868, was considered a notable success of the Freedmen's Bureau in this part of the state to the minority of whites that believed in its mission. Against the advice of several friends, Harper had accepted the challenge to oversee the Bureau's efforts in the region the previous year. The Freedmen's Bureau was the popular name of the newly established U.S. Bureau of Refugees, Freedmen, and Abandoned Lands that Congress created during Reconstruction immediately after the Civil War. The Bureau provided practical aid to more than four million African Americans in transitioning from slavery to freedom. As the local Bureau superintendent, Harper had taken pride in this tangible effort to provide basic education to freed slaves and assist in the difficult road to social recognition and economic self-sufficiency. Beyond providing education in reading, writing, and rudimentary math, the school was also a central site for providing medical care as well as government rations for the impoverished, both black *and* white.

This progress had not come easy. Most whites were hostile to the Bureau and its purpose and expressed vehement opposition to its efforts. Harper was constantly shouted down in Winston's town hall meetings when he made a case for aid and resources. Big Jim Bailey, the sheriff of Winston, and his deputies had begrudgingly guarded the construction of the school, distribution of rations, and other actions in the face of ugly resistance.

Some lifelong friends had deserted him and Susan, but not all. Lansford Hall and his wife, Lucia, continued to be loyal friends. Lans had come to Harper's aid on several occasions when Sheriff Bailey was nowhere to be found, and angry crowds gathered to disrupt the Bureau's work. Once, he had even ridden his horse into a mob armed with sticks and clubs to protect Harper and his meager team of agents as they were marking off a three-acre tract for a communal farming allotment to several families of former slaves. While there had been instances of violence in the past year, nothing approached that of the burning of Gaines School.

The next morning after the fire, Harper was waiting for the sheriff when he arrived at the jail. Without preamble, Harper said, "They burned down the school last night."

"What? Who burned down what school?" Bailey responded impatiently, avoiding Harper's eyes.

"You damned sure know what school, the Gaines School," Harper retorted while feeling his blood rise. "And, I know who did it...that Kiger boy and his ring of troublemakers."

"Settle down, Harp. Now, how do you know that? Did you see 'em?" Bailey countered.

"I did not, but the teacher, Ruth Miles, heard them say they *would see to that school*" when they came around last week."

"Now, Harp, you know I can't just go around arrestin' people for what they say. If I did that, we'd have to build a second jail," the sheriff chuckled at his own joke.

"We can't let this stand. This lawlessness has been building up to this and, you know it, Jim. It's past time to bring order to these acts and help these folks." Harper asserted.

Bailey swiftly replied, "These folks, as you say, get lots of help. You see to that. Hellfire Harp, they're free, ain't they?" He paused and looked as if he was carefully considering his next words. "Ok, ok. I'll go round to the Kigers and see what they have to say."

Harper stared hard at the sheriff and nodded. He knew there would be little help coming from that quarter. Without another word, Harper turned and walked out of the jail.

***

Levi Kiger was nineteen years old and the son of Johnson Kiger, a private that served in Harper's 1st Battalion, NC Sharpshooters. Johnson was killed at the battle of Chancellorsville almost five months after Fredericksburg. He had been a poor soldier, never mustering the discipline needed and even going absent without leave, which resulted in several months spent in the military prison in Richmond. Levi was only 14 at the time, and after the war, he, his mother, and four younger siblings went to live with an aunt on the eastside of Winston. Since the war, he and Billy Morris, another war orphan, had been in one scrape after another. However, burning down a school was a new level of mayhem.

It was late afternoon when Harper and Lansford approached the Bridle & Spur public house, taking notice of the four horses on the post. The Bridle & Spur was where Levi and Billy usually held court among their band of miscreants, calling out the world's problems and attributing nearly all of them to the black man. Entering the establishment, they immediately saw Levi sitting on the bar itself with Billy Morris and another two sitting in front of him. Jameson, the proprietor, kept a distance from Levi while nervously wiping down the other end of the bar. Levi caught Harper's eye briefly, smiled, and continued his oratory.

"Yep, we are head and shoulders above the negro when it comes to brains and virtue. Why, just think about it," Levi proclaimed while giving Harper a quick glance. "George Washington, Thomas Jefferson, Robert E Lee, …all Southern white men who wrote the things we live by. Hell, the black man can't even read books, let alone write 'em." The others snorted derisively even though it was safe to say none had ever read anything of the aforementioned if they could read at all.

"Is that why you burned that school, Levi? Just to keep them from reading and writing. I bet you'd hate those boys showin' you up, huh?" Harper said distinctly as he and Lansford moved closer.

With his hands, Levi abruptly pushed off the edge of the bar and snarled, "Clayton, what the hell do you know besides takin' up for the black man. And what if I did burn it down?

They got no right to schooling. They're here on this earth for one reason, and that's to do the white man's biddin'!"

By this time, Billy Morris and the other two had stood up and faced Harper and Lansford in defiance. "You boys have to answer for what you've done," Harper said deliberately.

"Old man, I did this town a favor, and you refuse to see it," Levi replied pompously while attempting to roughly shove past the two.

Harper then grabbed Levi and the next minute, was pandemonium. The gang all leaped toward Harper at once, with Lansford catching one of the crew with a lightning blow to his weak jaw knocking him over a small table. Harper held Levi fast as he attempted to punch and kick his way free. Before Lansford could intervene, Morris hit Harper across the back of his head with a clay bottle causing him to release Levi and fall to the floor. Flashing forward, Lansford caught Billy with a fist to the side of his head, knocking him to the floor, stunned. In the chaos, Levi ran toward the back and out the door but was dropped cold by a wooden plank across his face by an unknown attendant. The other hooligan, a scrawny beanpole with only one eye, scrambled over the overturned chairs and made his escape out the front door.

Harper rose slowly, feeling the back of his head and coming away with some blood. He saw Levi sprawled across the back door threshold and Billy Morris slowly coming to at his feet. "Well, Lans, it's always good to have you in a fight…just like I used to tell you in Virginia. Sorry, I brought you into this, but I sure am glad to have had you here," he said, smiling weakly.

Lansford, massaging his left hand, replied jokingly, "We need the exertion from time to time. Besides, you know you're losing some steam now that you're approaching thirty. Don't think I didn't hear him call you "old man." Then more seriously he said quietly while looking down at the broad figure slowly coming to on the floor, "Harp, I wondered who flattened Levi. He sure does have a pretty nose all busted and bloody."

"I don't know, but I sure thank him," Harper said. "Let's tie these two up and get 'em over to the jail," pointing to Kiger and Morris.

"What about this other one?" Lansford questioned while looking at the third member, who was on his knees and rubbing his swollen jaw.

"Leave him. These two are the instigators, and I aim to see them held to account for that school," Harper said with a sober voice.

With that, they tied the hands of the two hoodlums, offered apologies to Jameson, and marched them the six blocks down Main Street to the town jail. The evening sun was low in the sky as the lonely call of a great horned owl swept down the empty street.

***

Since Christmas, Phillip's young family had enjoyed a peaceful time together. One afternoon they bundled up Susannah and ventured down to the fishpond, now frozen thick. While Maria and the babe watched, Phillip had ventured onto the ice and performed a comedic ice dance for them, running and sliding up and down the frozen pond. He loved making his young wife laugh.

The unrelenting snow of the New Year had essentially shut down all activities on Phillip's small tobacco farm, creating a welcome hibernation with Maria and his little Susannah. His injured arm had become somewhat painful and swollen by the first week of January, but he had not thought much about it. Over the course of the night of the 7th, the arm began to throb, and in addition, his neck commenced to burn, which inhibited any sustained sleep. By the morning of the 8th, a high fever had come on, and Phillip knew he needed help beyond Maria's tender care. He was now worried but careful not to let his young wife see it.

"I have to try to reach Doc Hauser, mi amor," Phillip intoned while holding her hand. "I believe I'm gonna need some medicine for this arm."

"And your neck, too. Can't I try to find him?" Maria meekly replied. "You have no business venturing out like you are. And this unholy blessed snow…" she trailed off softly, turning away.

Phillip's face brightened as he looked at his delicate and pretty young wife. "Well, I can just see you now wandering around out there in two foot of snow, asking anyone you meet where to find the doc," he rebuked her gently. "I will be perfectly fine. Plus, I know just where his house is on the river. I've got plenty of wood loaded in to keep you and the babe warm, and I'll be back by nightfall."

Giving her and the child a reassuring squeeze, Phillip pulled on his boots and grabbed the leather coat and hat off the peg by the door. Taking exaggerated steps to navigate the deep snow, he made his way to the barn, where his two mares were settled into their stalls. Scooping the wooden bucket into the small well, he watered both horses and gave them a feedbag of hay each while he saddled his favorite, Sable.

"Alright, girl. Here we go," Phillip whispered to the filly while patting her neck with its coal-grey winter coat. He set off into frigid air, thankful that the snow had recently stopped. Sable struggled a bit to gain a footing but was soon making an even pace through the drifting snow on the winding lane from the farm.

What was a half-hour trek in normal weather took several excruciating hours. Phillip was shivering as well as burning hot by the time he arrived at the doctor's home on the main road into Bethania. He tied Sable to the post and, with much effort, made his way through the snow to the front door. Breathing hard, Phillip knocked with the edge of his fist, and within seconds, the doctor's startled wife opened the door.

He struggled to say, "G…good day Mrs. Hauser, is the…is the doc…?" At that moment, everything turned white, and he collapsed at her feet.

"Henry! Henry, come quick!" she cried.

Phillip heard voices in the distance and slowly opened his eyes to see Doc Hauser standing over him. How the little man and his wife managed to get him on the hardboard table was a mystery, but he was relieved to be in the doctor's home. His fever had climbed through the morning with the arduous trek and a heavy sweat soaked both wool and cotton shirts.

A Tennessean, Henry Hauser had come to Bethania in the 1870s after medical training at Knoxville College. Word had gotten to the school that doctors were in short supply down the mountains in the Carolinas. Hauser made the trek, finally settling in Bethania, where he met his future wife. In twenty-plus years, Doc Hauser had become a respected and critical community member.

Mrs. Hauser had taken the kettle off the woodstove and was stirring something in a large rounded mug. "This is willowbark tea," she said without smiling, "Will help with that fever. Let it set a bit, and then drink it down."

"This ague, tell me how long," the country doctor said quietly while raising his substantial grey eyebrows with an inquiry.

"Ague?" Phillip repeated.

"Yes, ague. It's a condition with sweats, chills, and of course, a burning fever," Doc Hauser answered in a patient manner seasoned over the years.

"Well, only a few days, I guess. This "ague" came on after my arm swol' up and got red and all. Here it is," Phillip said as he pulled the shirtsleeve up, bandage and all.

"Oh my. Oh my," Mrs. Hauser instantly uttered upon seeing Phillip's left arm. The infection had progressed rapidly, perhaps due to the exertion of the ride. The left arm was an unnatural red and noticeably larger than his right. The scabbing had now broken apart, with a yellow liquid seeping from the deep wounds.

"My neck needs tending to as well, I expect," Phillip interjected while sitting up and exposing the red and swollen lacerations on his lower neck and upper chest. With more than a little effort, he drank most of the bitter hot brew.

The diminutive doctor quickly took charge. "Ruby, I need two of my poultices from the shelves. And bring the oregano oil with 'em. I should have seen to these long before now," he admonished. Mrs. Hauser returned to the room and, without speaking, handed the grassy cloths to her husband, who had begun to clean the wounds as Phillip grimaced and held his breath. Placing the poultices saturated with the herbal concoction on both arm and neck area, he looked up and, again with raised eyebrows, asked, "Now, would you like to tell me how you got in such shape?"

Phillip inhaled deeply and responded, "A couple of weeks back, I got into a nasty bout with a mountain cat while hunting elk out on the Saurtown cliffs." He quickly retold the story as both the doctor and his wife's eyes grew quite wide.

When he had finished, Phillip laid back and closed his eyes. He continued to sweat heavily while shivering invariably. Doc Hauser said, "You will stay with us tonight while we get this fever under control."

With eyes closed, Phillip replied slowly but emphatically, "I have to get back to my family, Doc. I have to get home by nightfall. It's just my wife and little one, and they need me there."

"My boy, they need you alive and well is what they need. And you're not able to make that trip, not by a long stretch," the doctor quietly asserted. The doctor's wife quickly nodded and added, "Those wounds need dressing regularly. They're abscessin' something terrible, and poisons have to be drawn from the blood."

Phillip again said weakly but with conviction, "I have to get back. I appreciate your concerns, but I aim to get back. Send me with some of that willowbark and some poultices, if you will. My wife can nurse me back."

"I advise against it," Hauser repeated but then reluctantly added, "but I see that you're bound and determined. As soon as this damnable snow melts a bit, I will pay you a call to see how those wounds are progressing."

"Of course, Doc. I know you will," Phillip answered softly. "I thank you and Mrs. Hauser for all your help…all your kindness."

By late afternoon, the mare was again slowly making its way through the heavy snow, with Phillip guiding her through drifts and drooping evergreens. Ruby Hauser had prepared the aid package, and Phillip had loaded it into his saddlebag for the trek home. The mid-winter sun was brilliant and flashed off the pure white snow. He could feel his strength leaving him as the hours passed.

The twilight sky was a thin purple streak on the horizon when he finally came into the yard. He unsaddled Sable and, struggling, gave both horses some water and grain. Carrying his kit, Phillip struggled to the house and was met by Maria at the door. "Oh, Philli, I've been worried sick," she wept, tears streaming down her flushed cheeks as she reached out to support him. "I couldn't imagine what was happening. I've been so scared."

Phillip's eyes were dull, his face flushed and soaked. "I'm here. I'm back, mi amor," he murmured as from a distance. He then stumbled forward and collapsed into the big stuffed chair by the fire.

***

The wind was unmerciful. It blew imperiously through those gathered in the churchyard as if daring protest. Harp held Susan close as she shivered in his arms and sobbed softly. Eli and Jacob stood silently, staring across the half-acre churchyard. Eleanor supported the young new widow who had cried a thousand tears and whose remaining strength had essentially been depleted. The weather had again turned perfectly cold, with sub-freezing temperatures creating a hard ice shell over the ground. The previous day four church men had worked to dig a proper grave into the frozen ground. The same men stood by today, two on each side, waiting to lower the casket into the grave.

Phillip, in his fevered state, had drifted in and out of consciousness for six days before succumbing to the infection. In her panic and with the baby in tow, Maria had journeyed on foot to Eli and Katherine's house the day after Phillip had returned. Eli himself brought Doc Hauser to attend to Phillip, but there was naught the old physician could do at this stage. He pronounced the blood had become poisoned from the corrupted wounds. (Sepsis was little understood in those times). Over the next few days, Harp and the rest of the family had come to stand vigil. Of course, the whole family was distraught, but Maria was utterly in ruin. Wailing, rocking her body back and forth, and furiously digging nails into her arms, she was inconsolable. Susan, while grief-stricken, stayed close by consoling the young girl. Kat had taken the baby Susannah, and she and Emma made sure she was warm and fed.

The minister, Reverend Rinn, performed the Lutheran liturgy for the burial of the dead, with the assembly providing responses in unison. Jacob mumbled the replies from memory and thought of his brother, younger by less than a year. They had grown up almost as twins but certainly not identical. While Jacob was deliberate and circumspect, Philli was spontaneous and instinctive. Jacob kept his thoughts close while Philli shared his with friends and strangers alike. Opposite sides of the same coin, they were. And they were inseparable in their youth. Whether swimming or fishing the Yadkin River, hunting the foothills of the Piedmont, or teasing most of the girls of Bethania, the Clayton brothers were sure to be together.

He recalled, with a bit of emotion, the time when Philli, coming to his defense, had knocked down both Cooper brothers. Jacob, at fourteen years old, was small for his age, and Caleb Cooper had tripped him at the town harvest festival, causing him to fall into the ring where prize bulls were being shown. He had jumped up to retaliate, but the older brother, Samuel, had pinned his arms with both boys laughing. In a flash, Philli had delivered a blow to Samuel's eye knocking him backward. Then without hesitation, he pummeled Caleb across the head and body. Jacob smiled as he could still see in his mind both boys running for their lives that day. He could clearly remember Philli's wide grin and retort, "Well, I guess we won't be countin' on those Coopers for any more fun, will we?"

Harp stared at the coffin and felt the cold deep in his bones. His mind wandered to the summer days when he and the boys and sharecroppers would work as one in the red clay fields. It was tough work planting the seed, priming the leaf, and harvesting the tobacco crop, but Philli had made the days pass more easily. He was the family prankster, and his humor inevitably lightened the undertaking. Once at harvest, Harp reminisced, Philli had bet all within earshot a silver dollar that he could knot more hands of leaf than anyone within the hour. Of course, most took him on only to quickly see that Philli had devised a new method of banding the outer leaf around the bundle to cut the traditional tying time by half. Within the hour, Philli had clearly managed more hands than anyone. Smiling but saying nothing, he then produced a sheet of paper and the nub of a pencil and tallied his winnings expeditiously. Harp smiled to himself and, in his mind, saw the disarming yet brilliant Philli wink, the wink that usually accompanied his good-natured shenanigans.

Harp also thought about Philli going off last year to fight the Spaniards in Cuba. "Why?" he challenged Phillip at the time. "Why fight for something so removed from one's home and interest?" It had become all too clear. Philli craved adventure, and he sure found it with Teddy Roosevelt's bunch. He had been gone just over a year. Upon his return home, he said most of the time was spent traveling to the fight, and with the exception of the San Juan engagement, there were only a couple of scrapes of note. Even so, he returned with a young wife, an infant daughter, and a changed soul. The easy laugh remained, but there was something added behind it; something suggesting that one had been tested, that one now knew something of a broken world. "Not unlike me all those years ago," Harp mused. With that, Harp breathed deeply and raised his head to take in the melancholy scene and reassure the gathered crowd with his presence.

Three enormous ravens, perched atop the church roof, let forth their unnerving harsh calls breaking the winter stillness.

CHAPTER 3: SPRING 1900

The large transoms were fully open on both walls of the town hall auditorium, allowing a mild breeze to circulate. The day was bright and quite warm, betraying the late spring. Harper stood at the head of the large acacia wood table facing the assembled councilmen and various other local officials.

Shaking his head, he demurred, "In my opinion, this is not a workable solution. For the Flemings to take over the Williams and Davis concerns, well, that results in essentially a private monopoly of the water supply for the town. These two water reservoirs and pumping stations ensure a steady and affordable supply to both Winston and Salem. Both need updating. And, with the growing population, another reservoir is going to be needed pretty darn soon. With just one controlling private interest, I'm worried about the position this puts both towns in."

Seth Fleming, his lanky body, unfolding out of his chair, instantly retorted, "Get off your high horse, Clayton. You know as well as I do that this is perfectly legal. If I didn't know better, I would think you hate missin' out on a business opportunity. Both Davis and Williams here are just fine sellin' out to me, right boys?" Fleming turned to face the two men with a hard stare. Seth's brother Mathias, sitting beside the two men, forced a cough and scuffed his chair back and forth to break the silence.

Archie Williams, a white-haired Moravian, blinked as if brought out of a stupor and quickly nodded in approval. Orvil Davis just stared down at the polished wooden floor between his feet and slowly nodded. "See there, it's all proper and agreed to," Seth proclaimed while Mathias sneered nearby.

Harper replied, "Well, Fleming, it's not the legal case I'm making here. Technically, the legality is not an issue. It's more one of what's good business practice and perhaps even good ethics. The Board here asked me to look into this and give my two cents, and that's what I'm doing." He surveyed the crowded hall noticing Levi Kiger leaning on the back wall. "Yep, there's Fleming's bully boy," Harp thought. "I wonder just how much pressure he and his thugs put on Williams and Davis." He and Kiger had, since that brawl thirty years ago, over the school burning and Levi's subsequent jail time, a history of clashes, and the bad blood between them ran deep.

Seth Fleming responded, "Now you've said your piece. You can sit back down and let the council do the votin'. They know us Flemings are good on a promise and the best ticket for ensurin' good water for the future. Hell, we all know Winston's growin' faster than any town in the state, and it needs aggressive water management to keep up. Both Davis and Williams here don't have the means to keep investing to meet the need," Fleming recited to the gathering with deliberate attention paid to the nine aldermen seated around the front table. After a long pause, he slowly lowered into his seat.

Mayor Eaton then stood up and petitioned, "Anybody else have something to say before the vote?" After a few moments of low murmuring in the hall, he stated, "Ok, for the business of Fleming Water Works acquiring the Williams and Davis companies for the purpose of contracting the water supply and management for the two towns, all in favor say,

'Aye.'" Five 'ayes' sounded. "All opposed say, 'Nay.'" Four 'nays' responded. "The aye's have it. The motion is passed."

Harp met Alderman Lans Hall's disgruntled look with his own and immediately wished he had not given up his seat last year. They both knew this development was ripe for future trouble. The Fleming brothers were already shaking hands, slapping backs, creating a loud commotion while exiting the hall. He couldn't help but wonder which aldermen had been on the receiving end of a fat cash payment from the Flemings. Harp glanced to the back of the gallery to see that Levi Kiger was nowhere to be seen.

It was only midday, but Harp was depleted. He and Lans rode up Main Street and observed the bustle of the merchant stores. The newly enlarged firehouse had recently been built; a Jacob Clayton design, he reminded himself with pride. Winston had become twice the size of Salem over the past decade. While the Moravian town of Salem was thriving and sustainable with skilled tradesmen and the academy, it's younger "sibling" had become a fast-growing city with its burgeoning tobacco and textile industries. The town had recently adopted the aggressively optimistic slogan of "Fifty by Fifteen," meaning a population target of 50,000 by the year 1915.

Lans brought him out of his reverie with an admonishment, "Stay clear of those Flemings, Harp. They're just lookin' for ways to bring you down a peg or two. I'd hate to think what they and their dog, Kiger did to Davis and Williams to get them to sell."

"I'll be fine, Lans," Harper responded. "I'll admit I'm worried about them getting the city water contract, though. Lord knows what corners they'll cut to enrich themselves and what that will mean down the road. You know it, and I know it."

"Well, just stay clear of 'em; that's my advice," Lans replied. "Lucia and I will see you and Susan tomorrow at the celebration, right? I believe I hear the girls are planning a picnic for afterward at Grace Park."

"Uh, that's right," he acknowledged. In fact, Harp had forgotten about Winston's Fiftieth Anniversary Fair until Lans reminded him. "Let's meet at our house around eleven o'clock. Eli and Eleanor, and the others are meeting us there, too. We can walk over to the square."

"'Till then, Captain," Lans said with a good-natured salute and continued on up Main Street to his house close to the old reservoir while Harper turned his horse onto Fifth Street.

***

Seeing Levi Kiger today brought back a flood of unsettling memories. He wiped his face with the blue silk handkerchief Susan had recently given him, and his mind wandered. He mused about Tom Silver and how they had first met all those years ago. Kiger and Billy Morris had been given ridiculously light one-month sentences for burning down the Gaines schoolhouse…an unsurprising judgment from a plainly prejudicial judge. Shortly after the trial, Silver had approached Harper outside his office, which doubled as the Freedmen's agency, and offered his thanks for bringing some justice to the sorry episode. Harp smiled as he remembered what Silver had said next.

"Mr. Clayton, I suppose that busted nose on Levi will sure stay with him longer than any jail time," he had said, smiling modestly yet with a hint of mystery.

"I expect you're right." Harp had responded, eyes narrowing. "I don't suppose you know who laid into him. Because, if you do, I want to shake his hand right here and now."

Silver hesitated, then stuck out his hand. "Tom Silver's my name, Mr. Clayton."

"Harper Clayton," he said while holding the handshake. "My friends call me Harp."

Thus began a thirty-year friendship of mutual trust and support. It was a bond that had only grown stronger, with each man standing up for the other on a number of occasions. Harp had come to love Silver and his family and saw them as keen markers for the injustices suffered by blacks in an increasingly un-reconstructed South.

Silver had been born into slavery on a large tobacco plantation in the tidewater region around Williamsburg, Virginia. His father's father and mother had been brought as children from the western coast of Africa to the colonial port of Charleston and then sold to an agent representing the Virginia planter. The grandfather and his wife had a large number of children, with some being sold in the Richmond market to mostly white buyers but also to a few free blacks.

Silver's father was born late in the grandfather's life, and he would tell young Silver stories about the old man, like how he was the finest whittler for miles around and would make wonderful toys and pipes and flutes for the master's children and household. He also told stories about the old man and his musical skills. There wasn't an instrument around that grandfather couldn't play with accomplishment. Silver's own carpentry and woodworking skills, as well as his finesse with the fiddle and banjo, must have come from his grandfather, he often thought.

Silver and Sadie grew up close and married in their teens. Sadie worked in the big kitchen in the main house, while Silver became one of several carpenters on the plantation before and during the war. The war years were hard, with food becoming increasingly scarce. The master's three sons had all gone off to fight. Only one had returned. After the war and after the 13th amendment to the US Constitution was finally ratified, Silver and Sadie made their way into central North Carolina, hearing that freedmen were finding jobs among the German and Moravian inhabitants.

It was in Winston that they settled, with Silver finding work at the Fogle Brothers sawmill and woodworks. Silver was on the job those thirty years ago when the foreman sent him to the backdoor of the Bridle and Spur to deliver a finished set of solid oak two-by-four runners for the tavern's front porch. Silver had overheard Harp confronting Levi Kiger about the school burning and the resulting free-for-all. And, he was ready with one of the planks when Levi attempted to escape out the back door. He was too scared to introduce himself at that moment, but he absolutely knew that Harper Clayton was someone he wanted to get to know.

***

The central four square blocks in Winston, running north-south from Fourth to Fifth streets and east-west from Trade to Liberty, had been laid with Belgian blocks the year prior. It was here that the town set its fifty-year anniversary fair. The big event was an opportunity for the city leaders to showcase a city full of hope and promise and poised to grow in the new century.

The two new La France pumping wagons would be on display. The Reynolds and Hanes companies would demonstrate their innovative new rolling and knitting machines. Silversmiths, fine woodcarvers, quilt makers, stonemasons, and potters would be joined by painters and other visual artists, many from the Moravian craft guilds in Salem. The county horse show would be a main feature in the mid-afternoon with the finest Appaloosas, American quarter horses, Morgans, and Tennessee Walkers all groomed and ready for show.

A range of food and novelty vendors were contracted to offer specialties of the day, such as a recent delight to America called "popcorn." A company from Atlanta would be sampling its sparking beverage in a bottle called Coca-Cola and claiming it not only delicious but also a "brain tonic and cure for all nervous affections." Exotic cocoa beans from the southern climes were to be roasted and brewed into coffee right there on the street. These, plus a host of sweet treats such as flavored ice creams in sugared cones, elegant cakes, and pies, would tempt even the most particular patrons.

There would be, of course, musical and other entertainment. A fiddle group, Roger Moseby and the Muddy Creek Ramblers, would be on hand, as well as the Dixie Banjo Review, of which Silver was the bandleader. The Salem Brass Band and Winston Militia Marching Band, both longtime local favorites, were on the schedule. A number of strolling musicians would also entertain the crowd. Jugglers, magicians, and fortune-tellers would dot the sidewalks to entertain young and old alike.

Winston Fiftieth Anniversary Fair

The Claytons and Halls walked the few blocks to the fair, where a sizable crowd had already gathered. The entourage included Harp, Susan, and Nell; Eli, Kat, and their twins, Noah and James, with the two daughters, Emmy and Anna, pulling them along the street. Eleanor, Tom, and Tee were also part of the troop and in fine form. Maria, who now lived with Susan and Harp in Winston along with baby Susannah, agreed to join in. This was a pleasant surprise since the young widow had not ventured out whatsoever since moving into the house on 5th street after Phillip's funeral.

Lans and Lucia and their son, Lucas, arrived earlier that morning. Lucas was Hall's only living child and, at thirty years old, was thus far a bachelor. He and Eli were about the same age but were different souls and had never been close. While Eli was robust and craved the outdoors, Lucas immersed himself in books and could be regularly found at First Presbyterian Church library on Cherry Street. Calamity had struck the Hall family on several occasions over the years. Years before, Lucia had delivered two baby boys, stillborn. And a daughter, Lucretia, had tragically drowned at the age of fourteen while swimming with friends in the old rock quarry west of the town. In the face of such woes, Lans had stuck by his wife, strengthening her and refusing to be defeated. It was this fortitude that Harp had seen in Lans on the battlefields of Virginia and Carolina, really their whole lives. And he deeply admired his old friend for it.

The festival was a sensory experience unseen before in Winston. Children raced from one delight to another with family in tow. Women in an array of multi-colored dresses, men in their Sunday best, bands outfitted in smart uniforms, and many brightly colored booths and banners created stunning visual pageantry. The tastes and smells from the food roasters, blenders, and brewers were intoxicating. The incessant sounds of the barkers calling for attention, the jumbled mix of musicians, and hundreds of simultaneous conversations were all quite overwhelming.

After experiencing most of the fair, the Clayton-Hall faction gravitated to the bandstand constructed at the corner of Fourth and Liberty, where the Dixie Banjo Review was about to begin its performance. The "Dixies," as they were called, were a five-banjo ensemble with Silver, his son, Jeff, and three other members. They were attired in identical red-striped vests and new straw hats. Silver tipped his hat to the Claytons and Halls when he saw them arrive. Harp had heard Silver play banjo for family and friends many times over the years but had never heard this full band. Silver had told him that the banjo originated in western Africa, where his people came from, and he got much pleasure from keeping the tradition alive.

The Dixies opened up with Stephen Foster's *Oh Susannah*, and the audience clapped along. Maria even smiled weakly and bounced the babe on her knee upon hearing her name in the song. The band then played *Swanee River*, *Carolina Jig*, and several other familiar toe-tappers as the crowd grew in front of the stage. The next songs were not familiar and had an inherent sadness and sentimentality. The growing crowd was enthralled nonetheless. The band finished their performance with a lively rendition of *Camptown Races* to an enthusiastic reception.

Harp was so immersed in the music that he did not notice his son-in-law huddled with Seth and Mathias Fleming off to the side of the bandstand until the music had stopped and clapping died away. He was entirely surprised to see the three together as he had no idea that Tom knew the Flemings. Tom wasn't looking in his direction, but Harp instinctively knew something was afoot. Both Fleming brothers, heads tilted to Tom were deep in an animated exchange that Harp could not hear. Seth Fleming was obviously driving the parley, pushing his finger into Tom's chest for emphasis. Harp looked around to locate Susan, Eleanor, and the others. All were at the stage congratulating Silver, oblivious to the confab and Harp's growing sense of foreboding.

Swiftly walking to join the group, he called, "I tell ya, old friend, that was one of your best! You Dixies sure had the crowd going. Outstanding, Jeff. Just outstanding!" Harp exclaimed directly to Silver's son standing behind his father and Sadie, smiling proudly.

"Thank you, Mr. Clayton, sir," the young man answered shyly.

"Ah, it was just some ol' banjo music. We been playin' them songs for years," Silver remarked humbly but with an obvious note of pride in his voice.

"Well, it was topnotch, and we just loved it," Eleanor jumped in brightly.

"Indeed," Susan added. "It was first rate. I knew most of the songs but not those few in the middle. They sounded more like sad love songs, sentimental but almost mournful."

Silver looked at Sadie, then cautiously back to Susan and the others and said, "Those are some songs my grandfather played on that old plantation in Virginia at day's end at the cabins. Why, they go back generations, even to Africa, and we're keepin' 'em alive for the coming generations."

The group stood quiet for a moment, perhaps searching for a proper response. They could all see Silver's earnestness. After a bit, Susan broke the silence and said, "We do hope to hear them again." Then without thinking, she added, "We're going for a picnic at Grace Park. Sadie, you and Silver, and Jeff, please join us." Harper immediately winced, knowing how egregious, even illegal, that would be at the park reserved only for whites.

Silver smiled briefly and quickly replied, "Thank you kindly, Miss Susan, but we better get home. We're tuckered out after all that playin'."

***

Later that evening, after Eleanor, Tom, and the others had left the house on Fifth Street to return to their own homes, Harp walked out to the front porch to light his cigar. Exhausted from the day, Susan and Nell announced they were going to bed. As he settled into one of the porch rockers, Harp could not shake the image from earlier at the fair of his son-in-law engaged with the Fleming brothers. In his head, an alarm bell was sounding. He knew that the Flemings would go to any links to get what they wanted and, if they could sully the Clayton name in the process, so much the better. Deep down, he knew that Tom was now part of some Flemings' scheme. He reminded himself to be vigilant.

The late spring night was pleasant and mild, with a host of crickets and night birds creating a spirited background symphony. A hidden mockingbird sang a soothing aria as Harp rolled his lit cigar between his fingers. It was in these hushed and solitary moments where Harper Clayton's spirit was unbound, and his mind roamed freely to the past and future. A visual memory of Eli as a boy came to mind. The young lad was climbing the grand beech tree in the front yard of the home place with the agility of a young chimpanzee. Laughing, he cheerfully challenged his father and sister Eleanor to follow. Phillip and Jacob, only two and three, respectively, tilted their heads up sharply with looks of amazement. Harp could still hear young Eli's high-pitched exhortation to the group below.

Harper remembered Lans, Judge Mitchell, and other friends riding into the yard that same day in 1877. They had come to inform him that a compromise had been made in Congress, effectively ending Reconstruction in the South. It was a compromise to settle the fiercely contentious 1876 presidential election. After the disputed electoral-college vote, a commission of congressional representatives and Supreme Court justices voted to award Rutherford B. Hayes the presidency. Behind the scenes, however, allies of Hayes had met with southern democrats in secret and agreed to withdraw all federal troops from the South in exchange for an agreement from democrats not to block Hayes' victory. The removal of federal troops from the South was the catalyst to end Reconstruction and re-establish white control of state governments and society writ large.

Less than a decade earlier, under President Grant and with the influence of radical republicans in the North, the US Congress had passed the 14th (equal protection under the law for formerly enslaved people) and 15th (the right to vote regardless of race, color, or previous condition of servitude) amendments to the constitution. For the first time, formerly enslaved males could vote. And, vote they did. As new members of the Republican Party, blacks were elected to southern state legislatures and even the US House of Representatives. The dream of a color-blind democracy was becoming a reality. Grant deployed Federal troops located across the five designated southern districts to maintain order and subdued the efforts of violent white supremacist groups, notably the Ku Klux Klan, to great effect. The 1876 Compromise, however, brought much of this progress to an end. Racism was, of course, prevalent in both the northern and southern states, but racial violence sprung up like a grass fire in the South. The newly enfranchised black vote was suppressed with new laws such as literacy tests and poll taxes. Moreover, blacks were subjected to violent intimidation to repress their vote and run for office. The Ku Klux Klan reemerged, stronger than ever.

It was this part of his past that Harper loathed above all. His recollections were still sharp of the confrontations with enraged mobs as he, Lans, and others had provided a cordon of protection for the black men on their way to the voting polls. Reasoning with such fury was hopeless. He had tried before but was shouted down. Harper recalled wondering what drove people to such animus. Even now, he wondered.

One especially dark memory of those times stood out in sharp relief: Election Day 1880. James Garfield and Winfield Scott Hancock, two former Union generals, contended for the presidency. Thomas Jarvis was picked to finish Zebulon Vance's term as North Carolina governor when Vance was appointed to a seat in the US senate. This solidified a renewed control of state politics by the conservative Democratic Party.

Thomas Silver and other black men in Winston had exercised their right to vote that day just as they had done the previous ten years. Despite the expected insults thrown their way by white agitators around the polls, the vote had occurred without violence. In the local race for state representative, Silver had backed Malachi Jones, a black minister, for the seat.

Jones narrowly won by less than one hundred votes over a local bank adjuster, Egbert Adams. A party to celebrate the Jones victory was hastily planned for that night at the minister's Macedonia Baptist church.

The celebration was in full swing with barbequed whole pig on the spit and lively music from fiddles, banjos, and various percussion instruments. The well-wishers numbered about fifty or so and crowded around Malachi Jones, enthusiastically offering their congratulations. Sadie and her friend, Alice, had previously gone outside to the privy but rushed back into the church with eyes wide. "There's Klan outside with torches!" they shrieked. Silver and the others looked outside from the church windows to see a ring of men, many in Klan robes and hoods, encircling the small church. Most had torches and sticks or clubs. The only sound was the flickering from the burning torches on the cold November night.

The minister and Silver raised their arms to quieten the nervous party. Silver then exhorted them, "Now everybody just quiet down now and, me and the reverend will step outside to see what these boys want with us. It will be all right. Everybody, just calm yourselves now." Jones nodded in agreement and followed Silver out onto the church's front porch. Controlling a powerful urge to shake, Silver checked his fear and inquired of the hooded men, "What can we do for you men, might I ask?" No one spoke. No one moved. The torches blew and hissed from the cold wind. Silver recognized the tall form of Egbert Adams.

Earlier that evening, Harper had heard from a friend at the courthouse that trouble was brewing. Adams' supporters, incited by false claims of cheating from Seth and Mathias Fleming, were going to march to the little church and force Malachi Jones to concede his victory. In their minds, the fraud perpetrated on the good citizens of Winston would be answered for.

Harper made the rounds as quickly as possible, gathering up a small group of former Freedmen Agency friends. Lansford Hall, Dick Bennett, Taylor and Logan Murphy, and several others joined him to intercept the mob. The night was fast approaching by the time they headed east out of town.

Silver inquired again in a measured tone, "Is there something we can do for you?"

An ugly voice responded, "You can say that this election was stolen; Jones here cheated to win it. That's what you can do."

Silver's heart sunk at the recognition of Levi Kiger's uniquely hoarse voice. But, he and Jones turned to one another and silently knew they were not going to admit to cheating that did not happen. "There was no cheatin' done. All those votes were cast fair and square by men that have the vote," Silver announced. "We don't want no trouble. Mr. Adams and Reverend Jones can go to the courthouse tomorrow and have them go over the count again."

"We don't need no recount, do we, boys?" Kiger laughed cruelly while scanning the ring of torches. "We'll just take that victory here and now."

With that, he and most of the others rushed the porch to grab Silver and Jones. Some of the men watching from inside the church burst through the door to intercede. Within seconds a brawl had erupted in the yard. Fists, sticks, and clubs found their mark as men were knocked cold and blood flowed. Kiger and his ever-present abettor, Billy Mitchell, produced a rope and commenced to tie a noose around Jones' neck. Silver pulled Mitchell off of the minister but was blind-sided by a stick that came out of the night. He went down hard to the ground.

The rope had just been swung over a leafless poplar tree branch when Harper and the others arrived at the church. He fired his Smith & Wesson revolver three times into the air. At the sound, the fighting abruptly stopped. Dismounting, Harper walked straight to Levi Kiger and, without a word, hit him with a surprising and powerful blow. Kiger instantly went down and stayed down. Harper then commanded, "This stops now! You hear me? These people don't deserve this. Get the hell home, all of you."

The attackers slowly moved away, some grumbling, some limping and rubbing their injuries. The women in the church swarmed into the yard to attend to their men. Silver had come around by this time and, while sitting up on the ground, caught Harp's eye and silently nodded. Malachi Jones had removed the noose from his neck and began to help others that had been hurt in the melee.

CHAPTER 4: LATE SUMMER 1900

The plans had consumed the better part of the Spring and Summer. Jacob had spent countless hours researching the latest architectural designs of the gilded age as well as corresponding with his recent cohort at McKim, Mead & White in New York. The vision was to replace the grand but ill-fated Hotel Zinzendorf on that beautiful knoll at the head of Fourth Street, and Simeon-Stone had been retained to create the design.

The Zinzendorf, named after the European count that designed the Moravian settlement of Salem, had been constructed in 1890-91. Four stories and with over one hundred guestrooms, the hotel was briefly the centerpiece of Winston's drive to become *the* resort town of the South. But it was not to be. On Thanksgiving Day 1892, as hotel staff prepared for a sumptuous dinner, the cry was heard, "Fire! Fire!" While touted as "perfect in every way" with its 85-foot center tower and modern appointments such as electric lights, steam heat, and elevators, the hotel had been constructed almost entirely of wood. It burned to the ground in less than two hours. The cause of the fire was still a mystery.

This was an important moment in the history of the city as well as for Simeon-Stone. Jacob was determined to match, if not exceed, the opulence and design creativity of the Zinzendorf. Besides the new firehouse, he had designed several structures in Winston since returning to town, but nothing on this scale and importance. His reputation, as well as that of the firm, had grown over the recent years but would be put to the test with the new hotel. The Reynolds brothers and Pleasant Hanes, who essentially ran the West End Hotel

Development Company, had formed a committee to oversee the grand project and requested Simeon-Stone to present its plans at their August meeting.

"I envision a large conservatory on the scale of the Hotel Victoria in New York," Jacob announced to the committee while showing a photograph of the delightful glass structure. "The architect, Richard Hunt Morris, noted that this feature alone drew the best of the city to the hotel. Its rooftop garden is also an amusement for taking the morning air, and ours will be a calling card as well with its overview of the city and surrounding woodlands." The young man's confidence and enthusiasm grew as the whole West End Hotel committee group listened intently, and Samuel Stone looked on with affirmation. Jacob was well-prepared with multiple design boards. The three-story foyer and public rooms were stunning. Each guest room was to be appointed with its own bath with hot and cold running water, a rarity for the times. The kitchen, laundry, staff quarters, and other operations were expertly laid out in the cavernous basement space.

"Well done, Master Clayton," observed Hanes, "I see you have brought both an aesthetic and functional eye to the project, and I must say, it appears quite grand. But, what have you designed to prevent the kind of disaster that occurred on this site only eight years past?"

Jacob was ready. He knew the Zinzendorf fire would be a critical discussion point, and he had anticipated the question. He then revealed his last design board. "Sir, from the massive stone foundations to significant portions of the framing that will use high-grade steel, you can see that the structure will be largely fire resistant. We have also designed an innovative firewall made of steel that effectively buttresses the kitchen from the hotel's common areas and guest rooms." Pausing for effect, he continued. "And, let me add that in the event of fire, we have provided an innovative system of fountainheads throughout the building that will emit water from an on-site reservoir. This new fire suppression system is just now being installed in the splendid hotels of Boston, New York, and Chicago."

The room murmured approvingly, with committee members turning to each other and nodding. Will Reynolds announced, "Sam, you and young Clayton here have given us a plan to definitely consider. The committee will discuss this and respond promptly." With that succinct response, the meeting was obviously at an end.

Jacob's elation was throttled a bit. Based on their reaction, he thought that the committee would give their approval on the spot. He looked at Stone, who was giving him a reassuring look. With that, he quickly said, "thank you so much for your time today and for this unique opportunity."

The room began to clear, and Jacob packed up his design boards. Sam Stone, putting his hand on Jacob's shoulder, said, "That was one heck of a job, Jacob. I believe they're hooked."

"But they said they have to talk it over," Jacob responded.

"Oldest trick in the book, my boy," the older man chuckled. "If I know ol' Will Reynolds, he'll just use this to create a little doubt on our part. And with a little doubt comes a willingness to negotiate a lower price for final plans and oversight…a little doubt, a little lower price. That's the game…and it is a game to these boys."

***

It was a brief walk to the house on Fifth Street. Even so, the mid-day August sun was intense, and Jacob was flushed by the time he reached the front gate. He had told his mother that he would come by for a visit after the meeting with the committee.

Stepping through the wrought iron-scrolled gate, he immediately heard the most angelic sound; a soft modulating whistle coming from Nell's pursed lips. He could see his sister in the side rose garden in conversation with a handsome wood thrush. He always knew that Nell had a gift, that special prowess in connecting with the natural world. Between her books, flowers, and animals, Nell's world did not let many people in outside her family. Now fourteen, Nell was blossoming into a beautiful young lady with long raven hair and her mother's delicate porcelain complexion. He wondered, oddly, if his mother and older sister were taking a hand in bringing Nell out of her self-imposed, sheltered world.

Jacob walked slowly toward the garden, but the bird startled and quickly flitted away. This brought Nell out of her reverie, and she turned to see her brother.

"Jacob, my long lost brother," she called out while running to embrace him. "So you do remember your home after all."

"I hated to interrupt your charming recital with your little colleague," he said, smiling. "And you seem to forget that I have my own home these days."

"That boarding house? Why that's only a place for widowers and old maids." Nell laughed while pinching his cheek. They both turned toward the front steps.

Jacob inevitably smiled with satisfaction when he looked upon the Victorian home. He recalled offering his ideas through numerous telegrams to his mother during the planning and construction of the home while he was at school in Boston. He had suggested the gas-fired boiler in the basement, a new design from England. It kept the entire home comfortable with steam heat even during the record cold and snow from the previous winter. The styling of the turrets on the front corners was borrowed from an Astor home on Cape May. The design of the small formal garden in the rear was similar to one of Frederick Law Olmsted, the famed landscape architect of New York's Central Park and the new Vanderbilt Estate in the North Carolina mountains.

Opening the leaded glass front door, he called out teasingly and with uncharacteristic bravado, "Is there anyone here to receive the designer of Winston's newest and most elegant hotel? He is here to share a most promising reception from the committee."

Susan came through the dining room into the foyer and, with a wide smile, said, "Now wait for father so he can hear all about it as well. He just arrived from the office and is washing up. Of course, you must join us dearest." She continued, "I have missed you so. It seems as if you live in another land these last few months."

"I am sorry, mother," Jacob replied. "This West End hotel opportunity has wholly consumed me this summer. It is my chance to do something extraordinary."

"Did I hear "extraordinary"?" Harper exclaimed from behind while placing both hands on his son's shoulders. "We must hear all about "extraordinary," right mother?"

Jacob turned and smiled at his father and was immediately struck by the thought that Papa had aged since he last saw him; a bit more gray hair and wrinkles around the eyes. In fact, Jacob knew his father and mother had been thoroughly shaken by Phillip's death eight months prior. They both could not entirely hide the sadness behind the smiles. Jacob knew because he, too, still grieved deeply for his younger brother.

Forcing these thoughts aside, he continued, "I hope you don't think I'm getting beyond myself, but I believe this new West End Hotel is my best work yet. And, I believe the Reynolds brothers, Hanes, and the rest truly liked what they saw this morning."

"I've no doubt," Harper replied with conviction. He reflected on how swiftly the Reynolds brothers were buying up the smaller tobacco manufacturers and their energetic plans for the town's future. In fact, just this year, they bought out the Hanes' tobacco concerns. Returning his focus to his son, he added, "Jacob, my boy, you have a unique gift; an ability to visualize what most can't. This new age is set for the visionaries like yourself, those creative thinkers and builders that can take us forward."

Susan quickly joined in, "Your father is enthralled with this new century and all it promises, I assure you. He goes on and on about how America will move forward; the machines, the people, and the progress our society will make. But before he conveys all these favorable auspices, please give us more details on your extraordinary morning. Oh, and Nell dear, please bring the tea into the parlor." Nell caught Jacob's eye and turned to the kitchen with a mischievous roll of the eyes.

***

In a short impromptu meeting, the town council quickly approved the new reservoir for the city. The town was growing rapidly, and the need was clear above and beyond the existing two older reservoirs that served both Winston and Salem. The Flemings were granted the project yet had bypassed Simeon-Stone for the design and engineering plans. Instead, they had brought a Mr. Robeson up from Atlanta to do the work claiming that waterworks was his specialty. Sam Stone had told Jacob that there had been rumors of bribery of city officials, unsatisfied clients, and lawsuits surrounding Robeson's firm in Atlanta, but nothing official.

The excavation work had already begun, with foundations being poured the last week of September. It was faster than anyone expected, and the mayor and council were pleased. Jacob was surprised that the design and engineering work had moved so quickly through the approval process of Randal Shelton, the city supervisor for waterworks. Out of pure curiosity, he decided to take a look for himself at the site located up Trade Street at the Eight Street intersection. It was land that some said the Flemings had acquired for pennies on the dollar but had sold to the city for the full dollar and then some.

Riding up to the team of workers working their shovels, he inquired, "Where is your foreman?"

A young freckle-faced adolescent squinted into the morning sun and eagerly reported, "Bossman Rivers is havin' a chew with the muckedy-mucks over in the trees there," while pointing a skinny sun-burned arm in the direction of a few oaks adjacent the site. Scanning his companions, he muttered in a contrived serious tone, "Bossman has a shovel affliction, you know. If he picks one up, he gets afflicted."

At that, the group busted out laughing, drawing the attention of Rivers and the other men under the trees. Noticing Jacob, the foreman, Seth Fleming, and another man began to walk in his direction. Jacob dismounted to meet them. "Looks like some real fine progress here, gentlemen. How is the digging? Good bedrock?"

"Who's asking? And this is a private build site for your information," grunted Fleming. He had taken his slouch hat off and mopped his brow with a fine handkerchief. "If you must know, the digging is just right, and we're finding true rock for our footings. Isn't that right, Robeson?"

"Quite right, Mr. Fleming, quite right. Why, this is the ideal site for this kind of project. Excellent ground. Excellent contours. Excellent drainage. Couldn't be better," the sprite of a man responded.

John Robeson was a tiny specimen, not more than five feet tall, with a rather slender frame. There was something quite odd about him. His hair was oily and unfashionably long, and his eyes were two distinct colors: misty grey and golden brown. This distinction served to give him a fantastical visual appearance, somewhat like a creature of the forest. Jacob thought him to be well into his forties, but it was hard to be sure given his diminutive stature and overall countenance.

Gathering himself, he said, "My apologies, gentlemen, Jacob Clayton at your service. I design buildings and am always intrigued by the professional work of others in the field."

"Ah yes, you're Harper Clayton's boy. How is the old man?" Fleming asked with a fabricated smile that made Jacob hesitate. "And, I expect your mother is as lovely as ever?"

"Uh, they are quite well, thank you," Jacob replied automatically with apprehension.

"Well, as I said, this is a private building site for now," Fleming responded, signaling an end to the conversation. "Come back when we're near finished, and I'll give you the nickel tour myself."

With that, Jacob swiftly remounted his horse, tipped his hat, and said, "All the best with the build. I hope it remains a success for you and the town." He then spurred his horse forward onto Trade Street, heading south, but he could not escape an immediate feeling of dread. Maybe it was Fleming's spurious smile, or maybe Mr. Robeson's odd aura.

***

It had been ages since they had been off together, just the two of them. Eli and Kat Clayton had been married a dozen years, and their bonds of trust and love had grown deep in that time. With their 12th wedding anniversary coming up, they were keen to get away from the farm and children and share the day with each other. Nell had readily agreed to watch over the twins and the girls. She had a full day of treasure hunts, tree climbing, and apple picking planned, and all four children were eager and animated to be with their older cousin.

Kat suggested to Eli that they picnic at the Hidden Falls near the Hanging Rock. They had visited there when they were courting and had always promised they would return someday. Well, this was the day. Kat had packed enough to fill two saddlebags; smoked pork in a vinegar sauce, cabbage, summer squash, and a variety of fresh local fruit-blackberries, cherries, and fresh peaches from the Bethania general store. Eli knew the water at the falls was clean and fresh, but he also packed two canteens and a bottle of muscadine wine to celebrate the occasion.

The couple kissed the children goodbye in their beds just after dawn. Nell had come the night before so they could leave early and have the day.

Picnic at Hidden Falls

"So long, Nell," Kat said, smiling from the saddle. "Thank you again for this. And, make them mind."

Nell nodded and responded, "Today will be a fun adventure for them and me, and if they don't mind, I'll just have to get the birch switch after them" she laughed. "You two savor your time together. Everything will be fine here."

With that, Eli and Kat started out toward Bethania and on to the Hanging Rock as the sun was breaking the trees. They rode in silence for a while, enjoying the sounds of a late summer morning in the Carolina foothills. A pair of cardinals called to one another with that unique string of two-part whistles. The seventeen-year cicadas had recently emerged from their underground sanctuaries to create their unmistakable loud vibrations. The air was still, and the late summer flora was beginning to lose its fresh green display; indeed, the poplars were already shedding some of their hand-sized yellow leaves.

They continued the steady elevation climb and arrived at the waterfalls by mid-day. The clear water tumbled down from the Hanging Rock, gathering in a sizable pool before continuing down the mountainside. The spray from the splashing water created a rainbow mist above the pool.

Scanning the idyllic setting, Kat intoned, "More beautiful than I remember," as Eli helped her down from the mare. "It's surely a piece of God's artistry."

Eli lifted her up by her slim waist and, looking into her bright eyes, agreed, "Yes, more beautiful than I remember."

Kat cherished those expressions of love from her husband. She and Eli had been devoted to one another since they were young adolescents, and neither had ever had any romantic interest in another. She remembered Eli rescuing her from Luther Davis in secondary school when Luther had pressed her up against a tree and touched her budding breasts. From nowhere, Eli spun Luther around and knocked him down to the ground. He then jumped on the boy and began punching him repeatedly in the face until Principal Wilson pulled him off. She still remembered what Eli had then said to her with tenderness, "Are you alright, Katy? I just wanted to help you, that's all." From then on, it just seemed to be understood that Eli Clayton and Katherine Hauser were to be together. In 1887, they were married in the same little Nazareth

Lutheran church as Harper and Susan. Eli was twenty. Kat was eighteen.

Eli had spread the blanket across a soft grassy patch beside the pool where the sun cast fractured beams through the leaves of the overhanging beech and elm trees. Kat pulled the saddlebags and began spreading their lunch on the blanket while Eli unsaddled the horses to let them graze and drink from the deep stream. They savored the lunch and the soothing rhythm of the cascading water. Late summer monarch and swallowtail butterflies danced over the pool. Eli had placed the bottle of Madeira in the water to cool it, and they had surprisingly finished it as soon as the food.

Lying back with his hands behind his head, Eli spoke as if to his self, "We'll be needing some extra hands for the harvest this year." Without looking at his wife, he continued, "The growing season has been very good, especially after the last priming. With Philli…" he paused and then continued. "With Phillip gone and Jacob committed to that hotel doings, I'll be looking for help with the cutting and bundling. Tom said he would be there but, you know I can't count on him. I'm thinking Josh Evans' boys will be a big help, as well as some of Silver's friends in town. I believe if we…"

Touching his arm, Kat held a handful of plump blackberries to his face and said with mock scolding, "Eli Clayton, today is not for planning and working; it's for escaping to the mountains and celebrating us. Yes, just you and me."

"You are right. Thanks for putting me back square in the present," he said with a wide smile.

Not a regular partaker of spirits, Kat felt the Madeira's effects. Jumping up, she cried, "How about a swim? It's certainly hot enough!" She pulled her shift over her head and, standing there in her knickers with hands on hips, declared, "You heard me. It's water time."

Promptly pulling his cotton shirt and trousers off, Eli stood in his drawers as Kat laughed and shrieked, entering the clear water. He quickly followed and ran past her while lunging headfirst into the pool.

"Come on, slowpoke, err, I mean sweetheart," he joked.

"Yiiiii, it's cold, Eli! How can it be so cold when it's the hot August summer?" she challenged.

"Just all at once, that's the secret. You'll get used to it, you'll see," he replied while half swimming half walking to the waterfall. He crouched under the cascading water letting it buffet his head. He was sure this sensation was perfectly therapeutic and invigorating. When he emerged from under the falls, Kat had ventured into the pool and was lying back in the water with her chestnut hair splayed out behind. "She's still a beauty," he thought.

Wrapping his arms around her, they held each other close without speaking. It was a wonderful connection, wet yet warm and sensuous. Eli took Kat's hand and led her out of the water. Brushing the remains of lunch aside, they laid down on the sun-warmed blanket. Their cold lips met in a full kiss, and they pressed their bodies against one another for warmth. Within moments both were stirred with desire, and they made love eagerly in the heat of the afternoon. Afterward, they dozed--she with her head on his chest.

Newly emerged cicadas intruded with their rhythmic staccato of noise while a busy woodpecker hammered incessantly in the distance.

CHAPTER 5: AUTUMN 1900

"I-I-I don't know. I'm in this thing mighty deep already, and I can't see how I can do more," Tom said nervously as he gripped the glass of beer with two hands. He and the Fleming brothers had agreed to meet at the Burke Street Saloon, one of the Flemings' assorted interests, to discuss Tom's investment in the new reservoir.

"Whadya mean, Tom?" Seth Fleming quickly responded. "This reservoir's a no-lose deal. I know it, and you know it. Hell, we stand to more than triple our money. You know we got that bottomland for a song, and Robeson declares we're saving a bundle on brick and concrete through his mason. We just need to bring on the finish carpenters and pipe men to get this thing solid. Your part's just another thousand, and we'll turn the heat on and finish this build." The older man looked around the saloon and, putting his mouth close to Tom Moser's ear, whispered, "Hey, this is gonna put you on the map with the big boys." Seth Fleming knew exactly how to work Tom. He continued, "We couldn't have done it without you. And, with this last piece, I'm gonna put you in for a bigger stake of the profits."

"I just don't know, Seth," the younger man confided.

Fleming, losing patience, exclaimed, "What is it, your wife? Women don't understand business. She can't see this sure opportunity for what it is. Men like us, well, we know what's best for our wives, right? She's gonna thank you for your foresight and business savvy when this is all said and done."

Mathias jumped in with his customary vulgar tone. "So, who wears the damn trousers in your marriage, Moser? You don't have the guts to tell her what's what, do ya?"

Seth Fleming cast a murderous glance at his brother, commanding him to back off and let him handle the younger man.

Tom did not say anything. He just stared at his glass of beer, still in both hands.

"Hell, it's that old fool, Clayton, isn't it," Fleming blurted, his face reddening. "He's been telling you what to do for too damn long. It's high time you stood up to him and showed him how real deals are done and money is made in today's world. Maybe it's time we put him in his place for good." Realizing he was losing control, he put his arm around Tom and said cheerfully, "Heck, forget all that. What say we have another one and think about the profits comin' our way."

One became two; two became four, and the next thing Tom knew, he was weaving toward his Glade Street home. The October night was chilled and breezy. Dry, crispy leaves swirled along the sidewalk. He was trying to do the calculus of coming up with the additional money. Fleming was right, he mused. This deal would be the difference maker for him. He wanted to show Eleanor and his father-in-law that he could deliver; that he was the one who understood business in these modern times.

It was only five blocks from the bar to his home, so Tom had decided to walk there and back. He walked past the site for the coming West End Hotel and couldn't help but feel the jealousy rising up inside for the notoriety his wife's brother was achieving with such a high-profile project. It was quickly becoming the talk of the town since being approved to proceed last month. "Well, I'll show them how real money is made. I'll show them all," he asserted to himself as he opened the leaded glass front door to his west-end home.

Although it was not late, Eleanor was in her dressing gown on the brocaded couch. The striking young woman had her hair down and was reading a recent collection of stories, *Bayou Folk*, by Kate Chopin. Tom came over to kiss her cheek, and she recoiled slightly, "Tom, you've been drinking."

"Yes, dear. That's what you do at a bar." He laughed meagerly at his own joke.

Putting the book aside, Eleanor stood and replied, "Since you've thrown in with the Flemings, you've been spending more and more time at that place up on Burke Street. I have to say I don't like it very much and, you know, I don't care for those brothers very much either. I don't trust them one bit."

"You trust me, don't you? Heck, I don't like them either, but this is business, and I aim to make big money with those two," he declared. "We just need to put in a little more to ensure this reservoir gets done quick."

"Tom, we're out on a big limb already; all our share of the farm profits, all our savings. Don't you realize what will happen to us if this reservoir investment doesn't come through?" She was standing face to face with her husband searching his eyes for understanding.

"You have to trust me, El, and leave these business decisions to me. Seth says I'll get a bigger share of the profits with this last investment. You do still believe in me, don't you?"

Quietly she said, "Yes, I still believe in you. It's just, just…"

"What…your father? He's not the only one that knows what's what," he retorted spitefully.

She reacted with more emotion than she intended, "My father has been what's kept us in this house with his support. He and Momma have stood by us through thick and thin to the point of embarrassment, and I refuse to ask them for anymore!"

"Don't you know I know that? …that it eats away at me every day?" Tom cried. "I'm the head of this household. I want to provide for you and Tee. I want to give you all the things you deserve and more! I want the respect of this town. And I, uh, I want the respect of your father. The new reservoir is my chance to prove to you and him that I'm made of the right stuff…that I'm worthy."

"Tom, you don't need to prove anything to me," she responded while holding his face with her slender hands. "I love you, and I've loved you forever. I know you are a good man, and that's what matters to me. We'll work this out somehow, someway." With that, she took his hand and led him up the curved staircase.

***

The moon was up by the time Silver returned home. Unsaddling his dark mare, Rosie, Silver quickly brushed her down and put her in her stall. It was a still night with only a few night birds calling. Walking around the corner of the carriage house, he saw Sadie at the kitchen window. She was busy working on something out of sight, but Silver could tell she was singing and humming to herself as she worked. Silver smiled and thought just how much his wife loved to sing. Her voice was unmistakable, low and smooth, full of heart yet full of hurt. Sadie sang when she worked. She sang when she played. It was just one thing that made Silver feel so deeply connected to her.

"Where ya been, Mister Sir?" Sadie called without turning when he entered the door. *Mister Sir* was her pet name for him, and Silver knew she was in a light mood. "I have been tryin' to get these late beets canned all evenin', and if you plannin' to have some this winter, you come on over here and help, Miss Sadie." With that, she laughed heartily at her own jesting.

"You know I told you I had to help on somethin' with Harp. I just didn't know it would take this long," Silver replied while squeezing Sadie from behind. Quickly changing the subject, he asked, "You seen Jeff, Sadie Lu? It's late, but I believe I'd like to play a little fiddle music tonight." He called her "Sadie Lu" often, even though "Lu" was not Sadie's middle name. In fact, Sadie had no middle name. She liked it when he called her that, nonetheless.

"Jefferson ain't here," she replied while tightening the lid on a jar of dark red beets. "He's off with that Polly girl again. Those two becomin' quite regular. I won't be the least bit surprised if they decide to marry up. What do you think of that, our Jeff finally settlin' down? Silver, you hearin' what I say?"

Silver mumbled something in the affirmative, but his mind had already returned to the ugly business from earlier that day. Harper's daughter and son-in-law had come to the law office to appeal for the money for the incremental reservoir investment. Harper initially refused them and got into a fierce argument with Tom. Silver happened to be in the offices doing some needed repairs to the wooden window frames and heard it all too clearly. In fact, Christian Harmon, Harper's long-time secretary, Angelica Vogler, and several others were also subjected to the sharp words.

"Fleming is taking full advantage of you," Harper had said forcefully. "Can't you see he is using you, Tom? What's worse, he's using you to get at me. Why, he'd love nothing better than to embarrass this family or worse."

"This is not about you, Harper," Tom retorted, his voice rising and cracking at the same time. "Seth said you'd be jealous of me and with all the success of the new reservoir. Seth told me this would happen. And, what's more, he's made me a partner with a damn good stake in the profits. This is a sure thing…the town needs it. The town is paying for it. We're building it, and we make money when all is said and done." Tom's face was red, and he was visibly shaking, but he stood erect, facing his father-in-law. Eleanor was dumbfounded. She had never seen Tom confront her father with such emotion and, frankly, with any disrespect. She had never seen him…like this.

Looking at his daughter and then turning his eyes back to Tom, Harper thought about the young man's history of bad deals and poor judgment. Yet, he checked his emotions and said purposefully, "There's no jealousy, Tom. I don't know the ins and outs of this reservoir project, but Lans Hall is saying there's been trouble with the inspections and the town getting a good eye on what's goin' on out there. I don't know about that, but I do know Seth Fleming. I know he can't be trusted. I know he is looking out for the Flemings and no one else, period. I've seen it before on more than one occasion. Heck, Tom, why didn't you come to me before now to talk this through? I could have given you my thoughts on the matter. I could have told you about these Flemings."

"Why? Why? I knew you'd be on the naysaying side of this. I wanted to do something of my own making. I want to show you of all people that I can make my way, that I can provide mightily for Eleanor." But, now the fire was gone, and he looked rather spent and vulnerable.

Harper, no less adamant about his opposition to the deal, felt compassion for the boy; for that's what Tom looked like now, a young boy chastened and seeking approval. Looking again at Eleanor, he turned back to Tom and disclosed, "I'm going to loan you the thousand. I'll loan you the money with two conditions. One, you keep me abreast of all the developments and decisions made on the project. And two, you keep me informed on where the money is being spent and what Fleming has to say about it. Fair?"

"Fair enough," Tom replied hastily. "And, I thank you. You'll see the good in this," he said while holding out his hand but not meeting Harper's eyes.

"Oh, papa, thank you so much," Eleanor exclaimed while wrapping her arms around her father's neck. "This means so much to Tom... and me."

Harp looked at his daughter and knew it was at her his generosity was aimed.

After Tom and Eleanor had departed, Harper emerged from his office and looked to see who might have overheard the words between him and his son-in-law. Angelica looked at him sympathetically but said nothing. Everyone else seemed to be occupied with their own doings, with no one meeting his eyes. Silver continued with his window frames. Christian came out of his office and said, "Ahh, Harp, just the man I need. What do we want to do on the Snelling Farm matter?"

Harper smiled, relieved that the focus could turn to professional concerns. He answered, "I think those folks deserve to keep their farm, don't you? And you can help them do just that. Have them come in for an initial talk, and you take it from there. Ok?"

Before Christian could respond, Harper turned to Silver and said, "I think those windows are good for the time being. How about you and I take a ride north of town, old friend?"

Silver raised his eyes in question but immediately began to put his tools away and followed Harper out the door.

Both saddled their own horse in silence. Silver waited for Harper to tell him where they were headed and for what purpose. In his mind, Harper returned to the recent argument with his son-in-law and considered what Seth Fleming was up to. He thought there had to be some nefarious motive for him bringing Tom into this. "Fleming doesn't need Tom's money, and he sure doesn't take on anyone as a partner outside perhaps his dull-witted brother Mathias. Something is not right here, and I've got to smoke it out," he committed to himself. Leaving north by the Liberty road, Harper then told Silver what was on his mind and that they were going to the reservoir site to either find Fleming or at least find out more about the suspicious enterprise.

***

As they neared the site, Harp and Silver passed a gang of workers laughing and jostling one another on the road. Harp surmised the group had just finished work for the day. The work site was quiet as they approached, and the late October sun was low in the sky. In the encroaching shadows, they could see the imposing brick walls of the reservoir. Only a few workers remained cleaning their tools from the day's labors. Pale yellow shafts of light presumably cast from a gas lantern, emanated from the cracks in the walls of a small wooden shed to the side of the muddy grounds. Harper assumed the building was the foreman's station. Dismounting, Harp and Silver approached the door and knocked.

A voice growled from within, "Who the hell is it now? Can't I finish the day in some peace?"

"It's Harper Clayton and Tom Silver here to see Seth Fleming or someone in charge," Harper responded clearly.

There was silence for a moment, and as Harper started to knock again, the door abruptly swung open. "Who are you again? Mr. Fleming ain't here. I'm Rivers, foreman on this site," the man grumbled while staring at Harper and then at Silver from the doorway. He then stepped out into the dying light.

Oscar Rivers was a coarse-looking man with a heavy paunch and puffy, red-splotched face from an apparent long history with the bottle. He also had a long history with the Flemings, overseeing various schemes for the brothers over the years. Rivers had a dubious reputation in his dealings with the town as well as others in the building trade. He had even spent time in the local and state jails for past corruption. How Fleming managed to put him on as foreman on the new town reservoir tested any credible reason. Harper was sure bribery of some petty official was involved. Needless to say, Rivers was a confidant of Levi Kiger, with both being at Seth and Mathias Fleming's beck and call.

"I wanted to see Seth, but you'll have to do." Harper asserted. "Let's start with why the town engineer and council can't seem to get a straight story from Fleming, you, or anybody else around here about where things stand. Can you help me out on that, Rivers?"

"I don't have to tell you a damned thing. And who do you…?" Harper instantly slammed the scabrous man against the wall of the shed before he could finish, knocking the breath out of him. Silver stepped forward, but Harper held his hand up, signaling to hold fast.

"Yes. Yes, you do, Rivers," Harper whispered fiercely, close to the stunned man's face. "Otherwise, the town's going to hear about the shady goings on out here and that they better be checking up on their investment." With that, Harper released his hold on the man and watched him slide down the wall into a sitting position.

***

By the time Silver and Harper made their return, the streets of Winston were quiet and empty. Before going their separate ways, Silver warned his friend, "Harp, you need to be watchful now. It won't be long 'til Fleming hears about your little brush with that loathsome Rivers man, and I expect he'll come your way."

"I appreciate that, Silver. I'll keep an eye out," Harper responded absently. His mind continued to process what Rivers had told them. He was no engineer, but he knew that raising a structure of that size on newly set foundations was suspicious. He recalled that Jacob had visited the site a few months back, and he decided to confer with him. He also made sure to find out what Tom knew, if anything, about the actions surrounding the foundation work.

Tying his horse to the post outside the Vogler boarding house, Harper then made the steps and knocked on the entrance door --it being late enough to where the family had locked up for the night. Rye Vogler, the proprietor, quickly opened the door. With an instant smile, the tall, bespectacled man said, "Well, hello there, Harp. Come to see about our resident architect?"

Harp responded with a smile of his own, "Hello yourself, Rye. As a matter of fact, I am looking for Jacob. Is he here?"

"That he is. He had the evening meal with us tonight, which is quite rare, I must admit. Mrs. Vogler put out a fine meal I say, fried chicken with yams and beans and some blackberry cobbler. Why it was…"

Harper politely curtailed the obviously lengthy saga of supper and interjected, "Oh, I'm sure it was a delight, Rye. I'm in a bit of a hurry, and I need to see my boy. If you don't mind, I'll just head up to his room. Thank you kindly." He then made for the stairs to Jacob's room, leaving Vogler with his mouth still open.

Harper could hear classical music coming from room number 4. He smiled as he thought about his worldly son and his love for music and art. He rapped on the door loud enough for Jacob to answer. Jacob opened the door and, with curiosity in his voice, declared, "Papa, what are you doing here? This is a swell surprise. Do come in."

The boarding room was large enough for a double bed, nightstand, and a rectangular table and chair. On the table sat a new Victrola with a winding handle and several large design sheets that Jacob was obviously working on.

"That is some machine," Harper uttered with his eyes on the gramophone. "Now music goes with you, I guess. What a marvel."

"And public orators, too. It's called a gramophone, and you can hear just about whatever sounds you can imagine. The sounds are actually engraved, or recorded if you will, on a flat disc like this one," the younger man explained. "The needle on the gramophone arm plays back the sound which is amplified through this horn. I just received this last week from the Victor Talking Machine Company in New York."

"Simply genius," his father replied. "You must bring this gramophone to demonstrate for your mother and Nell!"

"Of course. I certainly will as soon as I can finish up these fire suppression system drawings for the hotel. Since the go-ahead from the West End committee, it has been an onslaught of deliverables and due dates, and quite frankly, self-proclaimed experts coming out of the woodwork," Jacob exclaimed.

His son was clearly on his way in the world, and Harper was especially impressed with how much he had accomplished in such a short time. "Needless to say, I am immensely proud of you. And I hate to interrupt your work, but I need your thoughts on what may be trouble on the horizon. I was at the reservoir site earlier this evening." Before Jacob could question why he was there, Harper told him about Tom's involvement with the Flemings and his run-in with Rivers.

"Why would Tom throw in with those two? I thought they might be breaking code to get this thing built in record time. When I was there in September, framing walls were going up on freshly poured foundations. That's highly irregular. Seth Fleming wouldn't let me get a good look and sent me on my way. Without the proper hydration concrete can't be properly set. But, surely Mr. Shelton is overseeing for the town and won't let this happen."

Harper replied, "We will have to see about it. I saw they had brick walls already up out there today." He stayed a little longer while Jacob showed him the plans for the new hotel's fire suppression system. He then bid his son goodnight and slipped out before Vogler could hold him up with more discourse about Mrs. Vogler's culinary feats.

Susan had already retired for the night when he returned home. Feeling suddenly spent, he checked the doors and turned down the lamps. Making his way up the stairs, he then looked in on Nell sleeping peacefully. He thought about Maria and the baby at the end of the hall and winced. Thinking of her always brought back a wave of sorrow about Phillip. Finally, he opened the door to his own bedroom and met Susan's eyes.

Without pause, she said, "Eleanor told me what happened at the office today." Checking herself, she said soothingly, "I can see you are totally exhausted. Come to bed, and we can talk about it in the morning." Harper nodded silently and changed into his nightclothes. After an exchange of light kisses and "Sleep wells," he was soon in a deep yet troubled sleep.

***

1st NC Battalion at Chancellorsville

Creeping forward in the steamy late afternoon, Harper, Lans and the others worked to position themselves within range of the Union pickets. The air was moist and the ground was still wet from the spring rains. Bands of smoke from the previous day's fighting continued to flow through the trees, obscuring their sight lines intermittently. The woods around the small crossroads of Chancellorsville were thick with sycamore, poplar, and other hardwoods crowded with scrub pines and heavy undergrowth. The dense undergrowth created good cover but inhibited significant troop movement. Harper signaled his men to hold their position. Above the distinct calls of woodland birds, they could hear the faint sounds from the Union camp as men were preparing the evening mess. Through the lifting smoke, Harp could see a few of his men to either side and knew Lans and his squad would be in position off to his left. A flashing fear of the coming fight coursed through his body, and he closed his eyes for a moment to pray for deliverance.

Leaving the 21st NC Regiment for the newly formed unit had been bittersweet. He had marched and bled with many of the men of the proud regiment. He was leaving a number of friends behind. Because of their reputation for superior marksmanship, Harper's Company E as well as Company B of the 21st, had been carved from the regiment to form the 1st Battalion NC Sharpshooters, Major Rufus Wharton commanding. Harp had been relieved to learn that the new unit would remain a part of Brigadier General Robert Hoke's all-North Carolina brigade along with the 21st and three other North Carolina regiments. Captain Upton was the officer in charge of the newly formed Company B of the sharpshooters, and Lt. Harper Clayton was his second in command. Harp had successfully lobbied for Lans to be promoted to the company's second lieutenant. After several months of training together as a sharpshooter unit, the men were proud of their place in the elite battalion and even exhibited a bit of swagger around the winter camp.

After the Union disaster at Fredericksburg the previous December, President Lincoln had forced yet another change in command in the Army of the Potomac. Disgraced, Burnside had been replaced by Major General Joseph "Fighting Joe" Hooker. After a rest and refit in winter quarters, the reinforced Union army opened its spring campaign in late April 1863. Hooker planned an enveloping maneuver around Robert E. Lee's forces still entrenched at Fredericksburg. By leaving a force facing the Confederate army across the Rappahannock River at Fredericksburg, Hooker then sent a larger force to re-cross the river north of the town to get behind the rear of the rebel army. Lee's "eyes and ears," Major General Jeb Stuart had set his cavalry brigades in a wide screen around the army to detect the anticipated enemy movement in force. Stuart's troopers conveyed the intelligence of Hooker's move, and Lee quickly responded in bold fashion. Knowing he was significantly outmanned (in fact, greater than two to one in numbers), Lee devised an audacious battle plan. He kept only one division facing the larger enemy force at the river and sent most of his troops northwest to meet Hooker's flanking maneuver. Moreover, Lee then split his forces a second time by having Thomas "Stonewall" Jackson's 2nd Corps flank the right side of the Union force that had crossed the Rappahannock. It was part of Jackson's Corps, of which Harp's 1st Battalion NC Sharpshooters was attached and set forward as the first wave of skirmishers.

Captain Upton came quietly to where Harp had just settled behind a giant oak. "Wharton says we jump off in ten minutes, five o'clock. Tell your men, "pickets first, then officers, then targets presenting," the young officer conveyed in a rich tidewater accent. "And for God's sake, no noise until then."

"Yes sir," Harp whispered while feeling slightly annoyed that Upton felt he had to rehash the directives he had heard at least a half dozen times. "We are in position and ready," he said, but the captain was already moving left down the line and through the mist to Lans' location. While Harp and Upton had not grown particularly close since Fredericksburg both knew they could count on one another on the field of battle. There was even a grudging acceptance of each other, and the captain had relented somewhat of the overbearing military protocol he had previously imposed on his first lieutenant.

Harper then carefully made his way to give the orders to the forty or so men in his close command. Man after man grimly yet silently acknowledged his words. He then came upon Johnson Kiger. Kiger was a poor soldier at best. After a thirty-day stint in the stockade, he had just rejoined the company for brawling in camp. Johnson was ten years older than Harp, had grown up in the small town of Lexington south of Winston, and carried a very large chip on his shoulder. He was not especially close to any of the men as far as Harp could determine and could never be counted on in camp or in the field. After hearing the orders, Kiger muttered, "I can't do this. I-I won't do this."

"Keep your voice down!" Harp hissed. "You will advance, Kiger, or I'll put a bullet in your brain."

With cold eyes, the man stared malevolently at Harp but said nothing. Harp repeated, "You will advance on the signal," and then moved on, leaving Kiger alone and silent.

After he had made the rounds, Harper returned to his oak tree. Within moments a pistol fired, and bugles sounded the advance. As one, the company jumped up and ran toward the enemy pickets, screaming and firing as they advanced. For a long moment, it appeared as if the Southern infantry was the only force engaged; such was the complete surprise on the right wing of the Union line situated along the Orange Turnpike near Wilderness Tavern.

Harper raised his rifled musket, took dead aim, and shot a Yankee picket as the boy turned to run. Only stopping to reload and rapid-fire, Company B and the rest of the battalion, with several Southern brigades in close order, soon reached the turnpike and Union camp. Harp spied a Union major trying to rally his men. He fired, and the major crumpled to the ground. The camp was in utter chaos, with men abandoning cook fires, knocking over tents and equipment, and trying desperately to load and fire weapons. Within minutes, the camp was overrun with the Union soldiers in full retreat.

The overwhelming force rolled up the Union line forcing Major General Howard's 11th Division back at least two miles. Within the hour, adrenaline began to fade to exhaustion. Harp searched for his men but could locate only a handful in his vicinity. He spotted Upton, Wharton, and several other officers in a small clearing in an animated discussion with Robert Hoke, the brigade commander, and moved there to receive orders.

Seeing him approach, the captain called out, "We press the attack. With the light remaining, we will send them scrambling back across the river."

"My command is scattered. We need to regroup," Harper shouted above the noise.

"Do what you can, lieutenant," Major Wharton asserted. "Our orders are to keep the pressure on. We've broken their line, by God. And, we have the chance for something magnificent here. The 6th and 54th will follow close."

Harper saluted both officers and ran back to the spot where several Company B men had stopped to hear what Harp had been told. "Ok, boys. Let's gather up as many of the company as we can. Heck, if a soldier has lost his unit, enlist him in ours. We're going forward. Check your cartridges. Grab some off the wounded. We go in shortly."

Coming out of the woods with a smile breaking through his smoke-covered face, Lans Hall yelled, "We caught 'em napping for sure! I've never seen such a stampede."

Harp met Lans with a small smile of his own, then soberly announced, "General says we press the attack. Gather your boys and any stragglers and link up on my left. We lead the attack again with the 6th and 54th on our tails."

The shadows were lengthening, and fires were burning in the undergrowth as the men moved forward. Harper guessed his command was now about eighty men between remnants of the company and stragglers that had been "recruited." The smoke formed a solid grey-white veil in spots making the advance disjointed and difficult. The plaintive cries of wounded men throughout the woods only added to the men's fear. After advancing a quarter mile, Harp could vaguely make out the enemy force about one hundred yards to the east. In the brief lull in the fighting, Howard's 11th Division had reformed and had been reinforced heavily.

Within seconds the Union line opened fire. A sheet of flame from a thousand rifles swept through the Southern ranks. Men went down in dozens. Harp heard what seemed to be a swarm of hornets blow by his head. His neck burned as if several of those hornets had stopped just to sting him. Instinctively, he went to the ground and sought cover. Rolling behind a fallen tree, he then scanned his surroundings for his men, alive or dead. In horror, he saw the two men that had advanced into the woods on either side of him were clearly dead, one with several holes in his chest. The other, no more than sixteen years, had been shot through the left eye. Harp flattened on the ground as a second volley ripped through the trees. He again tried to assess the tumult. Groups of men were behind cover, looking toward him for direction. Many more were bleeding on the ground and in need of help. Other bodies lay still where they fell.

Harp knew there was no chance of surviving another advance with his meager command in the face of such firepower. He began to move toward the others to organize a retreat when a thunderous hail of fire came behind him and a resounding chorus of rebel yells. The reinforcing southern brigade charged through their ranks and into the Union line. Quickly putting a Company B sergeant in charge of caring for the wounded, Harp stood and rallied those who could to join the renewed attack.

For the next hour until nightfall, the opposing forces battered one another, inflicting great casualties on each side. Harp had only a remnant of his original command left yet led them as well as any troops looking for an officer. Only by a strong will did he continue the fight. Even with his battlefield experience, Harp had never undergone such pandemonium and butchery. Only darkness slowed the fighting to a grinding halt.

The rest of the night was spent trying to untangle the disorganized mix of companies, regiments, and brigades. It was well after midnight when the battalion was finally reset. A preliminary count of casualties in Company B was eleven killed, twenty-eight wounded, and a host of men missing and unaccounted for. The company had numbered eighty-nine at the start.

Harp made his way to a gathering point about a half-mile behind the lines and then had one of the men inspect his burning neck and tell him what he saw. The man said it looked like a nasty burn, red but with little blood. Harp knew he was lucky only to have been grazed by the fusillade of fire. He then pulled a cloth handkerchief from his pocket and tied it around his neck. He saw Lans Hall come limping up to the clusters of men. "Ah, there you are, friend. This was a day of two fortunes, no doubt."

Lans had endured a similar fate after the early rush of success. He had been slightly wounded in the lower leg but had otherwise survived the carnage. They both were emotional from the realization of friends they had lost. His earlier smile gone, the smaller man intoned, "It's only by God's mercy we survived, Harp. Danner, Woodson, Pete Riley…all dead. And I heard they found Johnson Kiger a ways back, close to the original skirmish line. Seems like he tried to high-tail it and run, and an officer shot him dead."

Harp recalled Kiger's baleful defiance and just shook his head. He then added, "The captain is grievously wounded, Lans. Hoke's adjutant just told me about it…a severe head wound. I'm on my way to the brigade's medical tents in the rear to see him. Will you join me?"

Harp had secured a horse from the adjutant, and the two friends then rode double and slowly to the rear.

The night was strangely quiet after the tumult of the day.

CHAPTER 6: CHRISTMAS 1900

"Mama, that is for babies! We're too old to do that anymore!" Noah protested.

"I'm with Noah. Why don't you, Aunt Eleanor, and Aunt Maria just take the girls and baby Susannah to the Christmas play this year?" James added.

The twin boys were now eleven and would rather be in the woods than all dressed up and squirming in the Little Winston Theatre seats, Kat mused. Mustering an arsenal of arguments, she responded, "Only one more year, boys. You know we love to do this at Christmas to get into the spirit. This year is something brand new, *The Nutcracker and the Mouse King*. I think there are sword fights! I'm sure Tee will be coming. And, of course, Anna and Emma love seeing their big brothers there. Remember, they have sweets afterward!" Kat chuckled while thinking that was the full extent of motivations she could come up with on the spot.

"Oh, okay. One more year," Noah grumbled.

"Sword fights are good. I hope they have sword fights," James said brightly. "And, sweets!"

It was a cold and wintry Saturday. Kat and the boys were out on their annual Christmas shopping, which had become a holiday ritual. They were on a mission to find their father the perfect Christmas present. Eli happily agreed to stay at home with the girls, pretending he didn't know what quest was underway. Last year the twins had given him a Western cowboy hat, black with a leather band and silver medallion. Eli just loved it and now wore it quite often. James suggested they give him something he could have fun with this year, and Noah and Kat heartily agreed. So, they were off to *Sportsman Supply*, Winston's best merchant of "fun things" for boys and men.

Kat pulled the carriage up to the post on Trade Street, which was just a short walk to *Sportsman*. She hopped down with both boys anxiously waiting for her. The street was busy this December Saturday as many farmers and factory workers came into town to Christmas shop and see the sights with family. They quickly found their way to the store and joined a crowd already there.

The young boys were fascinated with the merchandise. Featured prominently in the windows and behind extravagant glass cases were firearms of various makes and models- shotguns, rifles, and pistols. There were longbows, crossbows, colorful fletched arrows, and targets along one wall. Knives of all varieties, including hunting and pocketknives, were proudly displayed in several glass cases in the middle of the store. Noah and James ran to the Rover and Schwinn new safety bicycles that had swiftly replaced the slow high wheelers of the late 19th century. These innovations allowed the rider to build momentum and speed through their rear chain drives.

With Kat catching up, they exclaimed, "This is the perfect present for Papa! He can master it and then show us how to ride it." Both boys were closely inspecting the captivating machines pointing out the various strange and alluring features.

Kat, knowing her husband but not wanting to deflate the boys' excitement, replied with a warm laugh, "You are certainly right. These machines are delightful, but I don't think Papa is ready to retire his favorite horse, Riley, just yet. Let's give him a few more years to appreciate these horseless conveyances."

"Conveyances?" James asked with a puzzled look.

"Means to get around, to travel," Kat explained. Changing the subject, she exclaimed, "Look! I see some fine fishing rods and reels over there. I bet they have the newest models."

Just the word "fishing" was enough to change the boys' focus from bicycles. If there was one activity Eli and his sons enjoyed above all else; it was fishing. They loved to accompany their Papa on his famous fishing trips to the Yadkin or Dan rivers or to the various other lakes and streams in the piedmont. Surveying the wonderful selection of shiny brass reels, sleek rods of willow and ash, creels, hooks, and lures, the twins quickly agreed on the ideal rod and reel for their father.

Excitedly, they insisted on both carrying the prized gift to the carriage for the ride home. But first, Kat knew a trip to the Winkler bakery in Salem was in order. Since it was Noah's turn with the carriage, she let him unhitch Jenny and take the reins. She then directed him down Trade Street to Fourth and then south onto Main Street to Salem. The streets of Salem were also bustling on this frosty day, yet, Noah steered the carriage toward the curb with skill. Just down the street, with its colorful painting of a Moravian yeast bun, was the artisan sign for the Winkler Bakery. The smells from the bakery were exotic and magical, and they all quickly had their fill of the baker's warm sugar cake. Of course, they ordered more sugar cake to take home to Eli and the girls. With that, they set off for home in Bethania, full and contented.

***

Rivers Enlists Levi Kiger

A gusty and cold wind blew the cirrus clouds across the morning sky. After making the journey to the south of town, Oscar Rivers arrived at the unkempt clapboard house. Approaching the door, he noticed the peeling paint and grimy windows. He thought about the indolent owner and pounded on the door. No sound. After the briefest of pauses, he pounded again and then entered unannounced. The three-room house was cold, with no coals in the small fireplace and no heat coming from the woodstove in the corner of the front room. Rivers could see his breath as he exhaled and approached the back room.

Lying on a bare mattress on the iron frame bed was Levi Kiger and a much younger, rather hefty woman with long red hair spread across Levi and the mattress. Both were dead to the world, partially undressed with a couple of empty gin bottles on the filthy floor. Rivers, with a disgusted snort, kicked Kiger's legs that were hanging off the bed.

"What the hell?" Levi Kiger slurred while trying to open both eyes fully. "I'll tear you up," he croaked as he tried to rise. He then saw Rivers looming over him and instantly changed his tone. "What in the world, Oscar? What are you doing here? And why are you here so early?"

Taking his eyes off the young woman, he grinned and said, "Get up. It ain't early. Boss man wants to see you pronto. And, for chrissake, cover yourself. You think I care to see your meager endowment?"

By this time, the substantial woman was wrapping a thin blanket around herself and quickly moving toward the kitchen.

***

Seth Fleming paced the room while Mathias slumped in the fancy brocaded chair. "By God, brother! Something has to be done about Clayton. What business of his is this? He'll be bringing every council member nosing around the build site to create trouble. Shelton assured me that he got things under control, but with Clayton makin' trouble, I'm not so sure. Hell, gettin' his son-in-law in on payin' those two off was supposed to keep this kind of thing from happening. Looks like it's done just the opposite," the older brother lamented.

Sliding up in the chair, Mathias sneered, "Relax, brother. I got Rivers going down to Southside to bring Kiger up here. We'll have ol' Levi, and his boys get straight with Harper Clayton. Knowing them two's *history*, he'll just love that!"

Pouring a shot of fine cognac in his morning coffee, Seth equivocated. "I don't know about that. We sure as hell don't want this to get out of hand. Now don't get me wrong. Nobody wants to see Harper Clayton be brought to account more than me. We just have to be smart. We have to do things facile-like, that's all." He smiled maliciously at Mathias' bewilderment knowing his brother had no idea what he was saying.

By the time Rivers and Kiger arrived at the Fleming mansion on the northwest outskirts of Winston, Seth Fleming had conceived a plan – a plan to knock Harp off his inquiry, yet one to keep the Flemings free from all attention and blame. Seeing the shape Levi was in and knowing Rivers' hygiene habits, Seth told the men to meet him at the reservoir instead of inviting them into the refined home with imported Turkish rugs and English furniture. He and Mathias then followed the two on horseback the four miles to the site.

The cold wind swept across the open field around the reservoir. It was Sunday, so no one was on site. The four men crammed into the small construction shed where King Rivers typically held court, supervising the workmen. Today, he wasn't even a prince and was totally deferential to both Flemings.

"Damn it, Oscar, get a fire in that stove. The wind blows through this shack of yours like a sieve," Seth grunted. "Levi, you look like the devil. Too much whiskey, huh? Hell, I need you fit and sharp. I got something for you."

Still trying to clear his head after a hard night of drinking, Levi replied, "Hell, I'm fit, boss. I'm fit for whatever you throw my way." Levi tried to muster the confidence and look Fleming in the eyes, but his own were much too blurry. "And it was gin, by the way."

Seth said, "What? Gin? Well, no wonder you're in such a state. Whiskey just gets you drunk, but gin…well, gin sets you on a whole other kind of misery."

"And you sure have a look, and smell of misery," Mathias cackled.

"Now listen. Enough about Levi's poor habits," Seth commanded. The smell of stale alcohol and body sweat was becoming unbearable in the tight enclosure. Staring at Kiger, he said, "It's high time to do something about Harper Clayton and his unwanted interference. And, here's what I want you to do…"

Levi Kiger grinned with clear malice and exhaled audibly through foul teeth as he heard Fleming's plan.

**

The Clayton Christmas gathering was more subdued and strained than in years past. Memories of Phillip and his good-natured spirit were on everyone's mind. From his playing hide-n-seek with the children and giving horsey rides on his broad shoulders to telling adventure stories that enthralled the whole family, reminders of Phillip and his easy smile were close at hand. Susan was not her usual playful self, and Maria looked as if grief had wasted her to a slender wraith. It was only when her attention turned to Susannah that any spark was present in her countenance.

The men's Christmas Eve day deer hunt tradition came off yet, without Tom and Tee. Tom had declined the invitation citing a sore leg. Of course, Phillip's enthusiasm and hunting prowess were missed. There was a success, however, in bringing home five deer; three bucks and two does. By this time, the twins had become more comfortable with the rifle, and James brought down one of the does. His Papa and Grandpa were equally proud. Not surprisingly, Jacob had taken two of the bucks, and Eli had shot a buck and a doe. Harper did not take a shot but relished the time immensely with his sons and grandsons.

At the Christmas day gathering, the strain between Tom and Harp was there, but both were passable actors for the sake of the family. There was no talk of the new reservoir. Eli, oblivious to the issue, enlisted Tom to organize outdoor races and other games for the children. Later in the afternoon, Eleanor tried to engage everyone around the old piano with caroling before the big meal but was only marginally successful. Only Nell, Kat, and the girls gave Eleanor a decent effort.

However, the meal was exceptional, as usual, with the women putting forth their customary splendid efforts. Two big tom turkeys, baked golden and crispy, were the main attraction; that is, if you didn't consider the full side table of cakes and pies, including Susan's pumpkin pies and Eleanor's hummingbird cake. Maria had asked if she could pitch in with a few dishes, and everyone was glad she did. She prepared a deliciously spicy side of rice and beans that her grandmother had taught her from growing up on the southwest coast of Florida. After borrowing a few ingredients from Susan, Maria also made a tasty custard flan dish that was consumed eagerly, quite entirely, and complimented freely.

Before the meal, Harper had read the good news from the first chapter of Luke, as tradition called with Emma and Anna pointing out the various players in the nativity. And, the gift-giving had been happy and hopeful. Eli was especially taken with his new rod and reel, to the delight of both boys. Jacob had given Nell a Botany Guide from the Smithsonian Museum of Natural History. Susan and Harper had a brooch made for Maria that contained a lock of Phillip's hair encased in it. The young widow was overcome with tears and thankfulness. All the siblings had gone in together to contract the building in the spring of an elegant garden gazebo for Susan and Harp. They presented the two with a wonderful watercolor rendering of the rotunda. All in all, it was a warm and loving family Christmas in the first year of the new century.

Yet, there lingered a sadness that could not be pushed aside. Their son, their brother, and their uncle, was gone.

***

CHAPTER 7: WINTER 1901

The New Year had turned raw with rain and sleet. A cold winter wind seemed to blow unabated down the near-deserted streets. Harper recalled the historic blizzard from the year past. This early January weather was sufficiently dreadful, he mused, but nothing on the scale of the *"New Century Disturbance."* The roads were passable, and, in any event, he had considerable business to attend to.

The Railway Committee

Winston and Salem town leaders envisioned the ambitious project of building a railroad over the mountains to Roanoke, Virginia. Harper was chosen along with Colonel Francis Fries to head the oversight committee. Fries was both a manufacturer and banker with successful careers in his family's textile business and, most recently, as a founding member of the first trust company in North Carolina, Wachovia Loan and Trust. With his business savvy and enthusiastic personality, Fries was a good choice to co-direct the project.

The primary purpose of the rail line to Roanoke was to open up the Virginia markets for the towns' manufacturers and facilitate the flow of goods in and out of the town. Through Roanoke, they could become part of the larger Norfolk & Western rail system providing access to a wide range of new markets from Richmond to Washington and beyond. Faster deliveries meant bigger profits, and everyone wanted in on the decision-making. Harper knew his role would be largely one of arbiter between the tobacco and textile heavyweights that primarily included the Reynolds and Williamson tobacco companies, Hanes Knitting and Shamrock Hosiery Mills, as well as the various other manufacturing companies like Nissen Wagon Works and Fries' Arista and Indira Cotton Mills.

The mid-January meeting of the governing committee was initially scheduled to begin at 9:00 am but had been delayed two hours due to the weather. Harp had enlisted Silver and his friends the day before to ride to at least twenty homes to get the word out. Even with the weather, Harper expected a large turnout. He saddled his mare and set out for the town hall in the early morning rain in order to arrive before the others. Shaking the rain off his jacket and hat, Harper entered the hall to find Quince, the caretaker putting out chairs around the big oak table in the central meeting room. Quince had been taking care of the town hall facility for as long as Harper could remember and always had a natural good humor for everyone he came across.

Seeing Harper, he beamed, "Now you done beat everybody here, Mr. Clayton. Mr. Eaton, he told me to make sure to be here bright and early and get things set up."

Harp replied, "Well, Quince, I didn't beat you, did I? I tell you what. If I finish with these chairs, can I talk you into boiling a big urn of coffee? I expect the group comin' in will be wet, cold, and ready for hot coffee."

"Oh, yessir. And I'll make it nice and strong so as to get all these boys to sit up straight," the old man winked at Harper and moved on to the kitchen area.

It wasn't long before the committee members, a virtual who's who of Winston's business leaders, started to arrive. The Reynolds brothers, RJ and Will, with a reputation for punctuality, arrived first. They were quickly followed by the Hanes brothers, Pleasanton and John. After selling their tobacco interests the previous year to Reynolds, both Hanes were aggressively moving into the textiles industry. Then came George Nissen, who, with his brother, William, had built their family wagon works into one of the most successful wagon manufacturing companies in the South.

Colonel Fries arrived, nattily attired as usual, and made his way over to Harper. "Harp," he said smiling, "This is going to be like wrestling a bunch of alligators. Everybody's gonna want their own issues catered to. Let's just you and I keep the group mindful of the overriding goal here to get this thing done on time and on budget."

Harper responded lightly, "I've never wrestled an alligator. Sounds like fun as long as you stay away from the teeth. But, you're on the nose. We've got to get this thing built before we can accommodate all the particular ins and outs of rates and loads and what all."

With that, Harper turned to the room of twenty or so and announced, "Alright, folks. Let's get started. Old Quince has made us some strong coffee, so please get yourself a cup and have a seat."

Both Harper and the Colonel stood at the head of the table. After the murmuring and shuffling subsided, Harper stated clearly and strongly, "This committee is tasked with developing the plan for building a railroad to connect our towns to Roanoke, Virginia. That's over one hundred and twenty miles and crosses some pretty rough terrain." Then breaking into a broad grin, he added, "Oh, and we need to do it without bankrupting the town." The group laughed at that, and most looked over to Mayor Eaton sitting at the other end of the table with his own somewhat sheepish grin.

"Well then, gentlemen, let's get to it." Harper continued. "Let's begin with our city engineer for Winston, Jacob Ludlow, telling us about the engineering firms that can give us the details of accomplishing our goal; the construction, the timing, the land rights issues, and a whole host of other matters. Sir, if you would be so kind."

For the best part of an hour, Ludlow shared his research on three different railroad civil engineering firms around the South. After a robust discussion, the committee unanimously decided on Parker Engineering from Richmond based on the firm's experience with other railroad construction over mountain terrain. A motion was approved to immediately contact Parker in order to brief them on the project and solicit a bid. It was also deemed practical to obtain bids from the other two firms to ensure competitive prices.

The focus of the remainder of the meeting was on the creation of a collective timetable that included goals for financing, the work of subcommittees, estimated build times, and future session dates for the governing committee. Harper and Fries then adjourned the meeting. In the informal discussions afterward, all were optimistic about the new railroad prospects. Harper and the Colonel were thanked all around for their leadership.

It was mid-afternoon, and the weather had cleared a bit when Harper began to make his way to the Clayton-Harmon offices. He realized he was quite hungry and decided to ask Angelica to go for soup at the Besset Eatery while he wrote up the summary notes of the committee meeting. Turning onto Main Street, he noticed two disheveled men looking his way from the small greenway across the road. Catching their stares, both men quickly turned away. He thought it strange that they would look at him without apparent conversation. Not recognizing them, he put it out of his mind and walked the mare to the small stable behind the office.

***

Work on the reservoir continued at a brisk pace. While other construction around town had dwindled in January, it was rumored that the Flemings were paying extra wages to the workers to entice them out into the cold. The target date for completion had been advanced yet again to March 21, the first day of spring. The water committee of the town council was ecstatic at the news as the town's water needs were ever-pressing.

Tom Moser had noticed of late a distinctive aloofness from the Flemings and Seth began leaving him out of key decisions. He wondered what had transpired to create this distance between him and his partners. In the few times, he had recently tried to engage the older man, he had been vague and dismissive. However, Tom decided to leave well enough alone since he was not really concerned about the project details and developments in spite of what his father-in-law had demanded of him. His focus was entirely on his future take from the profits. With windfall in hand, he envisioned taking Eleanor and Tee on a grand tour of the big cities up North, residing in top hotels, eating at the French-inspired restaurants, and immersing in the rich culture that only a New York, Boston, or Philadelphia could provide. Tom found himself increasingly daydreaming about the future, one where prosperity and respect came his way.

***

Harper had worked later than usual, and the sun had long fallen over the winter horizon. Earlier, he told Silver not to wait for him, that he would make his own way home. Leaving the office, he walked the short distance to the stable where Jenny would be waiting for him and the sugar cube he inevitably gave her. Opening the door, Harper reached for the lantern just inside. Lighting the gas-soaked wick, he instinctive felt he was not alone. The lantern cast flickering light across the stable. Harper immediately noticed that the mare was not in the stable. Instead, there stood four dark hooded figures, silent, with three holding clubs. Fighting the urge to flee, he stood facing the four.

After a long moment of silence, the one without a club taunted, "You just can't let things be, Clayton. Now, why is that, I wonder?" Harper recognized the distinctive chalky voice of Levi Kiger. "Mr. Fleming said we had to teach you a lesson so as you'd mind your own business. You know what I told him? I say, there's no teaching this one. No, Harper Clayton thinks he's all high and mighty and knows better. And, I'm thinking that's why you left my daddy, a wounded hero on that Virginia battlefield all those years ago…you thinkin' you're too good to be bothered with a poor man."

The stable was again quiet with only the stuttering flicker of the gas lantern. The dark-hooded men stood still.

"You can take that damned hood off, Levi. You're not fooling anyone. Is that what this is about, Kiger? Me, responsible for your pa?" Harper inquired in a steady voice. "Well, here's the God's truth, Johnson Kiger was a sorry soldier. He was not a hero. Your pa was shot trying to run *from* the Yankees. He was shot because he was a coward."

"You're a damned liar," Kiger sputtered, instantly enraged. "My daddy sacrificed his life for the South. He died fighting for the cause. Hell, you're the damned coward! For these long years, you've taken up with the black man and destroyed all what was good in North Carolina." Levi Kiger was incoherent with rage. Triggered were the years of resentment and bitterness from the belief that his future had been stolen. His hate had been self-nurtured over the decades, feeling every slight, blaming an unjust world.

"Seems like we've done this dance before, Levi," Harper intoned. "You, with the hood. You, with a gang and looking to exact revenge on the unarmed." Harper thought confronting Levi with this kind of direct talk would reduce the man's wrath to an exasperated fatalism.

He was wrong.

Jerking the hood from his head, Levi howled, "You've had your time in the sun, old man. It's time for retribution." Harper could see the wild red eyes of a man without control. He could see a deep hatred nourished for many years through a truly dark lens. Kiger turned to the three and, without speaking, motioned them forward with a sweep of his arm.

It was not a fight to be won, but Harper fought nonetheless. As the clubs were raised, Harper sprung into the chest of the nearest assailant, taking both he and the foe to the ground. After one solid fist to the man's face, blows rained down from the other two. Harper tried to gain his feet to stand and did briefly, viciously grabbing one man by the head. Another strike to the side of his head sent Harper to his knees. From there, he was aware of the kicks and punches, but as if from afar. Strangely, there was no pain. Before losing consciousness, Harper spied Kiger with an evil, satisfied smile on his lips.

***

From deep inside his mind, Harper could smell and feel and even taste the mud. After a weeks-long period of dry weather, the skies had opened up on July 4, 1863- and rightly so. It was as if God had said, "Enough! Enough slaughter, enough malice, enough blood. Enough!" The retreat of the Army of Northern Virginia from Gettysburg was another kind of hell. Wagons, as far as Harper could see, sinking up to axles in the viscous black mud of southern Pennsylvania, were loaded with tens of thousands of wounded men and boys. The cries and pleas, the moans and whimpers of the wounded, weighed heavily on his heart.

And, on it rained. As part of General Ewell's 2nd Corps, Harp's 1st Battalion made up part of the rear-guard of the army. General Hill's 3rd Corps led the bedraggled column, followed by Longstreet's 1st Corps, then Ewell's men. The fear of the Union Army aggressively following up on their victory and attacking the retreating southerners was intensified by the vulnerability of the slow, strung-out, and exhausted force. Their only goal now was to make it through Maryland over the Potomac River to the safety screen of the Blue Ridge Mountains in northern Virginia. Harper tried to find some reserve of strength to exhort the men forward, to keep moving. After three days of fighting, the battalion was virtually spent. Men actually marched asleep on their feet. Casualty rates from killed, wounded, and missing had reduced the unit to less than half its size when the campaign began.

Coming off his brilliant success at Chancellorsville, Robert E Lee had decided to take the fight to the North. After two years of defending Virginia from the Union's offensive campaigns, the land was ravaged, and food stocks were severely depleted. It was time to force the issue by marching north and, if God's will, put an end to the bloodshed. But, it was not to be. The Union army, under the new leadership of Major General George Meade, had grabbed victory from the jaws of defeat by crushing the noble but ill-conceived climactic Pickett's charge on July 3.

Harper walked the line of men on the Maria Furnace Road. "That's it, boys. Keep together. Keep moving. You've shown yourself to be the best damn soldiers in General Lee's army. If those boys in blue come calling, we'll give 'em a Carolina reception," Harp called out, sounding more encouraged than he felt. He knew they were mightily exposed. The two companies of the battalion numbered less than eighty men still fit for battle. They were his men, he mused. Captain James Upton's head wound at Chancellorsville was severe enough to have him assigned to the invalid corps. At the beginning of the campaign, Harper was instructed by General Hoke's adjutant to assume command of B Company.

He made his way over to Lans Hall, who was coaxing his own men forward. Lans actions betrayed none of the utter fatigue that Harper felt deep in his bones. Harper was amazed at how his friend could always carry on, seemingly unaffected by the strains and horror of the endless war.

"What did the quartermaster have to say? Any resupply coming?" Harper inquired.

"We're in luck," Lans responded. "Captain Higgins says we've been allocated the issue for the 26th. They're so shot up from yesterday's charge that there's hardly any fighting force left to muster arms. My fear is our boys holding up much longer through this cussed rain and mud." Harp could now see the strain in his stalwart friend's eyes but also the usual determination.

"Get the cartridges and shot passed through the company as soon as we get it, Lans," Harper replied quietly. "I expect we'll see some blue cavalry coming up on our rear before nightfall. General Jones' cavalry is supposed to be screening our retreat, but I guess we'll see the enemy today. This God-forsaken rain has almost stopped us cold, but my guess is the Union infantry is just as stuck. That's why we have to look for cavalry trying to cut us up piecemeal."

Lans removed his cap, wiped the rain off his face, and blew a long breath. "Well, nothing to do but get to it. I never thought it would come to this Harp. I really didn't. I thought we'd roll over those boys and head straight for Washington. Now just look at this," he lamented while looking up the long sluggish column. "Miles and miles of wagons with the wounded and miles of wagons with supplies captured here in Pennsylvania headed south with thousands of bone-tired, starving men trudging alongside. Hell, we're easy for the picking."

While Lans captured the reality of the situation, Harper was surprised to hear his friend so fatalistic. In fact, he had never heard Lans like this. Then he thought, "Well, we've never been so clearly beaten. Sharpsburg was a bloodbath with our army retreating back into Virginia, but we were still a formidable force and still filled with the fight. This feels much different. The fight is gone in these men, at least for the time being."

Coming back to the present, he exclaimed, "That's why we have to keep these boys moving. Have the sergeants take charge of their squads and check the flanks. General Hoke says we're to get up to that Monterey mountain pass tonight and then on to Hagerstown and the Potomac tomorrow."

The wagon trains and infantry slogged forward for the rest of the afternoon of July 4. Even though Harper and Lans continued to encourage the men, some fell behind or fell out, totally depleted from weeks of marching on reduced rations and three days of hard fighting in the summer heat. The able-bodied helped those into already crowded wagons to keep the momentum going. Late in the day, with thunder and lightning all around, a cavalry scout from the 1st Maryland Cavalry Battalion reined his big chestnut mare into close proximity to Harper and saluted.

The scout was no more than eighteen, with a smooth sunburned face. "Union cavalry spotted on the southern ridge below the pass," the young boy blurted. "Cap'n Emack says they're formin' up and probably goin' to strike the train at Monterey Springs pass. I'm to spread the word up the line."

"Thank you, private," Harper responded. "There's what's left of the 26th North Carolina and 10th Georgia just up the column. Try to find General Ewell on ahead and kindly inform him that the rear will hold, with Captain Clayton's compliments."

The boy nodded gravely, saluted again, and spurred his horse up the line. Harper momentarily wondered where the boy was from and if his family back home could ever conceive of the work he was doing to help Lee's army escape the killing fields of Pennsylvania.

The fading light was oddly beautiful, with small rays cutting through the heavy grey thunderclouds. "The devil's beating his wife," Harper mused as he recalled the old wives' tale his mother used to say when there was sunlight while it was raining. He tried to picture his mother and wondered if she even knew anything about this terrible battle that had taken place. It had been six months since he had seen his family…a half year since he had seen his Susan. In his mind, he could see her delicate face and hear her soothing voice. Harper declared to himself that if he survived this war, he would ask her to be his wife.

The volley of fire wrenched Harper back to reality. Ahead of his rear-guard position, the Union cavalry of Brig. General Custer charged the wagons and troops exposed in the narrow mountain pass. The small number of dismounted men of the 1st Maryland returned a ragged and uneven fire in the gathering darkness. Within seconds the Union troopers had broken the line and were among the wagon train, killing and capturing prisoners and destroying supply wagons.

Harper called out to his men. "Form on me and forward! The two companies of the 1st Battalion came to life and charged into the maelstrom. Adrenalin and the discipline of battle-tested men kicked in as the troops engaged the enemy. They fired at least one round and then, using their rifles as clubs, began taking riders from their mounts in the congested melee It was a whirling madness; horses and men screaming, wagons overturning in the mud, and a twilight battle at close quarters with men fighting for their very survival. Lightning flashed in the sky with close ground strikes around them. Harper reckoned this truly was hell rising from the depths.

Harper used his rifled butt to knock a bearded cavalryman from his saddle and then the bayonet to finish the job. Turning to assess the company's situation, he was met with a terrific blow to the side of his head. He went down and was momentarily knocked senseless but then realized how lucky he was. In the chaos, he had been struck with the flat, not the edge, of a Union sword. He could feel blood on the side of his head and heard a high-pitched ringing in his ear. Men were down all around him, and yet, the Union forces began to disengage. He quickly saw the reason. General Jones and his 6th Virginia cavalry were approaching the pass along with Brig. General Robertson's 4th North Carolina cavalry.

There was no time to rest and regroup. The order came down the line to continue the march. Harper struggled to gather the company. Wounded were quickly crammed into already full wagons. The dead were left where they lay in the pass, and the nightmarish march continued.

And still, it rained.

The next day, July 5, the remnants of the army made their way down the mountains into Hagerstown, Maryland, and then on to Williamsport astride the Potomac River. The word was that hundreds of wagons of stores and wounded as well as over a thousand men had been captured from the forty-mile train. By the time Harper's 1st Battalion arrived at the river town, they could see for themselves why progress was suddenly halted. The river waters were raging from the extreme rains of the past two days. The rising water, along with destroyed pontoon bridges, prevented any immediate crossing.

Lee ordered substantial defensive works be erected around Williamsport and Falling Waters in anticipation of Meade's army of infantry and artillery. Over the next days, Union cavalry continued to harass pockets of Confederate troops in the vicinity with hit-and-run raids, but Meade's pursuing army was yet to be seen. Reconnaissance patrols were sent out to locate any fordable crossings while a new pontoon bridge was hastily rebuilt. On the 13th, the Army of Northern Virginia made their escape across the Potomac before Meade could launch his attack against the fortifications.

Harper and Lans guided their men fording the subsiding water at Williamsport early on the 14th of July. As one of the last units to cross, they saw the Union army initiating a reconnaissance against the empty entrenchments. They looked at each other with weary but grateful smiles. The army continued to march for the relative safety of Virginia. Orders came down to stay on full alert for an imminent attack. Luckily, it did not come. Small engagements occurred in July at Shepherdstown and Manassas Gap, but Harper's men were not engaged.

Ewell's Corps made its way down the Luray Valley into the Blue Ridge Mountains beyond the reach of the Union army. Companies A and B of the 1st Battalion went into camp for an overdue rest and refit. The condition of both companies was dire, with less than sixty battle-fit and many more wounded and missing. Harper's orders were to reorganize his unit and muster arms and supplies as swiftly as possible.

The relentless rains had mercifully subsided as the summer sun returned in a hot and steamy fashion. It was late afternoon when Harper and Lans finally secured enough food rations for the company. With a section of smoked ham and hardtack, the two collapsed by the center campfire. Just now could they take stock of the disastrous northern campaign and mourn the friends lost on the fields of Pennsylvania and Maryland. Both young men, made prematurely old by an unceasing war, talked of home in Bethania and the keen hunger to return. They speculated just when that would be and what changes had occurred in their long absence…would they even recognize the place? ... Would friends and family recognize them? Afterward, they both slept on the ground. Harper had nightmares of explosions, concussions, and shrieking cannon fire.

***

"Thomas, I'm so worried. Harp didn't come home last night, and he has never done anything like this without letting me know," Susan sobbed. "Please find him, Thomas. Please bring him home." Her instincts screamed that something was wrong, and she had come to Silver and Sadie's door at first light. Her breath was visible in the crisp and frigid January air.

After sleepily answering the door, Silver was now fully alert. His bright eyes darted back and forth as he contemplated what Susan was saying and calculated the possibilities about where his old friend could be. He swiftly recalled the recent trouble with the Flemings and his warning to Harper but hid any expression of concern from the distraught woman before him.

"Now, don't you worry none, Miss Susan. I'm sure there's a good reason he's still gone. With this new railroad business, I bet he's caught up with that big committee," he said reassuringly without feeling the least bit reassured. In fact, Thomas Silver was worried, too. Not letting his concern show, he added, "Why don't you come on in here while I go find him? Sadie will get the coffee on the stove."

"That's right, missus," Sadie answered from behind her husband. She had come into the room upon hearing Susan. "I'll fix us some good hot coffee while the mister goes and finds Mr. Harp."

"Bless you, Sadie," Susan replied tearfully, "but I have to be home in case he returns. Just please find him Thomas. I...I have to get home." With that, she turned and briskly made her way down the stairs of the carriage house. The cold clear rays of the rising winter sun glistened across the frozen yard.

***

The chestnut mare negotiated its way down the icy streets as fast as Silver dared spur her on. He decided first to try the town hall, where he knew the railroad committee had met the day before. Pulling up to the front steps, he could see the building was deserted. Not even Quince had arrived to open up. From there, Silver spurred his horse up Main Street and onto Liberty Street to Harper's office. Using his key to open the office door, he saw the space empty. Silver, getting more agitated by the minute, tried to think where his friend could be. Almost as an afterthought, he went to the rear stable to see if, by chance, Harp's horse was there.

Opening the door, Silver immediately saw Harper on the ground face down. Running over to the still body, he exclaimed, "Harp! Harp! Can you hear me?" Kneeling down, he then carefully rolled Harper over. He could tell Harper was alive, taking shallow breaths. He saw the product of the beating from the night before, which filled him with an instant rage. Raising his friend's swollen and bloody head, he again cried, "Harp! Can you hear me? Oh Harp, Oh Harp!"

"Bring the company forward, Lans. Engage to the front," Harper croaked as in a dream.

"What's that, Harp? What is it?" Silver puzzled.

Harper then opened one eye in a narrow slit and croaked, "Silver, my old friend. I'm really cold… and thirsty."

Silver surveyed the damaged body and shook his head. Besides the lacerations and bruising on Harper's swollen face, he could see the evidence of a severe beating over his entire body. He closed his eyes briefly, then grabbed a saddle blanket from the side of one of the stalls and laid it across Harper. He then grabbed a bucket and dipped it in the trough.

Holding Harper's head and gingerly pouring water on his busted lips, Silver whispered, "You in a bad way, Harp. You need a doctor. Can you hang on while I fetch Doc Bryant?"

Harp nodded, and Silver continued, "I'm going, and I'll be back here with the doctor in no time. Here…take some more water," Silver said while bringing the bucket up again. "Now you think of Susan and Nell and all 'til I get back."

Silver raced to the doctor's house, which fortunately was only a few blocks down on Spruce Street. Hearing the banging on the door, Doctor James Bryant opened it to see Silver, wide-eyed and breathing hard, calling out, "You got to come quick, doctor! It's Harp Clayton! He's in a bad way and needs help!"

"What's the matter? Where is he?" Bryant implored. "Let me grab my bag. We'll take my surrey."

Silver directed the doctor back to the stable, giving him as much information as he could along the way. Entering the freezing enclosure, they could see Harper shaking on the ground. He moaned incoherently as Bryant knelt beside him to check his condition.

The doctor sprang into action and asserted, "We need to get him warm. See if there is another blanket. His left arm is clearly broken, and there are several broken fingers that I can see. I won't know how bad his head is until I can examine him properly. Help me get him up in the carriage. Somebody made damned sure he was bashed thorough and good."

Harper cried out in pain and then blacked out as the two lifted him up and carried him to the carriage. With one free hand, Silver quickly laid a thick saddle blanket on the floorboard. They then attentively laid him in the carriage and covered him with another blanket. As they slowly traveled the three blocks to Bryant's house and office, Harper dreamed of Susan tending her roses in the backyard garden.

***

It had been a full month since Silver had found Harper in the stable. Doctor Bryant had quickly determined that Harper's injuries required medical care beyond his capabilities and had the damaged man transported to the City Hospital. The first two weeks were frightening episodes where Harper was in and out of consciousness. The doctors were most concerned about the extent of traumatic brain injury and internal hemorrhage, yet they were limited in what they could actually do. He was administered morphine, and his head was cushioned with pillows to prevent movement. They had set his broken arm and fingers and stitched several of the deeper lacerations. Fortunately, he had not lost his eyesight; however, he could not hear from his right ear where he had taken a direct blow.

Susan refused to leave his side. She softly read Wordsworth and Emerson to him while he was both awake and asleep. Gingerly she soothed his face with healing lotions and warmed his legs with heated towels. The nursing staff was amazed at her devotion and kidded with her about taking their job.

After several weeks the swelling in his face had started to recede but was still a mass of black and purple bruises. The hospital doctors confirmed his most serious injury was a brain concussion, and Harper could confirm that from the fog and dizziness he was experiencing. His recent memory was essentially gone, and his thoughts were a jumbled mix of offhand observances and distant memories. The prescription was rest and more rest to let his body heal itself. Harper was increasingly more awake and cajoled the staff into letting him return home, where he said he could rest and recover more swiftly.

***

Eli and the others gathered in the Clayton parlor on Fifth Street. "I'll kill whoever did this! By God, this will not go unanswered," Eli raged while striking the air with his fist. "I will…I will…"

"Simmer down some, big brother. That's not helping the matter," cautioned Jacob, "don't want Papa to hear us. Yes, we all want retribution, but first, we have to help the sheriff find out who's responsible. Silver, now think back. Are you sure there was no one around that stable, anywhere on the street?"

Before Silver could answer, Eli reacted, "You expect Bolton to find these scum? You hear that, Tom? Jacob here wants to give it over to the sheriff and his useless office."

"Hold on there, Eli. Jacob's just sayin' we need all the help we can get to hunt down whoever is responsible. They'll make inquiries all over town and maybe see who's talking," Tom added deliberately. Since Harper had been found, Tom had an increasing sense of worry. Fleming's last conversation was fixed in his brain. Surely Fleming wouldn't go this far, he thought…surely not. He instinctively shuttered at the speculation.

Silver, still shaken at the image of Harper on the ground, spoke up. "It was early 'bout seven. The street, everything was deserted. But I damn sure agree with Eli. I want to beat down whoever did this to Harp."

The small man to the side had remained quiet throughout the agitated debate but now slowly stood. At fifty-eight, Lans Hall was still lean and hard; his intense blue eyes still bright. Only a few wrinkles around his eyes and greying hair gave away his years. With a determined voice, he said, "We'll give Bolton and his men a bit of time, just a bit. But, one way or another, we'll rain hell down on whoever did this. That's for Goddamned sure."

The others stared at the small older man, transfixed by his intensity while knowing his lifelong faithfulness to their father and friend. Eli nodded fiercely with affirmation.

CHAPTER 8: EARLY SPRING 1901

A sizable crowd had gathered on 8th Street near Trade in the early March afternoon for the official opening. The sky was a brilliant electric blue with threads of wispy cirrus clouds high above. Mayor Oscar Eaton, most of the town council, and various civic and business leaders were in attendance. Arista Mills, Nissen Wagon Works, and at least a dozen other local companies were represented. The governor's office had even sent a representative to witness what was billed as "the most modern and efficient water reservoir and plant in the South." As promised, with the novel theories of Atlanta engineer John Robeson, the Flemings had completed the build in record time to the delight of the town leaders. The combined towns' population, now estimated at twenty thousand, continued to outpace other cities in the state, and the need for a sufficient water supply was pressing.

Speeches were made from the temporary viewing stand built for the occasion. Mayor Eaton, with his trademark hyperbole, proclaimed the 20th Century as a new age for the city of Winston. He excitedly declared to the crowd, "This astounding new waterworks is proof positive that we are on the threshold of a great renaissance here. Our beloved city is on the move thanks to the unabated demand for the tobacco and textile products that only we can manufacture. Raleigh and Charlotte and the other fine towns in the state stand in awe of the march we are on. And, of course, we will bring our esteemed sister town, Salem, along with us for the ride!" The crowd clapped and cheered with enthusiasm.

The city waterworks supervisor, Randal Shelton, then spoke and showered praise on the Flemings Company and the foresight of the town council. He described the state-of-the-art pumps, boilers, and standpipe that could send up to 5,000 gallons per minute through pipelines extending into the city. Pointing to the giant brick reservoir, he revealed that the massive walls stood close to one hundred feet and had a storage capacity of one million gallons. The new complex was indeed an impressive site, and the people applauded approvingly. Shelton concluded with an introduction of Seth Fleming, saying, "Folks, please hail the visionary for this tremendous undertaking…Mr. Seth Fleming."

Fleming stood, basking in the applause. Looking out over the crowd with a self-satisfied visage, he raised his arms as if a Baptist preacher and proclaimed, "I know many of you had doubts about our claims to complete this magnificent plant and reservoir in record time. I can't say that I blame you…'cause it was a mighty tall order. But my team did it…we did it all in less than eight months…never been done…never." The crowd gave a hearty cheer, and Fleming took it all in. "Now, our beloved town is poised to grow into the future with a trustworthy and certain water supply. And, me, Mathias, and the whole Fleming Company are proud to have made it happen." The angular figure of Seth Fleming was an interesting site up on that platform. He strode mechanically across the stage as he exhorted the people gathered around. "Why, this is just the beginning. The Fleming Company is poised for even greater feats to assist Winston into the 20th century." Fleming was just getting warmed up, and the mayor knew Fleming was intent on grabbing most of the credit for himself. He then pushed the governor's representative forward, which interrupted Seth Fleming's exhortations. Fleming glared at the young man and then the mayor. With an exhaled sound of disgust, he reluctantly retreated to his seat.

Looking a bit sheepish, the young man unrolled a single piece of paper, quietly cleared his throat, and announced, "My name is Horace Byrd, and on behalf of our new Governor Aycock, I want to congratulate the towns of Winston and Salem on this state of the art waterworks. It certainly is a marvel and puts you fine people first in the state with this water pumping capability. The governor sends his most hearty congratulations to all of you, and he most certainly appreciates all your support in the recent election." With that, he quickly sat down as the stage contingent looked around for the next item on the agenda.

Tom and Eleanor Moser took in the scene. He was annoyed that Seth Fleming had told him there was limited room on the platform and that he would have to stand to the side. He thought he should have taken his rightful place on the dais with the other leaders receiving the praise of a grateful town. Tom even felt slightly riled that his father-in-law was not there to see his victory, although he was well aware that Harper continued to recover at home and was not traveling. He was nonetheless elated that, after months of stress and worry, his investment was finally paying off. Watching his wife's smile, he felt vindicated and, yes, victorious. The young man considered his invested stake and the large expected return and smiled. He and Eleanor had already begun making plans for their summer northeast tour. He resolved to approach Seth Fleming about the payout as soon as the festivities were concluded.

Standing back in the crowd, Jacob just shook his head at all the self-toasting and congratulations coming from the speakers' platform. Granted, the project had been completed in remarkably record time given the scope and complexity of a modern water plant. Still, he could not escape the disturbing feeling that shortcuts had been taken and there might just be structural issues with the reservoir. He promised himself that he would take a close designer's look at the walls and foundation during the tours that were promised after the speeches.

***

The silver tray etched with medieval Germanic figures had been in the Bostic family for as long as Susan could remember. She recalled her mother telling her the story of how it had been brought to the Pennsylvania colony by her own grandmother and passed down mother to daughter for four generations. It was a special keepsake to Susan; she had used it over the past six weeks to take Harp his meals in their upstairs bedroom.

Nell was careful not to spill the tray of steaming hot tea and strudel as she climbed the stairs. The weather was warm for early March, and after placing the silver tray on the side table, she pulled the clerestory windows open to let in the fresh morning air. Her father was still sleeping. Harper's visible injuries, broken arm and fingers, lacerations, and bruises had mostly healed since the attack, but his concussed brain continued to present headaches and dizziness on frequent occasions.

While the young girl had grown accustomed to her father sleeping more since he returned home, it still struck her as unusual compared to how she remembered the years past. Her father was always the first to rise in the household, whether to start the fires in the chimney or stove or just to "get a jump on the day," as he often told her with a smile. She sat down at her drawing board near the window to work on her latest creation of nesting bluebirds. Upon hearing his voice, Nell turned from the window.

"Now, this is a fine awakening," Harp declared while shifting up in the bed. "Tea and baker's sweets delivered by my sweetest girl."

Nell blushed and then admonished, "Papa, mama says to keep you from moving around too much. She says you're getting too careless with that walking stick. Here, let me help you to your lounger."

"You and your Mama have been fussin' over me for well over a month, doing every little thing for me," he chided playfully as Nell guided him to the chair. "It's high time I got back to doing for myself. Now, don't get me wrong. I have loved the tender care. However, I need to get back to the normal way of things. Speaking of, is the Colonel here yet? We're supposed to go over the railway doings."

"No, Papa, no one is here of yet this morning," she sighed while thinking of the constant visitors over the past several weeks. There had been a virtual train of callers from the mayor to both sets of Reynolds and Hanes brothers to a number of other well-wishers and plain curiosity seekers. Susan had enlisted Sadie and Silver to mind the front door and parlor to help regulate the comings and goings and maintain some sense of order. Naturally, the family had hovered in force the weeks following the incident until Susan convinced them that Harp's recovery should proceed with fewer attendants. With that, only

Eleanor remained a constant presence and source of strength for both her parents.

The assault of Harper Clayton had been the talk of the town over the past few months, with increasingly wild speculation being spread as to the culprits and cause of the heinous beating. Some said a roving band of hoodlums intent on robbery were the transgressors. Others speculated it was the Klan intent on revenge for Harper's past affrays against them. And, of course, some were sure it was a lawless gang of black men looking to make mayhem against any upstanding white "man of honor."

Certainly, Sheriff Bolton, Police Chief Smalls, and other law enforcement had made multiple visits in their efforts to have Harp assist in identifying the assailants and provide other clues with which to apprehend them. Harp had not revealed Levi Kiger as the perpetrator. He only said that there were four assailants, all hooded. Harp was not totally sure why he withheld this information. His instincts told him to keep this a private matter, yes, a private matter best settled between him and Kiger… and, of course, the Flemings.

To this end, he had asked Silver to arrange for Eli, Jacob, Lans, and Christian Harmon, along with Silver, to join in meeting with him one evening in early March. Knowing who had done this to him was why Harp deliberately excluded Tom from the meeting. While it was hard to conceive that Tom had a hand in the assault, he could not rule it out, especially with Tom's connection to the Flemings and the testy encounter about the reservoir deal he had had with his son-in-law. No purpose was given for the meeting, and all eagerly anticipated what would be discussed. He confided in Susan beforehand

and admonished her to keep the meeting secret, especially from Eleanor.

"I want all of you to just listen and remain quiet until I have said what I want to say," Harp stated evenly when the group had gathered in his study. Jacob noticed that calm intensity in his father's eyes, that look he had seen only a few times in the past, such as at Phillip's funeral. He suspected that something cold and sober was forthcoming.

Harper looked at each man in turn. Then resting his gaze on his oldest son, he began, "I know that all of you have been more than anxious these last weeks to get at the parties responsible for jumping me in the office stable. You are family and my dearest friends, and I am fortified by your loyalty. I've had this time to ruminate on making this right and how to press forward. Should I let the law run its course and put this in the hands of the sheriff and police chief?" At this, Eli began to protest but was stopped short by his father's withering look. Harper continued, "Or should I, bent on revenge, go hell for leather after the culprits? Yes, I do know both the instigator and perpetrator," he said acutely, his dark eyes flashing. At this news, the whole group leaned forward, alert. "I've come to the conclusion that both paths should be employed to get a proper resolution. Here's what I mean. As far as the troublemaker behind all this is concerned, a proper and sound legal case must be made. Christian, my friend, I will need your sharp mind for the law to bring this to the courts. There can be no question as to the outcome. The evidence has to be clear and unassailable." His trusted partner nodded intently while judging to remain silent until Harp had finished.

Harp continued, "Now, as for the assailant, this must be dealt with once and for all. This is nothing short of a blood feud that has stretched out over three decades; too long…much too long." A look of sad remembrance came over his face, and his eyes dulled a bit.

"This was Levi Kiger. He was the attacker along with three of his gang," Harp announced.

Eli jumped up, shouting, "I knew it! I damned well knew it! That scum has tried for you more than once. Well, now he will pay dearly!"

The others quickly joined in shouting over each other. "Kiger and his bunch been makin' trouble for good folks for years," Lans proclaimed. "He can't get away with near killing you, Papa," Jacob contended. Silver jumped in, saying, "I'll finish what I started all those years ago."

The racket of loud voices caused Harper to wince. Holding his hands high, he smiled ruefully and declared, "Now settle down. Susan and Nell will think there's a brawl underway in here. You're right, Silver. Now is the time to finish this…too much water under the bridge with Levi Kiger. And, since there were no other witnesses except his ring of cronies, I can't prove a thing. They all wore hoods, so I don't even know who his accomplices were. So, it's my word against his. There's no other way forward except to end this war now." His mind raced through the dark personal history with Kiger; the burned schoolhouse, the vicious attempt to violate the 1880 election, and the many violent episodes over the years led by the homicidal Klan enforcer.

"But, this is my fight," he intoned, "and I won't have my two sons and best friends caught up in this sorry mess."

Still, on edge, Eli responded quickly. "Like it or not, I'm in on this, and I assume that goes for everybody here. Levi Kiger has to be dealt with harshly and decisively. Otherwise, he'll come after you again. And, I'm not going to have that, plain and simple." He looked around the room as the others nodded in agreement.

Harp saw the serious resolve in all their faces and knew there would be no dissuading any of them. He felt a pull at his heart and was overwhelmed with emotion. Gathering himself, he responded, "No man could have better sons and friends. I am truly fortunate. But, to do this thing right, we have first to force Levi to reveal, with witnesses present, that Seth and Mathias initiated the plan. I want the Flemings, both of them, held to account. You notice that Tom is not here tonight. I can't imagine that he is in any way caught up in this but with his ongoing dealings with those two, I just think it best that we leave Tom outside of this."

"There's no way Tom would have been party to this, Papa," Jacob interjected. "I know you've had words with him and his involvement with the Flemings, but there is just no way he would do something like this."

"I agree," said Eli. "I think he has been used by those two crooks just to get at you."

"In any event, we'll leave Tom clear of this," Harp asserted. "Now let's put our heads together on how best to draw Kiger out on the Flemings…"

***

The railway committee had made progress in the three months since the attack. With Harper in recovery, Colonel Fries had graciously taken the reins, and momentum was building. The chosen Richmond engineering firm had already drawn up plans for the route with detailed individual 20-mile grade sections and material summaries. Bids had been submitted, and companies were selected for grading and blasting through the mountain segments. The arduous process of negotiating the land purchases was well underway. The goal was set for the inaugural run to Roanoke by the fall of 1902, opening a wide swath of new markets to the Winston and Salem merchants. Some on the committee even envisioned some passenger service into the Virginia Blue Ridge area, although others were opposed to the idea as economically unprofitable.

Harper's first official business meeting was the April monthly committee meeting. Silver drove him in the carriage to the town hall. Assisting him down from the carriage, Silver then stepped back, astute enough to know that Harp wanted no other help in making his way into the building. With a nod, Harper climbed the steps with a walking stick in hand, knowing Silver would be there upon his return. Entering the meeting room, Harper was met with enthusiastic applause.

"Welcome back, Clayton," boomed the Colonel. "I knew you couldn't stay away too long. Had to make sure things were ship-shape, eh?" he joshed while continuing the banter. "Why, I was recently telling these boys that what we needed was some good lawyering combined with sharp business acumen. Know anybody that fits that description?" the stout man teased.

"Glad to have you back, old man," added Will Reynolds. "With the Colonel in charge, this whole thing has gone completely off the rails…if you'll pardon the pun." Reynolds then joined in the laughter at his own joke. "Yes, it sure is grand to have a professional again at the end of the table."

"Alright, alright. That's quite enough," Fries returned. "My pride is now wounded most grievously, and I am going to need some boosting from some of you. You there, Nissen. You'll stand by me, won't you? Tell these boys how wonderfully smart and efficacious I am," he said with a broad smile. The older man just shook his head. "No? Well, then, I suggest we call this meeting to order and get on with it."

The session lasted over two hours as Harper reacquainted himself with the project and issues at hand. Under the supervision of Ludlow, the city engineer, reports made by the town's procurement agents covered the cost and supply of steel rail, creosote ties, and other required materials. For Harper, it all began to jumble together in a blurry myriad of details. By the end, he was feeling quite weak, and his head was throbbing. Making his goodbyes, he walked deliberately to his carriage, where Silver was holding a water bucket up to his horse. Harper would have preferred to make straight for home, but he had agreed to meet Eli in town for dinner.

"Harp, you have the look of a man that needs a lay down," Silver chided. "Should I go for 5th Street, or are you still set on dinner with Eli?"

"I just need something to eat. Take me to Besset's, if you will. Eli should already be there. I'll have a pot of your favorite stew and some soda water sent out to you," he said, knowing

Silver could not join them in the eatery. Harper let his friend help him up into the carriage and then eased his back on the worn leather seat back as the horse pulled forward.

Eli was indeed waiting for his father at the eatery that, as usual, was doing a brisk business on a Wednesday. Eli, seated at a table toward the back, was looking away and didn't see Harper at first. Harper noticed his son's dark countenance, a familiar look for him these days. He briefly questioned his decision to reveal the identities of those responsible for the attack to his son and the others. "Why have I overburdened those I love with this trouble," he thought. "Because simply, I can't do it alone. I need their strength, their abetment."

"Sorry to keep you waiting. Those boys sure do like to talk," he said with a faint smile as he approached the table. "So, what's good today?"

At that, Eli brightened a bit and responded, "Well, Massie's bragging about her pork tenderloin with stewed potatoes and cabbage. Sounds pretty tasty and filling to me." He stood up to give his father a quick embrace, then instantly felt a bit abashed at the gesture of intimacy.

"That'll do me just fine," Harper replied while taking the seat opposite Eli at the little square table. "Let's have her send some of the same out to Silver; oh, and a bottle of soda water, too."

Eli gave the order to the proprietor and promptly sat back down. "I have to say you look absolutely sold out. How's your head today? Are you having more dizzy spells?"

Harper regarded his oldest son, seeing an earlier cast of himself. He then replied, "Oh, it's nothing to write home about, and don't go telling your mother anything. She's already beside herself worrying about me. I'll go rest at home after dinner." Wanting to change the subject, he then inquired, "How're your seedlings coming along? Won't be long before they go in the ground, right? I guess you got plenty of help with the planting."

"I'd say just about all of the seedlings are up and looking spry," Eli replied, eyes now bright. "We'll get 'em in the ground in a couple more weeks. You know I'm filling out those twenty additional acres by the stream this season. James and Noah will be right there with me this year, and Jacob said he'd come over for at least a few days, that is, if he can get away from the West End. Plus, I've got Silver's chums from the north side of town coming out for day work. I gotta say they always act glad to have the work, and they show it by staying on the job 'til it's done. I'm just ready to get back to the green side of farming," he said with a chuckle.

Eli paused, quickly scanning the room, and then leaned in, whispering, "Kiger's been throwing money around the taverns, been loud and proud, and gettin' in people's faces. Lans has some boys watching and listening. It won't be long before we move." The younger man's eyes flashed fire, and Harper was startled at his abrupt intensity.

He, too, glanced around the room and advised, "No more talk here, but I want to know before any action is taken. You tell Lans and Silver that I want to be kept abreast of things."

Father and son then moved on to more mundane goings on, such as the warm early spring weather and the new season's prices at the feed and seed store. When their food arrived, they both ate heartily without conversation. Eli then insisted on paying the bill over Harper's objections. Leaving the little restaurant, Eli greeted Silver with a grin and the tip of the hat. "Looks like you were quite pleased with Massie's pork tenderloin as well, Silver."

"That's the truth, Eli. I thank you both for the lunch," Silver declared while wiping his hands with the towel on the carriage's front seat.

Looking up and down the street, Eli drew nearer to Silver and said in a low voice, "I told him about Kiger shootin' his mouth off. Time is near."

Silver's face set hard, and he replied swiftly, "Oh yes. His time is comin'."

Hearing this, Harper swiftly countered, "Not here on the street. Tell the others we need to get together. I want to know what's in the air and all that's planned before anything goes forward."

Both men nodded in agreement without speaking. Eli then departed for Bodenhamer's to pick up some iron fasteners and other implements for his largest plow before making the trip back to Bethania. Harper climbed into the carriage, and Silver clicked the horse forward to 5th Street. He helped Harper descend to the house and made sure he was good on the steps before taking the rig on to the carriage house and his home above. After unhitching the horse and giving him water and a quick brushing, Silver walked out into the afternoon sun without noticing the warmth. He wondered what the future held.

Harper entered the house to find it quiet. Only the soft, distinctive ticking of the Gustav Becker mantel clock in the parlor could be heard. He vaguely remembered that Susan, Nell, Maria, and little Susannah had planned a visit in the afternoon to Henry Simmons, the commercial horticulturist. Harper smiled as he thought of Susan buying seeds and perennial plants from a merchant. My Bethania farm girl has gone over to the city, no doubt, he thought.

Suddenly, he felt wholly exhausted. His stamina was yet lacking. Tossing his fedora on the front hall table, Harper headed straight to the sun porch and his favorite cushioned wicker chair. Easing down, he spied a family of purple finches feasting on early seeds from the big mulberry bush beside the house. He considered the thought of how finches, more than most other species, enjoyed their communal meals. The March afternoon was peaceful and mild, and he decided to rest his eyes for a moment.

***

Fight for Bridge at Bachelor's Creek

The railroad bridge across Bachelor's Creek was an impressive wooden structure built in the 1840s to give the people of New Bern access to western Craven County and beyond. Taking it would not be easy, and Company B of the 1st NC Battalion was assigned the task. After three years of hostilities, the men were worn down and ever homesick, longing for their families and an end to the fight. They were battle-tested, however, and Captain Harper Clayton was sure they would again rise to the challenge. He asked for volunteers to lead the attack across the bridge. Not surprisingly, 1st Lieutenant Lans Hall and his men were the first to do so.

In the mid-winter of 1864, the battalion, as part of Hoke's Brigade's mostly North Carolina troops, had marched from the killing fields of Virginia to eastern North Carolina with the objective of retaking the town of New Bern on the Neuse River. For almost two years, the burg and northeastern part of the state had been occupied by Yankee troops[*], now commanded by Brigadier Innis Palmer. General Lee determined that recapturing New Bern and expelling the Yankees from North Carolina would facilitate the flow of supplies to his starving army as well as boost morale in the Old North State.

With the intelligence of the Southern troop movement, Palmer had reinforced the pickets at the bridge with a company of infantry and a single artillery battery from the New York 32nd Infantry Regiment. Mid-day on February 1, the NC 21st Regiment arrived on the field and began to form a battle line behind the bare tree line just out of range of the Union battery. Harper and the men could see the reinforced picket line positioned on either side of the bridge as well as around a miller's block-house about seventy-five yards to the rear. With surprise out of the question, the young commander knew that speed and ferocity would be critical in order to take the bridge.

"Lans, the regiment will advance and fire across the whole line to engage the enemy," Harper asserted while looking directly into Lans' charged blue eyes. "You have to get across that bridge like a shot to establish a foothold on the other side. The rest of the company will be on the run to shore up your

---

[*] *Major General Ambrose Burnside, the disgraced Union commander at Fredericksburg, had captured the area with his successful North Carolina Expedition in March 1862.*

155

position. With success, the whole regiment will follow and on to New Bern. May God be with you, my friend," he said firmly, grabbing the smaller man's shoulder.

"We'll do it. We'll be over that bridge in no time, so don't you dawdle with the other boys," Lans replied with a slight smile.

Then with a brisk salute, Lans rejoined his squad of volunteers. Harper saw him walking among his men, encouraging each one, and thought how favored he was to have Lans at his side.

The afternoon dragged on as more of the brigade came up. Snipers on both sides traded fire, each targeting officers or foolishly exposed riflemen. Harp saw couriers dashing to and from Hoke's hastily set up field headquarters. "We need to go now," Harp anxiously thought. "We're just giving the Yanks more time to reinforce. Now, damn it!" Suddenly, the whole 21st Regiment opened fire all along the line forcing the Union troops across the creek to hunker down. Within seconds, Lans led his men to the bridge and over, screaming like banshees.

Harper raised his pistol, shouted, "Charge battalion!" and ran to the bridge. As he reached the edge of the creek, he saw several of Lans' men falling around him. From then on, it was chaos of rifle fire, smoke, and screaming. Minie balls flew past his head as he found the bridge and pressed forward. The fire was so heavy that Harper initially thought that the whole Yankee force was zeroed in on his 1st NC. Men were down, some moving, some still. But for a fleeting moment, as the momentum slowed, he thought the attack would fail. The troops kept moving, and some reached the end of the bridge and began to take a position to fire and reload. Both sides brought artillery to bear as the fight began to grow. Harper's men were now all across the bridge, and he looked to the rear to see if the regiment was pressing the attack. Sure enough, the first two companies were moving onto the bridge in rapid advance.

"Hold fast. The whole regiment is coming up," he yelled to no one in particular.

The fire continued steadily for several volleys. To Harp's surprise, the Union troops began to retire, falling back to the blockhouse. He began reforming the company to push on the house when a courier came running up. "Compliments from General Hoke, sir. But, you are to hold your position and secure the bridge."

Harp then nodded, sending the young boy back to the regimental staff on the run. He was not a little satisfied with holding in place. The attack across the bridge had been brief but bloody. Already the wounded were being attended to. He located Lans. Harp marveled at the intense young man as he directed his troops into a defense line around the bridge.

"It's a mistake not to press the attack while they are reeling," Lans shouted above the din.

"You're probably right, Lans, but Hoke's orders were clear," Harp replied. "Get the boys ready to receive fire. We're vulnerable here against the creek and without cover."

"Sapp and Hester are dead. Sam Ingram is shot through the lungs, and several others are bad," Lans said without emotion.

"Your men did their duty, Lans. They went forward just like they'd done before. The honor is theirs," Harp said clearly and evenly.

They both took in the late afternoon scene. Men were down around them, and at least thirty Yankees lay dead or wounded on the field. Smoke from the firefight hung close to the ground creating an odd spectral feel. Harp began to look for the company sergeants to organize the line. But, by nightfall, it was clear that the Union troops had retreated to the safety of New Bern. Hoke ordered the brigade forward, and over one hundred federal troops that got lost in the dense pine forest were taken as prisoners.

They continued the march through the night along the Neuse River pike until they reached the outer New Bern fortifications. There it was clear that the other Southern attacks planned had not been carried out, and the whole of the town remained heavily fortified. Hoke ordered a halt to the offensive and for the brigade to entrench, although there was little chance of General Palmer abandoning the advantage by vacating his heavy defenses.

At this development, Harp was struck with an unusual wave of cynicism. He wondered if anything really mattered at all now. Was the sacrifice worth it? Would this God-forsaken war ever end? Bringing himself up with a start, he gave Company B the required orders and went off searching for General Hoke.

The battalion remained in position at New Bern for three days before retreating westward behind the protection of the many creeks and marshes in the surrounding area. It was a very low time for the company and Harp as well. He thought engaging the enemy for the first time in their home state would inspire the men. It was just the opposite. Being this close to home without being able to return to their families and farms in addition to the ongoing campaigning with no end in sight had a dreadful effect.

The coastal winter weather was cold, wet, and miserable. For the first time, desertions became a problem throughout all the Southern units, 1st NC Battalion included. To make matters worse, the battalion was assigned the onerous duty of patrolling the rear to pursue and catch deserters from the ranks as well as provost guard duty. It was a commission that both Harp and Lans detested, and it reinforced the dispiriting time for the battalion.

It was a frigid morning, and Harp was compiling the muster roll for February as well as writing a summary of Company B's winter campaign. Seated by the morning fire with a makeshift writing desk on his lap, he winced when recognizing how spare the company ranks were now. The men lost from battle and sickness totaled more than half the rank. The number available for duty was now under fifty. He thought back to the summer campaigns in Virginia when the company was one hundred and forty strong and full of fight and spirit. It was now but a shadow of those times, and he closed his tired eyes at the realization.

The commotion of galloping riders abruptly brought him out of his musings. Sergeant Nissen dismounted quickly and saluted while still approaching. "A couple of deserters, sir, holed up in a barn off the Goldsboro Road. I left Hastings and Montgomery on guard. What are your orders, sir?" the slim twenty-five-year-old inquired.

"Orders, Sergeant? Our orders are to apprehend any and all deserters… without incident if possible." The words sounded harsh, harsher than Harp intended. "See if you can talk those boys into submitting. Tell 'em we ain't hanging deserters." Not now, anyways, he thought.

"Yes, sir!" Nissen responded and hastily ran his horse a few yards before remounting and leading his men from the camp. An eddy of brown dust swirled and followed the band across the dead winter meadow.

Between patrols and provost guards, the company was stretched fully and showing the strain. Harp briefly wondered how long he could keep his own men in the ranks and present for duty. He prayed that General Hoke would change his orders and put the battalion back in the line. There were the usual rumors coming out of the general staff headquarters that changes were afoot. Harp had long understood that most of the staff rumors were just hearsay and rarely resulted in active orders. Still, his intuition told him that something significant was in the works.

***

An insistent tug at his coat sleeve interrupted the dream, and Harp first thought it was Sergeant Nissen again wanting orders. Harp then woke with a start, only to see little Susannah looking up at him with a curious smile.

"Oh, my little Suzy, you are an angel to behold," he declared. He could always see Phillip in the little girl's smile. Gently tossing the child up above his head and then catching her brought uncontrolled laughter. It filled Harp with a wonderful feeling, and he forced the unsettled dream into the past.

"There you are, and I see that Suzy found your secret hideout," Susan beamed as she came onto the porch seeing her husband with his little granddaughter. "It's got to be chilly out here. Now come inside for hot tea and honey."

Harp just smiled at the mention of his wife's go-to remedy for almost everything and everybody. "I was resting a bit, and little Suzy here found me, didn't you, sweetheart?" he said while holding her gently. "What treasures did you find for the garden, Sudie?"

"Oh, do come see! Mr. Simmons has brought in the most wonderful perennials from down east. We bought pink coneflowers, a mix of water lilies for the little rock pond, and several colors of azaleas. We filled up the carriage for the ride home," she laughed. "Nell is over the moon and is out in the garden with Maria organizing where each specimen will go."

"Well, let's go see these specimens and see if anything else will fit in the garden," he winked at the little girl up in his arms.

The late afternoon sun was bright as it nudged the treetops creating elongated shadows across the yard. From the top of the backstairs, Harp saw the girls in the early spring garden bending low to arrange the new plants. He walked down the steps holding to the wrought-iron rail with one hand while holding Susannah in the other. Just as he reached the ground, Lans Hall came around the side of the house, a determined look on his face. Handing the little girl to Susan, he knew what that look meant.

"I'll be only a minute, Sudie," he quickly said.

"I'll help the girls finish laying out the plants," she confided. "Hello there, Lans. How are Lucia and Lucas these days? I haven't seen them in ages, it seems."

"Hi yourself, Susan. You're looking well", he responded with his easy smile. "Lucia and Lucas are doing fair to middling. We're all looking to the springtime after this winter we've had."

With that, Lans and Harp retreated to the side of the house out of earshot of the others. "I guess you've heard about Kiger; how he's throwing money around and shootin' his mouth off about his recent good fortune…just a matter of time before he's full of drink and brags about his hateful conquest. We need to grab him now while we can, Harp, and force him to give up the Flemings."

Harp closed his eyes and rubbed his hand over his face. "Is this the right course, Lans? Should we bring evil to evil? Our lives have seen so much calamity, you and me. You know what? I just dreamed about the bloodshed on Bachelor's Creek bridge all those years ago. Is this our ultimate fate, Lans, to wage war against an enemy unabated? Is this God's issue for us?"

Lans stared at his old friend for a moment before responding. "I'm afraid it is. The way I see it is that this world has had darkness in it since the fall... always has. There are those in the world that breed misery and suffering and those that are here to try to wash it away. And if that means we have to wreck the breeders to accomplish this, then that's the way it has to be. Simple as that."

Harp envied his friend's moral clarity, black or white, a total absence of grey. His own was cursed to be more layered, he mused, with a few more shades of grey determining right versus wrong. Was man essentially a brute capable of fantastic inhumanity? Or, was he more a fallen angel, prone to sin but perpetually seeking redemption?

Shaking his head, Harp refocused on Lans and disclosed, "I have my doubts, friend. I have doubts. Listen. I have spoken with Eli and Silver and want to meet again to discuss the matter."

***

A full moon coincided with the vernal equinox in 1901. This meant that Easter would be celebrated in early April. Home Moravian church on the square in Salem was celebrating its 140th anniversary with weeklong musical services and other observances. Augsburg Lutheran, on the northwest corner of 4th and Spruce streets in Winston, was a growing young church of only ten years and also well prepared for the Easter festivities. Harp and Susan, along with Tom and Eleanor, were part of the forty-six founding members. Claytons were long-time Lutherans going back to their heritage in southern Germany. After immigrating to the Pennsylvania colony in the mid-1700s, the Claytons had then journeyed south to settle the verdant piedmont area of north central North Carolina along with the Moravian brethren.

Eleanor and Tom exited the Good Friday service and raised their hands simultaneously to shield the bright sunshine from their eyes. Along with Tee, they descended the granite steps to 4th Street, where Harp, Susan, Nell, and Maria, holding little Susannah, were waiting.

"Wasn't the service fine, El?" Susan was enthused as she pulled her daughter toward her. "And Reverend Lutz's sermon on the cross and Christ's atonement was simply uplifting."

Eleanor smiled at her mother and replied, "Oh, indeed. The pastor does wonderful work. We are blessed at our little church to hear the word of God delivered so capably." With that, she quickly caught Tom's apprehensive look as he turned from the group. Eleanor had been troubled these past months as she watched her husband and father grow increasingly distant. She had tried to understand this development with Tom, but he was evasive by vaguely referencing the two's argument about the reservoir investment months ago. Instinctively, she knew it ran deeper than that. In fact, Tom had been on edge and in a dark mood since the Flemings had not yet delivered on their promises with the reservoir payout.

Trying to bridge the gap, she inquired, "Papa, has Tom told you about his and Tee's photo explorations? They've become quite the natural scientists in capturing striking images of birds and other animals around the city."

Harper turned to his daughter and, with a bemused look, replied, "Oh? I didn't know you boys were interested in photography. I hear the advancements have been extraordinary over the past few years."

"Yes, I purchased a folding box camera from the Eastman Company a few months back," Tom offered rather laconically. "And I just got what's called a Brownie Box for Tee. It's pretty amazing how Eastman has made the process more practical. Instead of the old tintypes and glass plates, the images are captured on a roll of flexible film that's coated with a light-sensitive emulsion. This makes it much easier to take photos almost anywhere. Henry Leinbach over on 4 ½ Street has shown me the film developing process, and I've set up what they call a "dark room" in our basement to develop our films."

Tee interjected, "It's amazing, Grandpa! I've taken pictures of all the birds in our backyard; cardinals, bluebirds, baby wrens in their nest, and even a red-tail hawk," the boy exclaimed enthusiastically. "Nell, let's put my photographs with your drawings, and we'll have a show for sure."

Nell smiled in agreement. "I think you may love the birds and nature as much as I do. Have you seen any redheaded woodpeckers yet this spring? Or should I say, have you heard any of that clamorous bunch?"

"Well, Tee, I sure would like to see your photographs, especially that hawk," Harper replied to the boy with a warm smile. "What a wonder to bring your imagination to life. And ol' Linebach is just the person to show you the ropes. He is, without a doubt, the most renowned photographer in the region. Did you know that he is the one that made that world-famous photo of those Siamese twin boys up there in Surry County? Yessir, he's got a big reputation in the photography world."

Tom jumped in, saying, "Linebach is mainly a portrait man, and he's good with that. But, I'm going to get out in this world and photograph more important things like new inventions and the people at work who invent them. I'm going to go to the big events, like the launch of that new motorized carriage down in Raleigh. While I'm there, I'll photograph the new Governor's house and other sites. Why, I'll bring this world to life for folks, I'll, uh, I'll…" Tom's voice trailed off as he turned away, looking down Spruce Street.

Harper met Eleanor's anxious gaze and frowned. He knew Tom wanted to stand tall in front of his wife and son. Harper sighed and actually felt sorry for the young man whose desire for riches and reputation weighed much too heavily on his soul. He also knew Tom was deeply distraught about not yet receiving any return on the investment in the reservoir. Yet Harper sensed there was more to Tom's disquiet and melancholy. He abruptly decided to privately approach Eleanor about the matter.

Susan then interrupted his contemplation by reminding everyone about Easter dinner. She said, "Now, let's all go on over to the house for dinner. Blanche will have things coming out. There's a nice country ham and potato salad and other goodies. It's just us this Easter. You know, Eli has been down lately with his back after that fall off his horse, so he and Kat and the little ones will be at the farm. And, of course, Jacob is away up in New York exploring some new architectural marvel to bring this way."

"There's nothing better than Blanche's Easter ham, right Tee?" Eleanor beamed at her only child.

"Yes, let's run all the way. I'm starving," exclaimed the boy while pulling Nell's hand.

Nell let Tee drag her a few yards and then pulled him back. "You know I can't keep up with you, Tee, especially with these Sunday shoes on," she chided.

As the group began to move forward, Tom quickly raised his hands and said, "Y'all go on. I'm not feeling much like dinner. Besides, I have to finish developing the rolls of film I took of the Winston fire team."

Masking her surprise, Eleanor looked at her husband and softly inquired, "Are you sure, dear?"

"Quite sure. Uh, have a nice dinner, everyone," he replied abruptly while cutting a glance to Harper and Susan. With that, he began to walk in the opposite direction.

Susan called after him, "I'll send a plate home with El for you."

Tom threw up his arm without turning. Harper, Susan, and Eleanor just looked at one another, silent. After a moment, they turned to follow Tee, Nell, and Maria toward home.

Above them in the budding red maples along 4th Street, a pair of Carolina chickadees pitched in with their distinctive four-note *fee-bee-fee-bay* whistle.

CHAPTER 9: SPRING 1901

The imposing glasshouse was well along in its construction. Situated on an open meadow north of the Bronx River, the conservatory was envisioned as an iconic piece of the recently opened New York Botanical Gardens. Its ornate Victorian design was inspired by the Palm House at the Royal Botanic Gardens at Kew and London's magnificent Crystal Palace. It was, in turn, to be Jacob's inspiration for his own planned glasshouse conservatory at the new West End Hotel in Winston. While his design was, of course, on a much smaller scale, he hoped to incorporate the new steel and glass material model as well as some of the elaborate ornamentation and copper flora designs decorating the dome's cupola and cornices.

Jacob stood alone in the muddy field and shivered, more from excitement than the cold. The brilliant spring sun shone through the recently installed large roof glass panels creating checkered prisms of color along the ground. The young man was certain that a similar glasshouse, with its striking geometric design, would help insure a reputation of Victorian elegance for the West End hotel. He had to admit to himself that he was more than a little eager to further his own reputation as well.

While in the city for more than a week, he had just now ventured north to the botanical gardens. He had already visited the Victoria Hotel in the city to see firsthand its conservatory, but most of his time had been consumed in consulting with his old chums at McKim, Mead, and White, deliberating the latest developments in structural steel design and fire suppression systems. Silas Gabriel and Robb Turner were friends from Jacob's earlier time at the firm. Silas was a true New Yorker, born and bred in Brooklyn Heights. He was solid, athletic, and quite good-looking, with thick copper hair and large brown eyes. He had been a light heavyweight boxer at Columbia but had put on more than a few pounds since those days in training. Still, Silas was obviously a young man to have in one's corner if there was trouble. Robb (nee Robert) Turner, on the other hand, was rather scrawny. The son of a saloon owner in Baltimore, he was simply brilliant and had gone to Harvard to study law but soon fell in love with architectural design and all its mathematical creativity. Jacob had hit it off with both young men during his two-year stint at McKim.

Then there was Anika. Anika Van Dijk was a Dutch beauty, tall and lithe with pure light blue eyes and long ash blonde hair. She had joined MM&W not long after Jacob departed for North Carolina in 1898 and quickly became an influential member of the firm. For a woman to rise to the position of senior architect and rank on par with men was quite unique in the early 20th-century culture of patriarchal dominance. Her obvious intelligence and confident manner quickly made her an effective partner as well as a formidable foe.

And Jacob was instantly and utterly love-struck. Beyond his racing heart and tingling nerves when in her presence, Jacob felt a strange familiarity as if they had already met and knew each other. Yet, he knew this was not possible since he had never seen her before this time in New York. It was a connection that he wanted to believe she felt as well. What other explanation could there be for her lingering gazes, her light brushes against his arm, or her easy laughter at his rather clumsy attempts at humor?

Over the course of the week, he increasingly was finding it hard to focus on the task at hand, with his attraction to Anika only intensifying day by day. He winced when he recalled Silas and Robb taking him aside after a group presentation on the new skyscraper design trend. With a good-natured poke in the ribs, Silas said, "Old pal, I do believe you are enraptured with our sweet Anika."

"Why, what do you...uh, is it so obvious, Silas?" Jacob sheepishly replied.

"Oh yes. Oh yes, my friend," Robb chimed in. "And, who can blame you? She is Aphrodite, come back to tempt us all. But let me be clear, she has made it quite plain to all the fellows here that she will not mix business and pleasure, so, alas, we poor mortals are fated to merely gaze upon her beauty."

Jacob stared at his former co-worker and smiled. "A bit theatric, wouldn't you say, Turner, or are *you* so smitten that you only quote the classics these days?" At this, all three burst out laughing, causing the others across the room to look their way with puzzled expressions.

He was jolted out of his reverie with the words, "She's a beauty, is she not?" asked the gentleman with the stylish high hat and cane. In his Anika daydream, he had not noticed the small group of well-heeled New Yorkers coming across the meadow.

"She certainly is that, sir," Jacob exclaimed, quickly recovering his focus on the extraordinary glasshouse.

"Nathaniel Britton," said the older man offering his hand in introduction.

"Jacob Clayton, sir; of, uh, Winston, North Carolina. And, I must say that your reputation as our finest botanist precedes you, sir."

"Well, I'm just a person who has always been fascinated by plants. And I'm fortunate enough to have made my living studying them," Britton said modestly. "This conservatory is just a marvel, isn't it?" he beamed while redirecting their attention back to the glasshouse. "It will house, most eloquently, I might add, thousands of common and rare species from all over the world's southern climes; African Fever trees, Bromeliads from the Amazon rain forest, and countless more. Now, accessible to all Americans!"

The eminent botanist's enthusiasm was clear, and Jacob could not but feel happy for him. He added, "your vision for the gardens and this conservatory do you honor, and it has been my great pleasure to make your acquaintance."

Britton was obviously enjoying the encounter with the young Southerner. He inquired brightly, "What brings you to New York, uh, Jacob, is it?"

"Yes, sir, Jacob Clayton. I design buildings, and I am looking for inspiration for a glasshouse I am planning to adjoin a new hotel in Winston."

"Well, then, I must introduce you to the man of the hour, our architect, Robert Gibson, who is the lead architect with Lord & Burnham," he said while extending his arm toward the party. "Bob, come and meet my new young friend Jacob, a designer of buildings from Carolina. He's here on this fine morning to admire your work and just maybe to offer some improvements," Britton announced playfully.

Gibson smiled and approached the two. "I'm only certain of one thing, and that is this glasshouse can be improved upon. What say you, young man?"

"Oh, oh no, sir. It is the perfect design," Jacob stammered as he felt his face becoming flush. "It is an inspiration for all designers," he exclaimed while feeling quite embarrassed at his rather common praise.

Noticing Jacob's discomfort, Gibson gently admonished, "No design is ever perfect. Perfection is a hopeless standard that we will never achieve. There is always some facet of our creations, no matter how small, that can be further optimized. Now see the sunlight coming through the dome panels?" he said in a matter-of-fact manner. "By changing the panel geometry from rectangles to hexagons, I could have filtered more of the sun to create a more even temperature under the dome and enhance the interior eco-climate. But that will be for another time, another design. But I will say that design optimization is a noble effort; however, chasing perfection is a fool's errand. That is my advice to you, from one creator to another," Gibson said with a flourish and continued walking toward the conservatory.

"Goodbye, young Clayton," Britton said with a broad smile. "May all your designs be just short of perfect!" the botanist said with good humor.

The small group continued onward to the glasshouse, leaving Jacob alone again in the field. He felt fortunate to have had such an amazing encounter and, with a spring in his step, made his way down to the Bronx River Avenue to hire a carriage for the trip down to Manhattan.

High overhead, a broad-winged hawk soared gracefully over the greening landscape.

***

Silas, Rob, and the other young architects, printmakers, and various staff promised Jacob a night of frivolity and fun on his last night in the city. Throughout the week, an array of reserved and restrained dinners and even a chamber concert filled the evenings. Earlier in the week, founder Stanford White had joined the group for the string concerto at the Lafayette Hotel, and afterward, Jacob had unabashedly engaged the older man on modern building design and, specifically, the backstory of White's design for the new Madison Square Garden entertainment center on 34th Street.

His last night was a night to remember or one to expunge from one's memory, depending on one's perspective. Jacob met up with the group at the Lafayette for toasts to kick off the planned affair. Silas then proclaimed that they would all proceed to the Haymarket, the infamous dancehall in the Tenderloin District on West 30th Street and 6th Avenue. Jacob had heard tales of the Haymarket, its raucous bands, high-kicking saloon girls, and heaven indeed for prostitutes and pickpockets. Against his better judgment, the young Southerner reluctantly agreed. With Anika agreeing to join in, the deal was done. Anika had brought her close friend and apartment mate, Valerie. Val Ryan had come to the city from Albany to become a professional singer and was a beauty in her own right with auburn hair, hazel-green eyes, and a pale rose-pink complexion. Valerie lived in the same hotel apartment as Anika, the Tremont. They had apparently become fast friends, although Valerie was easily five years Anika's junior.

The Haymarket was in full swing by the time they arrived. The group waded into the packed throng of gentlemen and ladies, respectable and otherwise. The clouds of cigar smoke burned the eyes and gave the hall an overwhelming and surreal sensation along with the clamorous row. Circling the main hall was a second-floor veranda of smaller rooms, all suggestively shrouded in velvet. Jacob could only imagine what went on behind those curtains.

Some of the group were already elbowing their way through the crowd toward the bar for drinks. Jacob, feeling unusually courageous, linked his arm with Anika's and put his mouth close to her ear to be heard.

"Stay close to me," he virtually yelled. "This madness looks as if a lady could be easily compromised."

Anika tilted her head to look at Jacob's resolute expression and confided, "I've seen it all before. Remember, I come from Amsterdam, where this kind of vice and debauchery is quite abundant." With an easy smile, she continued, "But sir, your offer as *mon chevalier* is quite charming and most welcome." With that, she squeezed Jacob's arm tight against her side. Jacob felt an electric charge flow through his body and knew his role as knight protector was set for the evening.

Beaming, Silas came toward them with two giant bottles of champagne held high, one in each hand. Jacob noticed the big man's tie was askew and shirt open at the neck. Behind him trailed several of the others carrying at least a dozen tall champagne glasses. Securing a small round table, Silas put both bottles down and went to work cutting the foil and twisting the wire loose from the oversized corks. Holding one bottle aloft, he slowly pressured the cork upward. The cork exploded into the thick air with an emphatic report easily heard above the noise. The group and onlookers cheered in unison.

Silas quickly put his mouth to the bottle to catch the bubbly overflow. Then with arms wide and with great demonstration, he scanned his company and announced, "Fill your glasses, gents and, of course, our lovely ladies. We are here to fete our Southern friend and confidant," he cried with considerable elan. "He will be bringing our Yankee sophistication and a new century of thinking to rural burgs South and will most certainly continue to cherish his most upright friends here in New York. To Master Clayton and the future!"

"Master Clayton!" the group shouted together. Jacob could feel his face redden as he held his glass upward in response while feeling Anika's eyes on him.

Glasses were filled and refilled, then filled again. The raucous revelry within the Haymarket continued to build. Painted ladies performed the can-can on a crowded stage with more than a little leg revealed to the appreciative audience. Of course, Silas, with Robb in tow, positioned themselves closest to the stage and led the audience in cheers.

Jacob, still with Anika and Valerie, laughed and enjoyed the show from a distance. "Well, Master Clayton, do you believe Val and I should take our turn on the stage next and perform the can-can?" she suggested playfully while smiling at her friend.

Before Jacob could respond, a raw voice with a ragged edge answered, "There's no doubt you should, pretty. And, you should pull those fine petticoats nice and high for me and my boys here." Jacob turned to see a gigantic brute of a man, his massive head just inches from Anika's face. Along with him were two hirsute and disheveled men, both leering at the unnerved young ladies with obvious bad intent.

Instinctively, Jacob pushed his way between Anika and the huge fellow and was instantly met with the stench of stale onions and tobacco. Standing only to the man's shoulders, Jacob swallowed his fear and smiled, saying, "I can understand your mistake, sir. You see, my girl doesn't know the can-can as she was only jesting me. We'll just move to the other side of the hall so you and your mates can have an unencumbered view of the show."

Reaching for Anika and Valerie, Jacob began to move away. With a snort, the giant laughed harshly, "Not so fast, little man. I say she wants to dance, and I say she dances for me right on the spot."

One of the other men crowed in a singsong Irish brogue, "Yessir, Big Finn. She sure looks like she's wantin' to dance right here, right now. How can she resist ya?" Then both sidemen laughed in disturbing high-pitched tones.

Both women were now terrified and looked around for help. Silas and the others were still fixed on the entertainment on stage, a good space away.

Jacob swiftly weighed his options to protect the young ladies and, hopefully, without getting himself killed in the process. He again attempted to politely reason his way out. "Big Finn, sir, we're surely in your way here. Let me buy you and your chums a whiskey, and we'll be on our way."

A dark countenance came over the man and, with a cruel laugh, shouted, "I have a drink. It's a dance I want." His enormous hand then reached over Jacob's shoulder, wildly grabbing at Anika and intending to shove him aside. Without hesitating, Jacob brought his knee up hard into the enormous man's groin. Caught unawares, Big Finn bent forward and swung blindly for Jacob's head. The smaller man easily sidestepped the blow and landed a fist in the big man's fleshly throat, sending him to the floor sputtering. His father's advice came to mind, "Avoid a fight if you can but if not, make it count and end it early." He then proceeded to kick the giant in the head and ribs.

Jacob heard Anika's warning scream but not before the two other thugs tackled him to the ground and began raining blows on him. Jacob was quickly overcome by what felt like metal pipes against his head and shoulders. Within a moment, however, both hoodlums were yanked off of him, with expressions of fear and surprise. Through a bloody eye, Jacob could see Robb and about a half dozen others holding the men fast while serving their own punishment on their heads and bodies. By now, Big Finn had come around and, with a roar, began to charge toward Jacob, still down. Just as he reached for Jacob, a grand champagne bottle came crashing across his head. Time stood still as Big Finn froze momentarily, seemingly perplexed at what just happened. This was followed by a broad fist smashing against the hefty jaw. The colossus then fell face-first onto the sawdust floorboards. Silas grinned with arms raised, standing over his conquest.

Ruckus At The Haymarket

The dancehall had quickly become strangely quiet, with hundreds of patrons watching the impromptu spectacle, all while keeping a safe distance. A barman broke the silence. Looking at Silas and the group, he blurted, "The coppers will be here in a blink. I'd make clear if I was you. We know these hooligans," he said ruefully while looking down at the three.

"And, we'll make sure the coppers reacquaint with them as well."

Robb jumped in. "A fine suggestion, sir. No time to waste, ladies and gentlemen. I believe our time has come to say adieu to this fine establishment," he urged the group. He and Silas then helped Jacob to his feet. In the interim, Anika had recovered her poise. Putting her arm in his and, with her perfect smile, whispered, "You are *mon chevalier* after all."

As the weary group headed hastily toward the entrance, the Haymarket crowd offered up a brisk round of applause. Turning, Silas performed a deliberate bow that brought more hurrahs. He then quickly followed the others out the door and onto the street. Within moments the boisterous noise of music and laughter of the dancehall recommenced.

***

He awoke disoriented, briefly unaware of his surroundings. He then recalled the night before and shut his eyes. Beyond the pain throbbing in his head, face and shoulders, Jacob felt a surge of guilt about the goings-on at the Haymarket. Thinking of his mother and her certain disappointment in him if she knew about his indulgences only added to his sense of regret and even shame. There was some consolation in that the fighting was to protect the two ladies and his honor.

Then realizing where he was, he instantly sat up on the chenille bed and gathered himself. His coat and vest hung over a nearby winged chair with shoes and socks close by. The realization of being in Anika's bed both excited and embarrassed him. He vaguely remembered arriving at Anika and Valerie's hotel and being helped up several flights of stairs and into a suite of rooms. Beyond that, his mind was blank.

"Well, look who is joining the living," Anika, with her head poking around the door, interjected brightly. "I've been checking on you from time to time. We cleaned you up, nursed those cuts a bit, and then let you sleep. Knowing you were in good hands, Silas and the other boys retired to their own respective lodgings. I'm afraid you're looking at a couple of scars on that splendid face. Not to worry, you're still quite charming. Besides, scars make for superb stories among the company." With that, her pale blue eyes danced, and Jacob's heart danced along.

She was wearing a saffron yellow oriental robe; made of silk, he thought. A storm of poppies and other flowers cascaded down the front of the loosely tied gown. The young man's attention was drawn to its gracious opening at its neck.

"I, I am very sorry for all the trouble, Anika. Last night spiraled down to the cellar, I'm afraid, and I regret you having to endure it," Jacob admitted. "You should not have been there. The Haymarket is no place for a lady such as yourself."

"I've seen it all before. I'm Dutch. And regret? You should have none of that. You were nothing if not heroic, my gallant protector! Who knows what that beast would have done? I am thankful however that you survived without more serious hurt. No, you were quite wonderful," she said emphatically, yet with a charismatic smile.

Jacob smiled meekly while tilting his head down in appreciation. He then noticed the strong aroma of coffee and cinnamon, and other wonderful spices. "What are those incredible smells?"

"Follow me and let's discover," she said with a coy whisper while motioning him to follow. Jacob quickly stood, and immediately his head swooned. Sitting back down on the bed, he held his head between two hands.

"Oh, let me help you, love," Anika implored while moving to the bed. She helped him again to stand while bracing his arm with her own. Jacob shook his head in an effort to clear it. He then saw a brief flash of her smooth white breast under the open robe as she moved to support him. Concurrent feelings of arousal and awkwardness ran through him as he let her help him forward.

They walked into an ample sitting room, and Jacob thought that Anika certainly lived more highly than he. This was quite a suite of fine rooms for a young single lady in the city. They then made their way into the kitchen, where he was surprised to see Valerie with her back to them. Valerie had her own oriental silk robe. Hers was white with a design of roses intertwined on a faint green trellis on the back.

Turning to face them, Valerie smiled and said, "I see my breakfast has brought you forth, young southerner. Let me entice you with a specialty... coffee with cocoa and cinnamon. Oh, and there's hot strudel, Anika's favorite taste of home. But first, delight in these fresh citruses from Florida. I weaseled these rarities from Dominic, our friendly fresh grocer."

"If they taste only a measure of their sweet aroma, they will be wonderful," Jacob professed. "And, I don't believe I've ever had such coffee…what a nice treat," he added and eased carefully into a chair by the table. Even while focused on the breakfast spread, he noticed Anika move to Valerie for a quick kiss on her cheek.

The next half hour or so was spent savoring the light meal. They each spoke of their upbringing in the diverse worlds of Holland, Albany, and North Carolina. Jacob learned that Valerie was preparing to sing an aria at one of the premier salons on Fifth Avenue. Anika urged the auburn-haired beauty to give them just a peak of her planned performance. With humility, Valerie consented and briefly educated the two on Bellini's Casta Diva, the famous soprano prayer from the Italian's tragic opera, *Normelia*. Then Valerie gave the briefest of performances, and the sparkling timbre of her clear voice was intoxicating. Jacob had never heard such a voice.

Afterward, Valerie retired to her own room to dress for the day, leaving Jacob and Anika alone in the kitchen. "So, you and Valerie live here together, I gather," he said cautiously.

"Yes, we initially had our own single suites in the hotel," she replied. "We have gotten on so well that we decided in the New Year to take this suite of rooms for the additional space and to share the expenses. It has worked out wonderfully as we so enjoy each other's company." Changing the subject, she said, "Now, let's get you properly dressed for the journey home."

Jacob wanted to find out more about the relationship but decided to leave it at that. Feeling stronger, he returned to the bedroom and finished dressing. Anika escorted him down to the Tremont lobby and out onto the busy street. Turning abruptly to her, he inquired, "Might I write to you?" The two looked directly into the other's eyes. Jacob knew for certain that he was in love with this wonderfully unique creature. He had never known a woman of such confidence and innocence all at the same time. Of course, her physical beauty was captivating. His heart had been stolen.

"Certainly, *mon chevalier*," she enthused. "And, I will write to you. We must keep one another appraised of our latest design brilliance," she teased, giving him a playful wink.

"More than that, I want to hear everything about you. I, I really do!" he stuttered more emotionally than he intended. He reached for her hand, and she moved close to his face and kissed him on the lips, soft and full. They stayed close, holding hands, for a long moment.

Stepping back, she said with a smile, "Farewell, Jacob…' till we meet again." He smiled and nodded silently. Anika turned and disappeared into the Tremont, leaving him on the sidewalk. He then hailed a cab uptown to his hotel while feeling quite lightheaded. He imagined the feeling was not from the fight the night before.

He was scheduled to return home on the night train from Grand Central. He took his seat by the window yet longed to stay with Anika and recklessly thought about how he could disembark and go straight back into her arms. He imagined the two of them holding each other and sharing a passionate kiss – even sharing a bed. He chided himself for not professing his love to her.

The train lurched forward, jarring him from his fantasy. His disciplined nature swiftly recovered, and he reminded himself of the work ahead in Winston. The West End Hotel was in its later stages, and now he had his plan for the glasshouse and other finishing touches. The train left the station with three short blasts of its whistle. Within minutes, it was rolling south to Washington, DC. There he would catch the morning train to Greensboro and onto Winston.

Settling back in his seat, Jacob felt for the bandage on his forehead and grimaced at the reminder of the previous night. His emotions vacillated between regret and triumph. What an odd dichotomy of feelings, he thought. Within moments, however, the gentle rocking of the passenger car on the rails lulled him into a restful sleep. He dreamed of yellow saffron and warm strudel.

***

CHAPTER 10: EARLY SUMMER 1901

Since the meeting with Harper two months prior, Eli, Lans, and Silver had debated the best way to carry out their plan to seize Levi Kiger and force him to give up the Flemings. They had tracked the outlaw's nightly habits for weeks; each taking turns with vigilance. Shadowing Kiger was easily done as he typically made for the rather seedy Sprague Street Tavern each evening around five or six o'clock. There he had his evening meal and drank quantities of whiskey and beer while holding court among the riff-raff that adhered to his brand of civil disrespect and racism. In Kiger's bitter view, corrupt men and institutions controlled a world hell-bent on holding the common white man down, all while coddling the rich, of course. He was also convinced the black man was responsible as well for the sorry state of the world. And no one could fan the flames of discontent more fervently than Levi Kiger. It was his stock in trade, and he had honed his hate speech over many years.

Kiger typically returned home around midnight, with female company or alone. In either event, he was invariably drunk. Their plan was simple. They would wait until Levi returned home alone. Once he was in his usual alcoholic torpor, the three would enter the house, gag, and tie him up. From there, the outcome was somewhat less predictable. After much cajoling, Harper had reluctantly approved of the plan.

The appointed evening was cool for late May, with a full moon casting its brilliance and creating distinctive light and shadow on the world below. An orchestra of crickets chirped their relentless symphony, disturbing the silvery night. Southside Winston was quiet. Tavern drunks had made their way to beds both familiar and new. That, of course, included Levi Kiger.

As expected, Levi had spent the better part of six hours at the Sprague, drinking and arguing and even getting into a brief shoving match with another patron. Eli's man at the tavern alerted him on Kiger's pending departure. Eli nodded grimly to the man and sent him on his way with a five-dollar bill. Eli, Lans, and Silver then kept to the shadows, following Levi to his ramshackle home on Rawson Street. Even from a safe distance, they could hear Levi singing a bawdy tune about a working girl named Clementine and how she finally met her match.

The moonlight revealed an overgrown yard and broken fence gate as Levi lumbered to the door. He pushed the door open with his forearm and stumbled inside, kicking the door shut with the back of his heel. The three watchers waited for thirty minutes, scanning the road for anyone that might be about at the late hour. There was no sight or sound of anyone on the street.

"Let's go," Eli whispered and moved forward toward the door. The three quietly listened to ensure Levi was asleep before slipping through the door. Loud gasping snores drew them to the bedroom. Standing above the bed, they stared momentarily at the pitiful creature at their mercy. Then Eli stuffed a rag in the open mouth while Lans and Silver firmly held his arms and shoulders down.

Levi awoke with a start. His bloodshot eyes were wild as he violently shook his head to expel the gag. Trying without success to rise, he kicked ferociously, not unlike a fish hooked, and landed on the stream bank. After a few seconds, Levi became still, only to try to escape the restraints again with all his strength. Eli smashed his nose with a harsh blow that stunned and subdued him. They then jerked him up, tied his wrists, and bound his ankles as well. Eli cinched twine around Levi's head to hold the gag tight. He was dragged to a hardback chair and forced down.

By now, Kiger was alert, and his captors could clearly see both loathing and venom in his rheumy eyes. Moonlight penetrated the windows giving the room an eerie illumination and allowing both assailants and captives to plainly see one another. No one spoke for a length adding to the tense atmosphere. Lans was struck by the condition his old enemy was in. Levi Kiger clearly showed the evidence of a life lived harshly. A thick, jagged scar traced his cheek from brow to chin and was pre-eminent among a company of other smaller scars and discolorations. His eyes were bruised, sunken deep in his head, and offset by a decidedly crooked nose. So that's the famous nose, he thought and laughed to himself while glancing at Silver.

Breaking the silence, Eli said evenly, "Did you think we wouldn't come for your sorry ass? Did you really think that I would not avenge my father? Well, that time has come, Kiger. The jig is up. You've enjoyed building yourself up as some hero among that rabble at the Sprague, haven't you? But we both know you're nothing but a craven coward."

The grizzled man just stared forward into space. Lines of sweat had begun to form across his broad forehead.

"You see Levi? Harp Clayton has loyal friends," interjected Lans. "We've been allies since we were boys in Bethania and the blood fields of Virginia. And, after you did what you did to him…well, you shoulda known I'd be comin' for you. Of course, you and I have our own history, don't we, Levi? …that little dust-up at the Bridle and Spur so long ago? … or, havin' to make right that election? I guess those affairs were just a taste for what this has come to."

Then Silver added quietly, "we have a history, too, me and you. I see your nose never quite straightened out since that time at the tavern. I want to tell you now that broken nose was my doin'. I laid you out with a two by four, you comin' through that back door. And, knowin' the meanness you've done over these long years, I have to say it was one of the best licks I ever done in my life." Silver delivered these words not with gloating but with solemnity.

At hearing this, Kiger jerked his head sideways at Silver, pure hatred in his eyes.

"Now you see it, don't you, Levi?" Eli jumped in. "A man gets beat half to death by four cowards with clubs, so his son and two oldest friends must make things right. They must, and they will. First, you have to tell us who put you up to it. Who paid you to bushwhack my father? Go ahead and take the gag out, Lans."

With the gag removed, Kiger coughed and spit, then vomited at his feet. Breathing in and out with resounding effort, he shook his head back and forth. Finally, he looked up and whispered intently, "I didn't beat up nobody. You hear me? Your daddy wants to put this on me. He's had it in for me for years. Hell, it's my word against his, and I got plenty of boys to say I weren't anywhere near the place. Hell, he may even be a little crazy after that thrashing," he added as a slight smile crossed his lips.

Like a shot, Lans punched the wretched thug with a fist to the mouth, knocking him and the chair over backward. Kiger was still. He seemed to be out cold but then slowly came to and attempted to stand. He spit blood as well as a couple of teeth to the floor.

"That's not going to work, Levi," Lans said bitterly. "You've been tried and convicted in the court of what's right. Now tell us how the Flemings put you in this, and we just may let you survive this night."

With his eyes darting back and forth, they could see Kiger weighing his options and trying to figure out the best outcome for himself. Taking his hand away from his bloody mouth, he revealed, "Them Flemings ain't gonna admit to nothin'. The law will never take my word. Ol' Seth Fleming will see to that for sure."

Silver and Lans looked to Eli for his response. Eli replied, "Levi, I expect you're right about that. I sure as hell wouldn't believe a word you say. That's why you're going to write out exactly what the deal was with Fleming, when he brought you in on it and what his orders were. Then you're going to sign it and make it official."

Lans picked up the chair and set it upright beside the table while Silver grabbed Kiger and sat him down hard. With his knife, Lans then cut the rope tying Kiger's wrists and kept the knife clearly visible. From his pocket, Eli pulled a piece of paper, unfolded it, and slapped it down on the table along with a pencil.

"Ok. Now write," Eli commanded.

"I don't write," the now subdued man answered with obvious resignation.

The three looked at each other, and Lans' eyes sparkled for a moment as he declared, "Well, here's what you're going do, Levi." Eli and Silver were puzzled by their partner's obvious amusement. "You will tell your story to Silver here… all about how the Flemings hired you and how you planned and carried it out. Silver's gonna write it all down, word for word. 'Cause you see? Silver can read and write and has for years. Hell, he can read the Declaration of Independence, a newspaper, or even a bill of goods to make sure he's paying for what he asked. And he can write out his order to the same seller. Heck, Silver can write long love poems to his sweetie if he's a mind to. In fact, Silver has seen to it that all his family can read and write. Isn't that right, Silver?"

The black man nodded with satisfaction and sat down at the table while pulling the paper and pencil to him.

Levi Kiger now just looked tired and defeated. He told his story, all of it, and then made his mark at the bottom of the page. Finally, looking up at the three, he stated without emotion, "I'm a dead man. Fleming will see to it. It's as simple as that."

***

Harper and Christian sat opposite one other at the round table in the meeting room. Eli occupied a chair and leaned against the windowsill. Harper told Angelica that they were not to be disturbed.

"Harp, you and I both know that this signed confession is going to be a problem," Christian warned while looking at the paper that Eli had provided them. "Unless Kiger testifies in front of judge and jury, the defense will say this was obtained under duress and is inadmissible. Even more so, it is not strong enough to implicate the Flemings. Again, Kiger would have to testify in court."

"You're right. I know it. Damn! And, Seth Fleming will see to it that Levi doesn't testify, one way or another." Harper stood and began to pace. He had recently abandoned the cane but still moved slowly. "Levi Kiger has done evil things in his life, but he is a pathetic soul whose miserable course was charted for him long ago. Yes, he could have tried to rise above it," Harper admitted while raising his hand to bar Eli's expected dispute, "but some creatures in this world are condemned to their fate, pure and simple."

Eli couldn't restrain himself and asserted, "Are you serious? Here's a man that has seized on the weak his whole life and has committed all sorts of malice to blacks and whites, to men and women. No, he is utterly irredeemable. Hell, he left you for dead, and you want to acquit him?"

Father turned to the son and said with a modest smile, "I feel some forgiveness, yes. I have to say that in these past months, my mind has evolved from hate and vengeance to a bit of grace and mercy." With a more lighthearted smile, he added, "It must be God seasoning me in my later stages."

Eli just stared at his father and pulled the chair up to the table. He put his hand to his forehead, resting his elbow on the table. Christian looked amused, understanding his long-time partner.

"Besides, Seth and Mathias Fleming are the ones I want. They are the real malefactors here. Kiger is just an instrument of their evildoings. Now, let's put our minds to putting these two away."

"It'll have to be our doing," Christian said plainly. "You know some in the sheriff's office are in bed with those crooks. I don't think it goes all the way to Bolton, but they've greased more than a few palms with their dirty money."

"Well, unless Seth or Mathias freely admit their crimes," Eli noted with a touch of sarcasm, "this will come down to Levi and him givin' testimony. Fat chance. I saw the pure fear in his eyes when considering the Flemings."

"If not Kiger, then who? Who can take these two down?" Christian wondered aloud.

Harper looked up and said, "What if they precipitate their own reckoning? If for little else, Mathias is well known for blowing his own horn at the expense of others, especially in the throes of good whiskey. Lans is acquainted with some of his circle of chums from around the mills. I wonder if Lans can find these boys and work a few into a scheme to bring Mathias and, in turn, Seth down by his own admission?"

Eli brightened at this notion. "I believe Lans will find this a real pleasure."

***

Tom Confronts the Flemings

Seth Fleming had agreed to meet him to finally resolve his payout in the reservoir affair and clear up Tom's apparent "misunderstanding." It was raining, and the twilight hour was steamy as Tom drove his surrey up the Danville Road to the north side of Winston. He had been to Fleming's house before, but tonight felt peculiar and a bit intimidating. He wished that he had brought support with him to strengthen his resolve, but thinking about it, there was no one. After a few miles beyond the town boundary, Moser pulled the horse up in front of the large, imposing manor. He thought how out of place it seemed in the undeveloped woodlands outside the town.

A tall man with a curious van dyke beard opened the door and, taking his hat, led Tom into the large parlor with several gas lamps burning, emitting their distinctive odor. There, Mathias Fleming sat with a half-empty bottle of fine whiskey at his side.

"Come in, Moser," the large man gestured with a wave of his hand. It was obvious he was well into the bottle. "It's about time we came together on all this. Big brother will join us in a bit. How about a whiskey?"

"Uh, sure. Why not?" Tom responded with more confidence than he felt. The large room was bathed in low flickering light, and the air was thick, conferring an uncomfortable, disorienting feeling. After pouring the whiskey, Mathias said nothing as he stared at Tom with his familiar malicious face. This added to the younger man's apprehension. To break the tension, Tom pronounced, "My man at the pumping station tells me that the reservoir is delivering almost five hundred thousand gallons a day. And, once the city lines are enlarged and extended south, then a million gallons are gonna flow. They still marvel at the speed we got this deal up and runnin'."

At that, Mathias crowed, "Yeah, I had to crack a few heads down there at the town inspections office, but I got it done. I didn't have to pay out half as much as I thought to get those boys to play ball. Yep, I worked the superintendent to good effect. And, I…"

"I, I, I. Me, me, me." Seth mimicked his brother as he strode into the room. "Why, to hear you tell it, brother, this deal was a one-man show," he declared while smiling and giving Tom an exaggerated wink. "Tom, aren't we ever so thankful we had Mathias here to pull this off? I would have thought that we all played a role, but I guess it was all Mathias."

"Brother, we all had our role to play; that's true enough. Mine just involved putting the right amount of pressure in the right places," he disclosed with a loathsome grin. "One of my better endeavors, if I say so myself," he added, quite taken with himself.

"Tom, we had better defend ourselves before Mathias makes a claim to the whole thing," Seth stated facetiously with a straight face. "What say we get down to business? Now, Tom, I know you're looking for more out of the deal," he started. After a long pause, he continued. "That's not going to happen, and here's why. As you know quite well, we had to push hard on all parties to accelerate their normal timetables; Robeson, the Atlanta architect, the masons, the pipe men, hell, everybody went balls out to meet the schedule, and that meant a boatload of extra cash out of our pockets. Your job boiled down to keeping the inquiries from the town and inspectors to a minimum and to keep that meddling father-in-law of yours at bay. Well, of course, that didn't happen, did it?"

Mathias jumped in, proclaiming, "and then we had to take care of that."

Seth immediately cut his eyes to his brother with a vicious look of reproach that caused him to sink back in his chair. The older Fleming continued, "So Tom, the way I see it, right is right, and fair is fair."

Tom vaulted to his feet and blurted, "I sunk more than twenty-five hundred into this goddamned venture, and you said I would triple my money." He was shaking with anger.

"*Could*, Tom, *could*. I said you *could* triple your investment. Not, *would*. But as I just said, we had unforeseen costs, and quite frankly, you didn't perform up to par," the gangly rogue dissembled with a look of some satisfaction. "Besides, you didn't lose that much. You got a nice piece of your investment back. All things considered, not the worst outcome, right?"

"And, how did you and Mathias come out, huh? I bet you put a considerable amount in your own pockets," Tom replied, still shaking but now feeling despondent.

"Oh, we did ok," Mathias rejoined with a hideous grin, displaying foul and missing teeth. Again, Seth silenced him with a sharp eye.

His outrage rekindled; Tom took a step toward the brothers and shouted, "You swindled me! You made me believe I was a partner in this affair…that I would share in the profits. You're nothing but shysters, and you're not gonna get away with this. I'm gonna get what's owed me. You'll see."

Mathias rose quickly out of his chair and stood nose-to-nose with the infuriated young man. "That's sounding like a threat, Moser, and my brother and me don't take kindly to threats. I suggest you get the hell outta here before something ugly happens. And I strongly suggest you keep all this to yourself. You sure don't wish misfortune on that pretty wife of yours or that boy."

With found strength and contempt, Tom continued to stand face to face with the hard-featured brute. "How dare you threaten my wife and son!"

Seth quickly inserted himself into the situation. "Now, Mathias, let's keep things gentlemanly. I'm sure Tom knows what's at stake. He knows that he's as much a part of the whole deal as anybody, and the last thing he wants is the authorities to be lookin' into things. Isn't that right, Tom?" With a furtive look, the conman swiftly continued, "And, to show you there are no hard feelings, here's a hundred-dollar bill. Go buy that pretty wife of yours something nice," he purred while extending the crisp bill to Tom.

Tom took the bill, slowly crumpled it in his hand, and deliberately dropped it at Fleming's feet. He then turned and walked out the door.

The ordeal with the Flemings had triggered a range of punishing emotions that shot through his head with a disorienting intensity. After sending word to Eleanor that he was all right but needed some time to "sort things through," Tom had spent the night wandering the roads in a state of growing misery. He castigated himself for being so utterly duped by Seth Fleming. A bottle of Irish whiskey fueled his desire for revenge but also served to deepen his despair. He thought about taking Eli or Jacob into his confidence but quickly decided against that action. Wouldn't they only reject and rebuke him as well for his naivety? Wouldn't they excoriate him for putting their sister in this situation? He was pretty damned sure Eli would. Jacob, perhaps not, but he was not ready to confront either brother-in-law.

Then there was the other matter. What had Mathias said, exactly? Even is his clouded state, he could still see Mathias' detestable face and foul declaration of "having to take care of that as well." Taken care of what? Were the Flemings behind the assault on Harper? It didn't take much imagination to arrive at that conclusion. The more he pondered the possibility, the more he was convinced the Fleming brothers had been behind the terrible beating of his father-in-law. He had to tell the Claytons. It was the right thing to do, but moreover, it would go a long way to put him in a favorable light with them. Tom felt a wave of shame wash over him at this obvious self-interest. But, the guilt was transient. He began to piece together his plan.

***

Harper's vivid dreams, especially as a young lawyer with the Freedmen's Bureau, had become more frequent since the assault. He surmised they were triggered by the past winter's violent rendezvous with Levi Kiger. He had battled the miscreant and his gang so long ago in his efforts to assist North Carolina's former slaves. And this dream was no different.

"Without a doubt, there's been improvement since Grant was elected," Bureau agent Thomas Campbell pronounced. "Hell, with President Johnson, the Klan was runnin' wild, takin' the law into their own hands, burnin' and killin'. Everybody knew Johnson wouldn't turn the lawmen out to chase them down. Everything the Bureau did in North Carolina was subject to being overruled by Johnson's

Democrats. And Clayton's experience with that school burnin' in Winston was just a prime example of the lawlessness and mayhem we've seen across the state. With Grant puttin' Federal troops in place, arrests are up, and the violence has dropped dramatically," Campbell said with enthusiasm.

The gathering of the North Carolina Freedmen's Bureau was well attended. Assistant Commissioner Franklin Marshall, reflecting the Bureau's renewed energy and a sense of purpose, had called the meeting in June 1871 to communicate the new direction and potential support from the federal government. "I know our successes to date have been spotty and inconsistent, but Grant pushed the "Klan Act" through congress and has promised us more dollars for land acquisition, labor disputes, and medical aid. It's a new day, gentlemen. I'm asking all of you agents to provide a list of priorities to get on with the Bureau's work in your respective districts."

Harper smiled at the irony. President Grant now his benefactor, while only six years ago, General Grant was his tormentor in Virginia. He remembered the ordinary-looking soldier on his mud-splattered horse at Appomattox in April 1865. This appearance was in contrast to General Lee, resplendent in his clean dress uniform astride his striking iron grey American Saddlebred, Traveller. In these disparate images, one would have thought the roles of victor and vanquished were reversed.

Breaking out of these musings, he spoke up. "Mr. Marshall, I'm sure I represent all present in being ever thankful for the new support from Washington; however, we all realize the barriers we continually face in the local and state courts.

We are being blocked and overruled time and time again by magistrates that are clearly biased against the freedmen. Our ability to argue fair labor contracts and land settlements has been greatly diminished by the Black Codes that continue to spring up and are readily endorsed by the judiciary. The new constitutional amendment for equal justice seems to be all but ignored in our districts. Real equality, with these judicial obstructions, is a pipedream."

"I agree, Mr. Clayton, that the deck is stacked against us, but we must continue the push," Marshall added plainly. "And you, sir, seem to have a mind for the law. I would think you would be inclined to take up the mantle of jurisprudence. God knows we need critical thinkers in this battle."

The assistant commissioner paused for a response. Harper looked around at the others, considering his response. "Thank you, sir. I might just do that. But how does that change the present?"

Marshall responded with a smile. "Whoa, there son… first things first. We do what we can with what we have. Provided these new resources come through, I expect we'll have more leverage in these types of labor and land cases. Now, if there's no other business, I say we move to adjourn and all get to work."

As the agents and other attendees started to file out of the capitol building, Marshall took Harper aside and confided, "I was serious about you exploring the law. I'm sure you know our U.S. Attorney, Darius Starbuck, there in Winston."

"I do know of him. He was a representative at the 1865 state convention bringing North Carolina back into the union, correct?" Harper replied with respect.

Nodding, Marshall added, "Not only that, but he was also a leader on a group that petitioned the state not to succeed from the union in 1861. Grant recently approved his reappointment as U.S. Attorney in the Piedmont, so I would say ol' Starbuck would be an excellent mentor for you in the law."

"But, would he have me?" Harper wondered.

"He will. I will recommend you as his new clerk, and he will agree. Know why?" Marshall continued without waiting for a response. "Darius Starbuck and I have known each other for near thirty years, and we trust each other. Plus, he has a soft spot for what we're doing here with the Bureau. He's a Quaker, you know."

"I thank you most sincerely, Mr. Marshall. I will not let you down," Harper said with clear humility.

"I know you won't, Harper, and my friends call me John."

Harper's dream progressed as disparate images of Starbuck, Christian Harmon and those early cases from so long ago passed through his sub-consciousness. It then unfolded into the nightmare that was the tragedy at Hooper's field.

June 1872—Congress had just defunded and dismantled the Freedmen's Bureau. News of that sort traveled swiftly throughout the South, empowering disenfranchised poor whites to take action, often violent, in taking back lands that had been deeded or contracted to former slaves.

The high summer afternoon was hot without a cloud in the sky. Uriah Rawlings, with his large family and friends, was working the tobacco field on the old Hooper farm. It was serious work priming tobacco, especially with only rudimentary tools. By the end of the day, one's back was bowed and rigid and aching most powerfully. Yet, Uriah and the others went about the task with spirit and humor.

Rawlings had petitioned his former master, John Hooper, to contract the land to him and his heirs in return for a sizable share of the proceeds. Hooper, in an effort to escape the disorder in the South, was moving his family to Indiana to join a brother in a successful agricultural auction house. All in all, Hooper was a fair man. He agreed to lease his ninety-five acres to Uriah with the potential for the former slave to own it outright in seven years. Harper Clayton, legal apprentice, drew up the contract at the request of Tom Silver, who was a close friend of Rawlings. That was in the Autumn of 1871 after the cash crop had been harvested and sold at the Piedmont Leaf market in Winston.

This summer was Rawling's first growing season, and it was a good one. With the seed beds up and planted, the spring rains had been easy and regular, with the rich riverside acreage producing a fine crop. The day was actually the second priming, earlier than the typical year.

The group of thirty or so was spread across the bottomland close to the Yadkin River. This section of the farm was known as the "river patch" and consistently yielded a fine tobacco crop. Silver's wife, Sadie, and others from the black community joined in to help Rawlings get the priming done in a few days and be rewarded as well when the crop was sold later in the summer.

Jonathon, a large man with a cherub face, led forth with a field holler, a loud musical shout rising and falling and breaking into falsetto. His cry was echoed by the boys and men and girls and women around him:

"There is a balm in Gilead

To make the wounded whole;

There is a balm in Gilead

To heal the sin-sick soul."

The spiritual song chant in the field uplifted the group and helped the arduous work pass more easily. These call and response work songs had been passed down across generations of slaves throughout the South and had their origins in the music of West Africa.

The hot Carolina sun beat down fiercely, and the work slowed in the late afternoon. Silver and Sadie volunteered to go for water from the nearby cold spring. Reaching the shade of the woods where the gently flowing stream flowed to the river, Silver put his buckets down and took Sadie's from her. The rippling sounds from the nearby stream were soft and pleasant. Pulling her down in a small grove of bluebells, he revealed, "I think this shade and patch of flowers are our heaven-sent reward for our endeavors today. Why, Uriah's workin' us like field hands in the old days." Silver chuckled at the irony.

Sadie stretched out beside her husband and sighed, "This is heaven sure enough, but we got to get these buckets filled and back soon. So, don't you go thinking on something else, Mister." She smiled at him affectionately, touching her forehead to his.

"Well, aren't you the dutiful one, always thinking of others' necessities? That's just one of the reasons you're the girl for me," Silver replied with a grin as he helped her up.

"Just one? I want to hear about all those other reasons when we get back tonight," she laughed merrily and followed Silver on to the creek to fill the buckets. The water was clear and cool. They both dipped their hands in to splash their faces and then filled the four buckets. Suddenly, they heard gunfire erupt from the tobacco field.

Telling Sadie to stay put, Silver dropped both buckets and ran from the woods while hearing the screams and cries of the workers in the field. From a distance, he immediately saw five or six bodies down on the ground as a group of mounted riders was galloping hard away. Arriving at the scene, Silver recognized his friend, Uriah, lying on the ground with his daughter, Liza, already attending to him. He observed the big man, Jonathan, motionless on the ground as well as several others nearby. Young girls and a few of the women were wailing with pitiful cries while others began to reassemble after running in panic.

"God almighty, what happened?" Silver implored.

Zeke, one of the younger men, answered excitedly, "Riders came up on us sudden like…said we need to clear out…this here's Hooper's field. Mr. Uriah told 'em that he had a legal contract with Mr. Hooper to work these here fields, and they need to leave us be."

"They just pulled guns on us and started shooting," a woman called out, weeping. "God help us. Jonathan is killed dead, and so is Hiram and Esther. God, oh God."

Silver then moved to Uriah, where his daughter held his head in her lap. The older man had two bullet wounds, one in his shoulder and a more serious one is his belly. He looked up at Silver and said softly, "Never thought this would happen…knew they was goin' to raise cane with me working Hooper's land… didn't believe they was this hard."

"You rest easy, friend," Silver responded. Turning to the group, he shouted, "Somebody run and get Doc Everett here quick-like. Tell him to come as fast as he can…that we got several wounded with gunshots that need his attention." Silver looked around wildly. He spied two boys about twelve or so and yelled, "Go for the doc now! His house is on the Davidson Trail, almost in Winston. Run!"

With that, the boys took off running. Silver noticed that Sadie was now on the scene and helping some of the other women attend to the five other wounded. Three looked as if they were only slightly injured and were already standing. Two others, a boy no more than ten and a young man who looked to be about twenty, were more seriously harmed and remained on the ground. Turning back to Uriah, he noticed his friend's breathing was shallow, eyes closed.

"Stay awake, Uriah," Silver said abruptly. "Stay with us now. The doc is comin' soon. He'll fix you up". He looked up and met the daughter's desperate look.

With conviction, Uriah replied with eyes open," I don't want to leave this world just yet, mind you. I, I don't want to leave my children in such a cruel place. But, if Jesus is calling me home, who am I to linger?"

The young girls and women continued to sob and weep. Some of the men had already huddled together, their rage clearly evident as bitter oaths filled the air. Silver stepped over to where they stood and asked, "Who was this? Did you recognize any of 'em?"

One of the younger men with eyes ablaze professed, "I hate to say it, but no. They came up on us quick, and they was wearin' masks. Hell, at least one of the devils was a black man…a black man! How could a black man do the white man's biddin' and shoot down other black folks? It don't make no sense." He looked incredulously around at the others shaking their heads.

The sun was now low on the horizon. Doc Everett had not arrived. Besides the three that had died instantly, one of the wounded expired in the field. Silver and the others had carried Uriah and the other wounded in a mule-drawn cart to the Hooper house, where they were tended to as best as possible. Uriah and the other seriously wounded man lasted most of the night. At dawn, Uriah's daughter called the remaining family to his bedside to say farewell. By daylight, both had succumbed to their wounds which set off renewed mourning, loud and pitiful.

Silver and Sadie had stayed with the group providing what help they could. By mid-morning, the doctor finally arrived, claiming other urgent needs in town as his reason for the slow response. Silver highly doubted that story but remained quiet nonetheless while Everett went about tending to the four other wounded.

Making their sad farewells, the couple then walked the five miles to Bethania, where they immediately made for Harper's house. Susan, unaware of the trouble, directed Silver to Darius Starbuck's office in Winston.

After hearing Silver's recounting of the killings, Harper immediately sought Starbuck for counsel. As U.S. Attorney for the region, Starbuck was the key source of justice for these criminal acts. The case was officially opened, followed by a lengthy investigation of more than six months. Starbuck deployed federal agents and coordinated with local law enforcement, but after months of probing local gangs and known troublemakers, no suspects were ever identified. With wide-ranging interrogations, no witnesses came forward except the victims of the tragedy. Consequently, no one was ever charged, and justice was not served. It remained a sharp painful memory for both Silver and Harper and a lingering open wound for everyone there that awful day in Hooper's field.

***

CHAPTER 11: SUMMER 1901

Lansford Hall was highly respected at the Arista Cotton Mill, both by Francis Fries, the owner, and the one hundred and fifty or so workers. It was a respect that was earned. Lans had joined the mill soon after its inception in 1880 and was forever grateful to Fries for giving him his start after several failed attempts at farming and shop keeping. Lans had taken on more responsibilities over the years, culminating with his elevation to Shift Foreman several years back. With Fries' increasing focus on the new Wachovia Loan & Trust and, of course, the Roanoke railway, Lans, along with several other supervisors, essentially oversaw the running of the spinning and weaving mill. He was tough but fair in managing his employees, and everyone knew, from spindle operator to sweeper, that Lans Hall was true to his word and appreciated those who gave their best day's effort.

It was not uncommon for Lans to pay visits to the mill's break room to catch up with the workers and their issues of the day. The rank and file knew they could trust their foreman and had little difficulty in opening up to him. Whether it be problems on the floor or something about company pay or hours, they relied on Lans Hall to give them the honest take.

It was Friday, and Lans had a specific interest in Charlie Boyles and Howard Gunter, two of his machine operators and sometimes confidants of Mathias Fleming. The two were known to organize regular Saturday night card games with Fleming. While technically illegal in the state, gambling among private citizens was not a priority for law enforcement, who generally looked the other way. These "private" games were often the lively subject of break room conversations at the mill on Mondays – who won and lost big, who started a fight, or who made an embarrassing ass of himself. Scanning the lunchtime group, Lans spied Boyles and Gunter sitting at the corner round table with several other men. He made his way over to the table, greeted the group with a nod, and said, "Boys, it's been a good week. Looks like we will make a year's best eighteen hundred pounds of finished goods. I thank you all for the fine work. Charlie, Gunter, your machines have run a swell efficiency rate for this whole month. Well done!"

"Why, I thank you for noticing, boss man," Boyles replied and beamed with pride. Charlie Boyles was a big man from Kernersville in the eastern part of Forsyth County. His large baldhead, quick wit, and easy smile made the gregarious thirty-year-old a unique and likable presence at the mill. It was not unusual to find Charlie spinning an entertaining yarn with an appreciative group gathered round.

"Yes, yes, uh, thank you, sir. Thank you." the other man joined in. Howard Gunter, called Gunter by just about everyone, was a stark contrast to his friend, both physically and in personality. Slight of frame with a ruddy complexion and also about thirty, Gunter's small slanted eyes gave the appearance of a perpetual squint. His constant nervous movements suggested one ill at ease in the world.

Lans continued, "Well, it's my pleasure to tell you, boys, that Mr. Fries has agreed to give our whole shift a day's extra pay for the superior job you are doing. Everyone can pick up that cash bonus at the end of the day at the payroll window."

"Hurrah!" erupted the table in unison as hands were shaken and backs were slapped.

"Now that's the best news I've heard all week," exclaimed Charlie. "The work is hard enough, but ol' Fries and you bosses put the money where your mouth is. Ain't that right, fellas?" he implored as heads around the table shook enthusiastically. "I'd say we got us some ante money for tomorrow night's game, eh Gunter?" The wiry man's hands fidgeted while his narrow eyelids blinked rapidly.

At the end of the shift, Lans sought out the two friends who were still quite jolly about the unexpected bonus. As they exited the mill with other workers, Lans took them aside, conveying, "I say again, good for you boys on a job well done. Hey, by the way, are you fellows getting up a game Saturday night?" Boyles and Gunter exchanged furtive looks, and Lans quickly followed up. "Hey, it's no problem with me. I just know that Mathias Fleming is part of your crew, and I would like to have you listen out for something. There're some stories goin' around about that new reservoir and how it got done. I'm just interested in what Mathias may or not say about it. Heck, I've heard he may have been bragging about it before now. Any truth to that?"

Again, the two looked at each other. Slowly, Boyles said, "I can't recollect Mathias saying anything, but, uh, uh, we'll be sure and listen up for something, right, Gunter?"

With the attention quickly shifted to him, Gunter blinked wildly and stammered, "w…w…we will. We will, for a fact."

Lans felt like they had something to reveal but decided not to press the issue. "This stays strictly between us, boys. I don't want anybody else to be aware of this conversation…anybody.

Are we straight?" he said forcefully while staring straight at the two men.

"No doubt, Mr. Hall. We hear you loud and clear," Boyles responded stiffly. Gunter nodded, head bobbing rapidly.

With that, Lans marked a quick end to the conversation. "You boys have a grand time this weekend. Enjoy that bonus, and I'll see you Monday." He watched as the two quickly made their way down Brookstown Avenue without looking back.

***

It took all the nerve he could muster, but Levi finally made his way north of town to the Flemings mansion, having sent word of his arrival ahead of time. The whole way, he had considered just how much to reveal to Seth and Mathias about the encounter with Eli Clayton and the others. He now truly wished he had refused to confess anything that night, no matter what kind of beating would have been forthcoming. Having it all down on paper made him shudder in the saddle. And, having it written by that damned black Silver was too much to bear—of course, he would not say anything about that.

By the time he pulled the big doorknocker, he had essentially decided to tell the brothers what he had confessed that night. In his simple mind, all should be told so as to concoct a plan of reprisal preventing any evidence of their crimes from coming out – a violent plan of reprisal.

"Come in, Levi, and let's hear all about this regretful episode," Seth Fleming stated evenly as he met Levi at the door. He led the disheveled rogue into the front parlor, where Mathias sat with undisguised cold contempt. Kiger's swelling and bruising from last month's encounter were still evident, as well as the missing teeth.

Shaking his head, Mathis sneered and demanded, "What in the hell did you tell those boys?"

"Ok, brother. Just settle down. I'm sure our friend here didn't let them in on anything. He knows how to keep his mouth shut. Ain't that right, Levi?"

Kiger was silent, and the fear in his tired, red eyes was indisputable. After a moment, he declared, "I thought they was goin' to kill me. I…I didn't have no choice. Yes, I told them about what I did…what you and Mathias told me to do. Hell, they even wrote down my words. But, but listen now," he stammered. "I know I can make things right. I can get some boys, and we can make sure those three don't say nothin'. My boys and me can take them down right quick. Just give the word, and we'll be on 'em. Just say it. You know I'll do it and end all of it." At this point, Levi was wild-eyed with spit emitting out of his swollen mouth.

Seth looked carefully at his brother and then at Kiger. In an eerily calm, matter-of-fact tone, he replied, "I need some air. Let's walk out back and think about this some more. We have to think this through." He guided the shaken man with his arm around him out the back kitchen door. Levi didn't notice Mathias hanging back. Fleming led him down the stone steps onto the grassy yard, confiding, "Levi, this world is cruel and exacts a cruel justice on those that don't measure up. It's the way of things. When the Romans dealt justice, it was clean justice... with honor. Nowadays, people just want to survive whatever dirt they drag along with them." Glancing over Levi's shoulder, Seth added, "I'm afraid, Levi, we have to exact justice here. Now."

From behind, Mathias grabbed Kiger roughly by the greasy hair pulling his head back. With a swift motion, he slashed the wretch's throat from ear to ear with an enormous hunting knife. Bright red blood gushed freely as Kiger dropped to the ground. His body moved slowly in a strange rhythmic fashion as the lifeblood poured out of him.

For a moment, the brothers stood over the body, both silent. Then Mathias spoke while wiping the blade with his handkerchief. "What do we do with this garbage?"

"Throw him in the burning pit," Seth said without emotion. "And, use kerosene to make sure the body is burned completely. They've got nothing on us without a witness."

***

It was a fine June Saturday, not a cloud in the sky, and the air was fresh. Tom had sent telegrams to Eli and Jacob asking them to come to his house on Glade Street saying he had something important to tell them. Both had responded they would come.

"I've asked your brothers to join me here at the house today. There's something I need to tell them," he said to Eleanor while reaching for her hand. "I've been a fool, a blind fool, but I have a chance to make a little right out of it."

Eleanor's penetrating dark eyes narrowed, searching her husband's face for answers. "What is it, Tom? My family knows how the Flemings swindled you. You told them yourself, and they don't blame you for what those horrible men did. You know that."

"It's not that, El, although I'll never forgive myself for being so damn gullible. No, it's not the swindle. It's something else…something worse that I have to tell them and, then, I'll tell you. I promise. Now, don't worry. Everything's going to be ok."

"Alright," she said gently. "Tee won't be back from the farm for a while. I'll go see mama and give you some privacy. Just, please tell me you're not in danger."

At that moment, Tom realized he would do just about anything to make his wife proud of him. Smiling weakly, he asserted, "No, I'm ok but it's time to make things right. There was danger, lots of it. But, just maybe, it's time to put an end to it." Squeezing and releasing her hand, Tom then walked into the back garden. Eleanor was fearful but sensed the need to let the matter go for the present.

Eli and Jacob had agreed to meet up at the Fifth Street house and then walk the few blocks to Tom and Eleanor's. It gave them some time to anticipate what one another thought Tom was going to tell them. Believing, like Eleanor, that it must have something to do with the reservoir deal, they both were wary of the conversation. "You don't think he wants more money, do ya," Eli had groused. "Hell, don't say anything to Harp if he does."

"Perhaps he has dirt on the Flemings about the reservoir," Jacob pondered. Little did they know what was coming.

They met Eleanor coming up the walk with her sun umbrella as they were leaving to meet Tom. "Well, fancy meeting you here, sis," said Eli. "We're just on our way to meet with that husband of yours…don't know what's on his mind, do you?"

"Hello, you two. No, he's keeping the mystery. He wants to tell you before I'm let in on anything. I guess his wife can't keep a secret," she joked. "Hopefully, see you later? We can have a hard lemon punch on the porch."

"Now that sounds quite enticing on a nice day like today," replied Jacob with a laugh. "See you later."

The brothers made their way to the unique beaux-arts house on Glade Street, where Tom was sitting at the top of the front steps. Jacob thought Tom looked especially nervous. Eli wondered idly how Tom and his sister could afford such a house with all of his brother-in-law's financial stumbles.

"Come on up," Tom said while quickly rising. "I thought we'd sit in the back garden since it's such a fine day. How about something to drink?"

"Uh, have any soda water? Maybe with some lemon or lime?" Eli asked.

"Coming right up. I'll join you. How about you, Jacob?" Tom inquired.

"That sounds good to me. Thank you," he responded.

They followed Tom into the kitchen, where three bottles were fetched from the icebox and lime wedges cut. They then proceeded to the lovely garden, where multi-colored roses, blue hydrangeas, and a dense patch of daisies framed the cross-patterned brick walk.

The three settled into cushioned chairs around the wrought iron table. After some idle talk about the good summer weather, Eli broached the topic at hand. "So Tom, this is a ducky time to enjoy the weather, but we are wild with curiosity about what's on your mind."

Tom nodded and swallowed the last mouthful of soda water. Taking an exaggerated breath, he then proceeded to tell them about the encounter with the Flemings and how he believed they had orchestrated the attack on their father. "Mathias as much as admitted it, and I could see it in that lowlife's face. I would bet this house that Mathias and Seth Fleming were behind the assault on Harper." Stopping to survey Eli and Jacob's reaction, Tom was astonished to see the two brothers remain calm at his news. He expected them to be jolted out of their chairs – especially volatile Eli. Instead, the two looked at each other and nodded with grim affirmation.

Eli then told Tom of the recent business with Levi Kiger, his written admission of guilt, and the Flemings' criminal role in the matter. At that information, it was Tom that jumped up and exclaimed, "Hell, we have to get the sheriff out there. Those two lowlifes must be taken to jail and stand trial for all this treachery. They can't get away with such an atrocity no matter how much money they have...no matter how many lawmen they've bought." All the guilt and offense he had cultivated over the past months came pouring out as tears streamed down his face. "They about killed Harper and, and they damn ruined me. I'm sorry for all this…I'm the reason for all this. I hold myself fully culpable. Lord, what I've done to my wife. My God…God, help me."

By this time, all three men were standing. Putting his arm around Tom, Jacob tried to console him. "No, Tom. Evil is on the hook here. I put it all on the Flemings and their corrupt desires to rise by destroying anybody in their way. I'm sad to say that you got in their hateful path. So did our father. But, things are going to be put right."

Jumping in, Eli declared, "Damn straight things are going to be put right. But here's the thing. It has to be done legal. Harper and Christian know about the Flemings. They are working on a proper strategy to make sure this all sticks and those two crooks are put away for certain. So, you have to keep this quiet for now. I'm sure Papa and Christian will want to hear your story but no one else. Well, maybe El. You know she can keep a secret," he confirmed with a big smile.

***

The Card Game

The Saturday night game was always well attended. It floated from house to house just to keep the police from getting too interested though there was little chance of that. In fact, a sergeant and several patrolmen were regulars. Men with jackets and ties gave the proceedings an almost sophisticated air... almost. Cigar smoke filled the air, and spittoons were conveniently at hand. Several ladies in frilly aprons kept the ashtrays clean and the drinks coming. They were paid in tips and customarily from the winners' take of the night.

There were actually three tables running with varying minimums. The low-stakes table, with a quarter ante and minimum bet, was always popular, especially with the younger men still learning the fine art of poker. Additionally, there was a medium-stakes game with dollar minimums for those players willing to risk a bit more. Finally, there was the high-stakes table. This game attracted fewer players, a much bigger party of onlookers, and of course, much attention from the waitresses. With its five-dollar ante and unlimited raises, the stakes could get large in a hurry. The high-stakes table had been the place for paycheck-size losses and gains depending on one's luck and skill. Consequently, it was a raucous spectator favorite with emotions running high.

The game was well underway when Mathias arrived, drunk. His bragging and bullying were typically in proportion to the amount of Tennessee whiskey he consumed, and tonight, he was fully loaded with Jack Daniel's finest. Of course, Mathias went straight for that table where Charlie Boyles, Howard Gunter, and three other men sat engaged in a late-stage hand of Texas Hold 'Em. Pushing several onlookers aside, he blared, "Come on, boys. Don't sleep over those hands. Let's see 'em. Hell, that's nothing but a pauper's pot, anyway. Let's go."

As obnoxious and ill-mannered as the loathsome man was, the crowd knew better than to try to check such crude behavior. Fleming was famous for his vicious temper. On occasion, he had initiated fights with players and onlookers and even drew his big hunting knife one night when he believed another player had cheated him. As a result, the abhorrent bully was tolerated at best.

"That's it for me. I'm out," declared one of the men, who then swept his meager holdings away and stood to leave.

"Ok, ok, Taylor. Move on along. Better luck next time," Mathias stated with a sarcastic laugh while easing his bulk into the available chair. "Now, let's play some real poker, boys. I hope y'all brought plenty of dough 'cause I feel extra lucky tonight. Charlie, what's the game?"

Boyles, holding the deck, smiled pleasantly. He'd seen the show before. Then looking around at the players, he declared, "We're gonna stay down in Texas, boys. Two down, five up, and don't be shy on the river."

At this, Mathias impulsively sprayed whiskey across the table while laughing uproariously and slapping the table, causing chips to scatter. "Well, deal my big ass in Charlie ol' boy, and I'll start whittling down that stack of chips in front of you."

Gunter sat next to Charlie and replied, "Yeah, it's high time I had a hand. I'm snake bit tonight." He pulled on his charcoal derby as he looked forlornly at the few chips in front of him.

"What did beady eyes say, Charlie? Hell, he mumbles so as I can't hear a word," Mathias expressed with faux concern while grinning at both players and spectators around the table.

Unruffled, Charlie proceeded to deal two cards down each to the five players around the table. Bets were made, and everyone called. Boyles thought about what Lans Hall had told him and Gunter the previous day and casually said, "I hear that new waterworks is pumping water by the wagon load. There's a lot of jubilant people now that they got runnin' water to their houses." Gunter turned and stared at Charlie, who cut a quick glance his way and smiled.

Mathias couldn't resist the opening. "Yeah, we did it, didn't we? Just about everybody doubted us, but we proved 'em wrong. Brother Seth and me made a pretty penny on that deal. Just goes to show that fear is a great motivator."

"What do you mean, Mathias?" asked Charlie innocently.

Looking up from his cards, Fleming paused and grinned wickedly, "Let's just say that some people didn't see the big picture that Seth and me were seein'. Some people had problems with our way of doings and I… uh… well, let's just say I helped them see their way clear of those concerns. Let's just say some now know better than to hold up progress. Hell, if we'd listened to some of those naysayers, we'd still be diggin' in the mud out there. Besides, the town bigwigs are tickled pink to have their water…keeps them safe in their jobs for a while. They could care less how we got there."

Mathias then looked around at the staring onlookers, slowly exhaled, and then growled, "I thought we was playing cards. Damn, Charlie, throw the flop on the table. And, darlin', pour me another stout one," he said to one of the attending ladies.

Charlie dealt the next three cards, "the flop," face up adjacent to the pot in the middle; the Jack of spades, ten of hearts, and seven of spades.

To his left, Gunter opened with a two-dollar bet that was quickly called by the two following players. The bet was to Fleming, and he raised it by twenty dollars with a proclamation, "You boys gonna have to dig a lot deeper to see these cards.

You too, Charlie." He then laughed obscenely at the other players.

Boyles took another look at his own two hole cards and exhaled. "Well, too rich for me. I'm out," he said as he tossed the cards in front of him and looked to Gunter on his left. The little man was fidgeting noticeably, looking first to his own hole cards, then to those face-up on the table, and back again to his hand. Blinking repeatedly, he slowly pushed most of his chips into the pile. "I...I'm in," he said, barely audible. Mathias looked at Gunter, eyes narrowed,

The man to his left, after some deliberation, also called Fleming's raise albeit somewhat reluctantly. The remaining player quickly folded his hand like Charlie.

"Ok, pot good? Here's "Fourth Street" fellows," said Charlie as he dealt the sixth card face up... ace of hearts. "Bet to you, Mathias."

With a self-assured smirk, Fleming threw another twenty dollars of chips onto the pot, drawing whispers from the crowd. "Like I always say, you gotta pay to play," he blustered.

The other player to Gunter's left immediately said with exasperation, "I fold," and threw his cards on the table. There was a buzz throughout the crowd as more gathered to see the outcome of the biggest hand of the night.

"Well, little man. Looks like you don't have the chips to cover," Fleming jawed while grinning across the table at his edgy opponent. Gunter didn't meet his eyes but rather looked down at his remaining chips on the table. "Likewise, you wouldn't have the guts to stay in anyway, right?" Fleming was obviously enjoying this — him being the center of everyone's attention — him winning at others' expense.

As he began reaching with both hands to drag the pile of chips, Charlie interjected, "Hold on there, Mathias. Now, if Gunter wants to call you, I'll stake him the other ten dollars."

"That's bullshit, Charlie. Every man has to be able to pay his own hand to stay in the game," snorted Fleming, now agitated.

"Says who? You makin' up the rules on the fly, Mathias? This has been done before, and you know it," Charlie replied evenly. The gathered crowd murmured with approval.

Sensing the congregation against him, Fleming quickly changed tactics. In an oily tone and manner, he responded with control, "Ok, I'll be fine with that. It's just that now I'll be takin' all of his money and some more of yours, Charlie ol' boy." With that, he laughed coarsely, downed the whiskey in his glass, and called for another.

Charlie slid two five-dollar chips Gunter's way and winked at his friend. Gunter nodded and cracked a thin smile in return. Looking around the table and then meeting Fleming's watery eyes, he called, "And now, gents, the river card." He slowly revealed the last card face up…seven of hearts. "Bet to you, Mathias."

Fleming, fully inebriated, remained silent for a considerable moment. All three tables and attendants were now fixed on the proceedings. A hum passed among the crowd. With great drama, Mathias then reached inside his tailored coat, produced two twenty-dollar bills, and slapped them on the table to the gasps of the onlookers – exactly the reaction he desired.

Gunter sat frozen, looking down at the table. Charlie groaned inwardly. He barely had forty dollars left between his winnings and what he had in his pocket, and he sure didn't want to lose it all to the blowhard across the table. Plus, considering the fact Fleming was a notorious poor loser, Charlie knew he was in a no-win position. He looked sideways at Gunter, who was still staring at the cards on the table, blinking uncontrollably. "Gunter, I'll stake you if you want to stick." He knew his friend was holding a strong hand, or else he would have folded long since. That much he knew.

Without looking up, Gunter nodded slowly. Charlie sighed, pushed his remaining chips into the middle of the table, and then fished another twenty dollars from his pocket.

Fleming was enjoying the scene. "Look, folks. It's taking two of these rascals to match up with poor ol' Mathias. Now, let's see you beat this!" He dramatically turned over his hole cards, revealing two tens. Laughing loudly, he exclaimed, "Full boat, boys! Tens over sevens!"

All eyes turned to Gunter. By now, he was visibly sweating and looking as if he may jump out of his skin. Then looking straight at Fleming, he slowly, almost apologetically revealed a pair of Jacks. There was a momentary silence then Charlie erupted, "Full house! Jacks over sevens! By God, what a hand!" The crowd cheered wildly, releasing the built-up tension.

Mathias sat silent, his face flushing a dark red as Gunter deliberately gathered the pile of chips and bills from the table. All eyes were on Fleming as the room waited for the explosion they knew was coming. But to everyone's surprise, Mathias didn't erupt in a fury. His famous temper was held in check to the relief of all watching. Instead, the hardened rogue shook his head in mock disbelief, stretched his meaty hands toward Gunter, and bellowed, "You little bastard. You sucked me right into that. I would accuse you of cheating, but I know you don't have the nerve," Mathias asserted with a twisted grin. "Darlin' pour us all a strong drink," he cried. "Now that was one helluva hand of poker!"

Charlie smiled broadly and was not a little relieved. Gunter's head was twisting every way to keep from looking anyone in the eye. The timid man was euphoric, but one would never know it by his nervous manner.

***

CHAPTER 12: LATE SUMMER 1901

"I don't see why I have to wear this monkey suit," Eli grumbled as he stood before the round mirror, attempting to knot an acceptable cravat for the fourth time. "I'm just not a tuxedo man. Besides, how much did you say this thing rents for?"

"Now, that's enough of your fussing," Kat smiled as she unfastened the lopsided tie. "You know that Jacob wants us all to look smart for the grand opening." She then tied a perfect bow just as Susan instructed and stepped back to survey her work. "You look ever so handsome, dear!" she exclaimed. "You may not be a "tuxedo man," but you play the part beautifully. Now, if you can help me with the necklace, we will be presentable and ready."

Eli savored the compliment and had to admit, at least to himself, that he felt rather special for his first occasion in formal wear. He took the gold and silver necklace from his wife and carefully fastened it around her slim neck. The piece was an inheritance of the Monroe family dating back four generations to the ancestral home in Edinburgh, Scotland. It held a distinctive Asscher-cut sapphire with brilliant cerulean coloring.

Turning her and standing back to appraise the effect, he declared, "All eyes will certainly be on you, my dear." She had splurged on the turquoise and navy gown after seeing the modern, more narrow pattern and gorgeous satin material in Stockton's Dress Shop. When the high summer date for the grand opening of the West End Hotel was announced, Susan had decided that Sunday dresses would not do. She then escorted Kat, Maria, and Nell to the thriving shop on Liberty Street to select proper new dresses for them all. Taking ahold of her arm, Eli pulled her abreast so both could look in the mirror. "I must say we are quite a pair…ready to hobnob with Winston's movers and shakers. Papa has always told me that we Claytons are no better than anyone else but certainly just as good. So, put your back straight and hold your head high, lovely Kat. That's the confidence we bring to this wingding. Besides, you must know that you'll be the most exquisite lady on hand tonight," Eli revealed while squeezing her waist.

Eli and Kat then left the guest room and descended the staircase to the waiting party below. Susan had insisted that they come to the house in Winston to dress for the gala and then stay the night as it would be a late evening. In the parlor stood Harper with Maria and Nell. Kat couldn't decide which of the two young ladies was more uncomfortable in their new dresses. Maria wore a dark red dress with a high lace collar that drew attention to her olive complexion and dark hair. Nell's ball gown was patterned after the Scottish Highlands style with a cinched waist and flowing skirt. It was in pure sky blue with puffed sleeves and woven snow-white flowers around the middle of the skirt. Eli thought his little duckling sister was quickly growing into a captivating swan.

He remarked with enthusiasm, "You ladies are the perfect picture. Wouldn't you agree, Papa?"

Harper replied while straining his neck for more room in the stiff white shirt, "Why yes! Three more beautiful daughters could never be found. And, if we can coax your Mother to join us, I'm sure we'll have a fourth charming lady."

"Of course, I'm here, dear," came the quick reply from Susan. She stood at the top of the stairs in her silver-blue gown with long lines and Chantilly lace around the bodice and sleeves. Her silver hair was caught up with a dazzling silver comb. She looked extraordinary. Those in the parlor were momentarily speechless. Then Kat jumped in, "Mother Clayton, you're an absolute vision!"

Deflecting attention, Susan responded playfully, "I believe we all look rather presentable. We Claytons can be well turned out if pressed, right husband?"

Watching his wife come down the staircase, he continued in a lighthearted tone. With mock seriousness, Harper added, "I guess we'll do in a pinch. I just hope Jacob is not embarrassed by us ne'er-do-wells."

"Speaking of, just where is the man of the hour?" Eli interjected.

"He had to be on-site early to squire the VIPs around," Susan answered. "Why, did you know that Governor Aycock is expected tonight? And Senator Simmons will be there. Oh, and the author, William Porter, is supposed to be there along with a host of other artists."

"Well then, we will fit right in," Eli teased, rolling his eyes.

Harper laughed out loud and, with a sweeping gesture toward the door, solicited, "Shall we? I expect Silver is already in the drive with the carriage."

***

Since Jacob had returned from New York, the press was on to finish the grand hotel. It was all-consuming work for Jacob and the whole Simeon-Stone firm, with non-stop meetings with contractors and town engineers. Finish carpenters, boilermakers, plumbing fixture manufacturers, industrial kitchen fabricators, brick and stone masons, mechanical engineers, interior designers, woodworking craftsmen, structural engineers, iron and steel workers, fire suppression experts, glass artists, landscape architects, and the list went on and on.

Like the Zinzendorf, The West End Hotel was four stories with over one hundred rooms and many of the same appointments of the old hotel, such as hot and cold-water private baths for each room, electric lights, multiple elevators, and eighteen foot-wide porches for shady relaxation.

Building design and technology had advanced in the decade since the Zinzendorf. Jacob employed his knowledge and expertise acquired at McKim in New York to ensure a more durable structure. The latest steel frame construction along with brick and stone materials, gave the new hotel a much more fire-resistant promise. While the Zinzendorf was made primarily of wood, The West End used wood only in finish materials, not the structural core.

And what a finish it was. Craftsmen and artists from up and down the East coast were employed to ensure the design was original, exceptional, and yet, reflecting the varied European heritage of the region. Intricate Swiss cornices adorned the entrance and three-story welcoming hall. Stained glass artisans had created ornate geometric patterns for the multiple transoms throughout the main floor. The curved

German Rococo-styled lines in the hall, while certainly not Moravian, added a touch of exuberance to its pastel color palette. The renowned muralist Robert Henri was brought south to create a massive canvas depicting the history of the area in his distinctive modern realism style.

Situated on the southeast corner of the hotel was the glass conservatory. It was placed to capture the morning sun creating a more stable ecosystem within while throwing a mosaic of light refractions across the space. The building of the conservatory had only recently been finished, with its twenty-four glass panes being set the previous week. Jacob had sweated every detail of construction, ensuring his design vision was realized. While simulating Gibson's glasshouse of New York's Botanical Garden, The West End was unique with two small and one larger dome using the hexagonal glass panes to allow optimal light as Robert Gibson had offered.

Sam Stone had confided to Jacob that the hotel was clearly the finest from Washington to Atlanta. To a man, the West End committee was enthusiastic, Pleas Hanes calling the finished structure a "masterpiece." They eagerly set the grand opening for July 30 to present the triumph to the town. At the cost of $655,000, the West End Hotel was easily the most expensive hotel in the state. However, the committee and other investors were confident in a healthy return on their investment as guests across the southeast were expected to keep the hotel in demand.

***

Jacob was in a hurry. He knew he should have sent someone to attend to Anika and the others at the station since he was scheduled to pick up the governor and his wife. His excitement in seeing her again was like a low-grade current running throughout his body. They had corresponded frequently over the past four months, and he had been overjoyed when she wrote back, saying that she would come to Winston for the opening and that Silas and Robb had agreed to accompany her. He borrowed Stone's opulent double brougham carriage that was large enough to accommodate the three guests and their baggage. The summer sun was peaking in the sky when Jacob pulled up to the carriage park at the railroad station between First and Second Street. He prayed that the train from Greensboro was on time.

He paid the attendant a half dollar to hold the carriage, then entered the station and proceeded to the boarding platform. Jacob thanked his good fortune as the passenger train chugged into the station with hisses of steam filling the air. The train was crowded with travelers, and he surmised that more than a few were traveling to Winston for the grand opening.

Scanning the disembarking throng, he first saw the big frame of Silas Gabriel. Waving, he caught Silas' attention, who then turned to inform Robb and Anika. His Dutch beauty was nothing if not more radiant than the last time he saw her. Smiling broadly, he rushed to meet his friends with handshakes, back slaps, and a warm embrace for Anika.

"I could not be more pleased to have ya'll here!" he exclaimed. "I consider you three the most esteemed guests of all that will be there tonight. I hope your journey was satisfactory…not too long and hot?"

The three stood there smiling, and Jacob knew he was carrying on a bit too much. Silas jumped in, "Of course, we had to travel to the southland to see for ourselves what magnificence you have created. And, I sure hope it reflects all the brilliance you gleaned from Robb and me," he added with his trademark waggishness.

Robb Turner, adding his two cents, chimed in, "Yes, I guess it is high time to bring a few of our superior ideas down south." Looking around the station platform, he teased, "Why I believe we could fit the whole Winston station into the north terminus at Grand Central...think so, Silas?"

"Ok, boys. That's quite enough," Anika chided good-naturedly. "Can't you see they've missed you, Jacob? I can tell you that they both have been excited as school children to see their southern friend once again."

Jacob laughed and realized how much he, too, had missed his "northern" friends. "Let's get you settled so you can rest up a bit and get ready for the big to-do. Tonight you will have rooms at my boarding house, but tomorrow you will be my guests at the West End Hotel."

He picked up Anika's bag and led the group to the carriage where the attendant was waiting. Assisting her into the coach, Jacob then bowed with an extended arm and quipped, "Gentlemen?" He then jumped up on the driver's seat and clicked the reins to make the short ride to Vogler's.

When they reached First and Main Street, thousands of starlings in the distance took flight, creating an eerie murmuration with their whirling, fast-changing pattern in the sky.

***

He barely had time to change into his rented tuxedo before the appointment at the Granville Hotel. Climbing back onto the carriage, he made his way to the east end of Fourth Street. Jacob was nervous. He had never met anyone as notable as a governor. Governor Charles Aycock had been elected and sworn in within the past year and had a reputation as a no-nonsense politician. He wondered what he could say to entertain such a man.

Pulling the brougham up to the entry steps at the Granville, he quickly made his way inside, hoping that the governor was not waiting on him. Relieved that the lobby was essentially empty, he took a moment to observe the surroundings of Winston's traditional luxury hotel. He was struck at how old-fashioned the interior appeared compared to "his" hotel. With its heavy oak front desk and stairwell, gaslights, and worn carpets, the Granville was positively ancient in contrast to the West End. This realization boosted both the young architect's confidence and excitement in escorting the governor and his wife to the grand opening.

Within moments the governor and his wife descended the staircase, followed close by several young men, apparently aides. Jacob took a deep breath and approached the group, and extended his hand. "Governor Aycock, please allow me to introduce myself. I am Jacob Clayton, with the Simeon-Stone firm and your escort to the festivities this evening."

"Ah, very good, Master Clayton," Aycock responded brightly and obviously well accustomed to such encounters. "May I present my lovely wife, Cora," he said, extending an arm toward the smiling young woman. Jacob bowed slightly and wondered offhandedly if Mrs. Aycock was any older than he. Aycock then conveyed to his aides, "You see, Spencer? We are well in hand here—no need for you and Samuel to accompany us. I'm sure Master Clayton will take the lead. We will see you at the festivities."

Jacob relaxed a bit at the governor's friendly tone. Perhaps he wasn't such a curmudgeon after all. He led the distinguished couple out the door to the carriage, where a valet had been arranged to drive them to the West End. Helping both Aycock and his wife up into the coach, Jacob then followed and sat opposite them. The valet urged the horse forward to make the length of Fourth Street from east to west end.

"Master Clayton, ol' Pleas Hanes tells me you're the shining star of this new hotel. He says it's your creativity and vision on display here tonight." Turning to his wife, he said, "Cora, we are in the presence of the new generation of North Carolinians. Master Clayton and his comrades will be taking us proudly into the 20th century with their new ideas and fresh thinking."

Jacob felt his face warming. "Thank you, sir, but there have been major contributions from a whole bunch of people, including my boss, Samuel Stone, and of course, the many builders and artisans. Speaking of, I am excited to show Mrs. Aycock the glass conservatory, and its geometric design pattern. We are still in the process of bringing in flora specimens from tropical climates, but we do have several palms and exotic flowers installed.

The governor's wife smiled generously and responded, "Why yes indeed, Jacob. I've heard how you patterned it after the one at the New York Botanical Gardens. I'm most interested to see it and the flowers." She reached over and patted his hand, re-triggering his flushed feeling.

Aycock leaned back, obviously pleased at his wife's interest. The carriage made the journey down the street with the two-beat rhythmic cadence of the filly's working trot.

The late July sun was setting at the tree line when the carriage arrived. The new hotel created a stunning first impression. As the Zinzendorf, it was set on the ten-acre knoll that overlooked the town to the east and the undeveloped forest to the west. A striking rock face made of granite from the Blue Ridge Mountains created a dramatic entrance. That and the twelve towers anchored the unique architectural lines. The effect was a fine European manor house.

"My, my! What a marvelous structure!" Governor Aycock exclaimed as they pulled onto the brick drive. "From what I've heard, this has to rival Vanderbilt's new castle in the Blue Ridge Mountains around Asheville. Cora, my dear, I believe we are in for a treat here tonight."

Smiling, Jacob helped the governor and his wife down from the carriage. A crowd was swiftly gathering to welcome the governor.

Twenty or so young men from the community had been hired to direct the carriage traffic and handle the livery needs of the many horses. Several now took the reins from the valet to convey the carriage and filly to the impromptu livery stable set up nearby on Burke Street.

"Governor, welcome. Welcome! It is an honor to have you and Mrs. Aycock here with us," proclaimed Pleasant Hanes. He and several other West End committee members moved forward to shake the governor's hand. "I hope Mr. Clayton has provided a warm re-introduction to Winston."

"Oh, yes…without a doubt. Master Clayton has been the most gracious host. And, I must say your hotel is visually stunning."

Hanes responded, "Just wait to you see the interior and our glasshouse…nothing like it in the South. First, let me introduce you to some of our other members and special guests." With that, Hanes steered the party to a larger group of guests.

Jacob, left alone on the drive, felt a surge of satisfaction and accomplishment. His duties with the governor concluded, he decided to go in search of Anika and the others.

Lans, Lucia, and Lucas Hall stood nervously on the hotel's elaborate front veranda. Lucia wore a pretty yellow beaded tea-dress with fitted sleeves. While not as formal as the hourglass design ball gowns Susan and Eleanor had made, it still stood out with its fresh color and simple lines. Lans was wearing a black suit and sky blue tie, his dependable standby for weddings, funerals, and any formal affair such as the one tonight.

The three were relieved to see Harper, Susan, and the others coming up the drive. "Let's go meet them," Lans whispered while reaching for Lucia's hand. "Heck, we don't know most of these folks, and it's good to see some familiar faces."

Before they could make their way to them, Harper and Susan were intercepted by Mayor Eaton, Seth Fleming, and a few others. "Well, Harp, Susan. The big day is finally here," declared Eaton. "Now tell me you're not tremendously proud of Jacob. This hotel and his design will be the talk of the state. Governor Aycock is clearly impressed and quite taken with Jacob, I do believe."

Before Harper or Susan could respond, Fleming broke in, "Good to see you finally up and around, Harp. No cane tonight? Ah yes, that boy of yours is the talk of the gathering here tonight," his false flattery obvious. "And Susan, might I say you look lovely as ever? Heads will certainly be turning your way tonight." Harper contained his animus toward the villain yet couldn't help but notice Fleming's obsequious tone, which made his blood boil while taking him back to another painful memory long ago.

Susan abruptly replied with a manufactured smile, and Harper knew the memory was stoked in her mind as well. "Well, thank you, Seth. And, that "boy," as you say, is a fine man, and we couldn't be more proud of him… with or without this hotel. I'm sure he would be the first to tell you that a great many people are responsible for the West End Hotel. Jacob is not one to seek attention, you see. Let's enjoy the party, shall we?"

Fleming stared at them for a moment, obviously at a loss for a response. He then scoffed and made his excuses as he moved on to another group. Harper thought he saw the hesitation in his eyes, or maybe it was a touch of fear. Regardless, he was surprised and amused at how Susan jumped the lanky rogue. He chuckled at that, especially the obvious dig at the huckster's ego and vanity. He then spied Lans and Lucia coming their way.

Susan and Lucia complimented one another on their dresses and surveyed the gathering guests with Lucas while Lans pulled Harper aside. "The nerve of that bastard," Lans bristled. "How dare he engage with you as if all is right with the world. It's time to take that bastard down, Harp."

Harper looked around to ensure they were not overheard. "Not quite yet. We need the evidence to be clear-cut. We need witnesses that will stand up to scrutiny."

"I've now got some first-hand accounts of Mathias shooting his mouth off about their intimidation efforts on the water plant," Lans continued.

"Not here," Harper replied. "We'll convene with Christian and Eli on Monday to see where all of this stands, and then hopefully, we will move on them. But, tonight let's enjoy the festivities. Enjoy your pretty wife, and let's celebrate. Looks like Hanes, Reynolds, and the others have spared no expense with the gala. I would say they are eager to show off," he added teasingly. "Now, why don't we find Jacob and toast him with a glass of that fancy French champagne I see floating around?"

***

Jacob spied Anika from across the spacious lobby near the table where champagne and other wines were being poured. He felt his pulse quicken as he gazed at the Dutch beauty. She was wearing the latest A-line gown of light pink silk accented with golden flora designs that ran from the bodice to the bottom hem. Her light porcelain skin was highlighted with pink rouge. Unlike the traditional formal up-do, her long cool-hue blonde hair was loosely braided and flowing down her back.

Anika, as usual, had an enthralled audience of young men around her, including Silas and Robb. Obviously the center of the conversation, she tossed her head back in laughter and toasted the group. Her confident manner was clear even from across the room, and he smiled as he thought of how she always seemed to make an extraordinary statement – in her dress, in her demeanor, in her presence. He chided himself lightly in realizing that he was content to even watch her from afar – simply beguiled by her singular beauty.

She then noticed him and waved merrily. Jacob held his glass up in her direction. As she smoothly floated across the floor toward him, he knew this was one of the truly special moments in his life.

"There's the man of the hour! We've been searching for you," Harper declared, jarring him out of his reverie.

Jacob turned to see his father and mother. Off balance by the interruption, he quickly looked back to Anika, who was now close, and replied, "Uh, hello there... I'm glad you made it. Uh, this is my friend, Anika," he said, sweeping his arm around toward her. His hand collided with her glass of champagne, spilling it on her silk gown. "Damn, I'm so sorry. I didn't mean to..."

Unperturbed, Anika answered, "Well, of course you didn't mean to, silly. It's only wine and not the first time I've had a champagne bath." She then offered him a playful wink.

Susan interjected to Jacob's obvious relief. "Hello, Anika. I'm Susan, and this is Harper. We're this embarrassed son's parents. And, these are the Halls...Lucia, Lansford, and Lucas." After quick introductions, Susan continued, "Now, let's find you a napkin." She then led Anika back toward the serving tables. Anika looked back at Jacob and smiled merrily.

Harper put his arm around his son and smiled. "Well, that was an interesting way to introduce your friend, though I'm not sure your mother would be so calm and composed if I had done that," he quipped while squeezing his shoulder. "No doubt Sudie will get her all taken care of."

The Halls moved closer to Jacob and Harper, and Lucia declared, "Jacob, the hotel is simply astounding! I've never seen anything so grand! The exquisite décor and the immense ceilings create a grand impression."

Lucas stepped forward and offered his hand, "Congratulations, Jacob. This is remarkable! I had heard from some of the craftsmen the new hotel was superb, and now, I see it for myself. You have done an incredible job with the design."

"Thanks so much, Mrs. Hall and Lucas," Jacob replied. He was glad to change the subject from his awkward moment with Anika. "Why don't we take a quick tour of the main floor and the conservatory? I'm sure mother and Anika will catch up."

Just then, a bell was rung toward the entrance. "Ladies and gentlemen, if I may have your attention?" Pleasant Hanes announced, holding a fat cigar while standing on a small stepstool just inside the substantial leaded glass doors. "This is a momentous day in the history of Winston. I want to thank the governor and his lovely wife for joining us in this celebration. And, our new US Senator, Furn Simmons…thank you, sir, for being here on this festive night. Please give them a hearty Winston and Salem welcome." Hanes gestured to his left, where the governor and senator were standing. Aycock and Simmons responded to the applause with raised hands and appreciative nods.

"Also, we have some other VIPs I am excited to recognize," Hanes continued. "Esteemed author and native son, William Porter, although you may know him better by his pen name, O.Henry…and, notable architect from Charlotte, Louis Asbury. Also, it's my pleasure to welcome Captain Thomas Shippley, hero of the war against the Spanish in Cuba. Finally, give a warm welcome to North Carolina's acclaimed artist, Stella Aubrey, just in from our nation's capital. We are most grateful to all of you for joining us tonight to officially open the new West End Hotel." The crowd met these introductions with a great round of applause.

"Now I promise to keep this short," Hanes chuckled, "as I'm sure you all want to enjoy the food and drink and festivities, but I must say a few things about what our town has accomplished here. When the Zinzendorf Hotel met its demise, the community felt a bitter deflation of spirit. There was almost a consensus that the town should just move on and turn our civic attention elsewhere," Hanes conveyed and paused for effect. "Well, here we are now, nine years later, and this splendid hotel is like a spectacular phoenix rising from the ashes of the Zinzendorf. I and the whole West End Hotel committee, could not be more proud." He paused to survey his brother, John, the Reynolds brothers, and other committee members with brief bows of affirmation. Continuing, he added, "This grand hotel is a testament to this community's resilience and vision to be an acclaimed destination for travelers, both business and pleasure. Finally, I must toast the team that created this fabulous design…Samuel Stone of the Simeon-Stone Architectural firm and his brilliant young protege, Jacob Clayton. Ah, there you are, Sam. Where is young Clayton? Jacob, where are you?" From the back of the crowd, Jacob humbly raised his hand. "There he is, folks. The visionary for the new West End Hotel…raise your glass and another round of applause, please."

Jacob felt his face redden as the crowd turned his way and offered a hearty ovation. He was both thrilled and flustered at the same time. Before he could react, Hanes concluded with a flourish. "Now, enjoy the festivities, everyone. I've heard the food and drink are excellent…and free!"

Within moments, family and friends surrounded him, offering congratulations and all manner of good will. The string quartet resumed their playing. Amidst the well-wishers and vigorous hand shaking, he tried to locate Anika to no avail.

Silas and Robb pushed through the press of people and intercepted him. "Well, Master Clayton, Turner and I have been inspecting this quaint little inn of yours, and we have a list of improvements for you…right, Mr. Turner?" Silas expressed with a facetious grin.

"Yes, quite right, Mr. Gabriel. We surmise that Master Clayton's beam designs are a bit off-center and in need of adjustment. Of course, that means your floor-to-ceiling ratios are off," he whispered in mock seriousness. "Moreover, we must say you've gone way overboard on the design décor…unless your goal was to fashion a most elaborate whorehouse." With that, both chums burst out laughing, unable to continue the jape. At once, they both slapped Jacob on the back, laughing. "All joking aside here's to our southern prodigy!" Silas held his champagne glass high. "You have designed a masterpiece. In fact, I may have to borrow some of your ideas on some future Gabriel marvels."

Jacob raised his glass in response and grinned. He was glad his friends were here with him to celebrate the grand opening. Still, he wondered where Anika might be.

The celebration continued late into the night, growing louder and smokier. Jacob spent time with Eli, Kat, Eleanor, and Tom, introducing them to his New York friends and other guests. He grew weary, however, of repeating the same stories of how he came up with the various design ideas for the glasshouse, rooftop lounge, elaborate lobby space, and others. He longed to be with Anika.

And then, he saw her. Standing alone in the glasshouse, she was a vision under a palm artfully backlit by electric lights specially installed for the gala. She was watching him with a contemplative look, a gaze that said, "I've been studying you from a distance and have made a decision."

Jacob lifted his head in recognition and smiled. He then made his way to where she was waiting. "I had lost you for a while, and it was not a pleasant feeling."

She replied naturally, "Tonight is your night. Yours. The last thing I wanted was to intrude on any of that. You have a wonderful gift, Jacob. You see possibilities that others only recognize after you have shown them. You deserve the spotlight tonight. This hotel is a creative treasure; I can see how the city's leaders are so excited. You provided that excitement. So, bask in the glow of that, Jacob." She put her arms around him and kissed his cheek. He felt a wave of pure emotion.

Stepping back, he held her hands in his and said, "Just having you here tonight is all the treasure I desire. I have to tell you that I love you deeply. I have never felt this for any other. I knew this in New York and wanted to tell you before I left. Seeing you now, here…I'm sure of it. I'm madly in love with you, Anika van Dijk. I don't even know if you feel the same. I just have to tell you how I feel."

"You flatter me, certainly. And I feel love for you, too," she replied with an unusually soft tone. Releasing her hands from his, she continued, "But you don't know me, Jacob. I live a complicated life in New York, of which you've only seen a glimpse. How could you know me? We've only had a taste of each other's lives."

Jacob stared at her wide ice-blue eyes, a jumble of emotions running through his head. "I believe I do know you. I feel a sensational connection to you. I know it sounds mad, but I feel I know your true self, your spirit. It's quite strange to be this sure, I must say."

Anika hesitated. Then pulling him behind the palms, she kissed him full and long. Jacob eagerly returned the kiss, and they found a nearby wicker settee. For the next hour, they embraced and shared stories, filling in some of the unknown spaces. Only when Mr. Leinbach, the hotel manager, came through did they take their leave.

Jacob Spies Anika in the Conservatory

It was well after midnight, and only a few guests remained when they left the West End. The impromptu grassy stable was dark. Jacob noticed a lone constable slowly patrolling the area, but the attendants were gone for the night. Jacob hitched the filly to Stone's carriage and helped Anika up on the driver's bench. The summer night was hot and still as they traveled to Vogler's boarding house. He walked her to her room and parted with a final kiss promising to see one another at lunch. Jacob returned to his room on the upper floor, his head spinning.

Outside his window, a whip o' will tendered its soulful trill breaking the stillness.

***

That night Harper had a dream. Perhaps it was the opulence and sensory experience of the gala. Perhaps it was simply seeing Susan in her finery. Whatever the stimulus, Harper was transported back to that day in May 1874 to the wedding of President Grant's only daughter, Nellie.

Harper had been taken by surprise when his mentor, Darius Starbuck, offered up the opportunity to travel to Washington to meet with the President, some of his cabinet, and members of Congress. The purpose of the trip was to discuss ideas for preserving the progress that had been made in supporting the black population in southern states now that Congress had defunded the Freedmen's Bureau. And the President had graciously invited the group to attend the large outdoor reception after the White House wedding of his daughter.

The grassy lawn behind the White House was overflowing with businessmen, lawyers, and congressmen. Elegant wives in colorful dresses, hats, and parasols mixed throughout the crowd. Other advocates of more modest means were on hand to ensure a democratic representation. Some even looked as if they had eluded the handful of policemen patrolling the grounds to attend the festivities. As for Harper, he wore his best suit, although it paled in comparison to the morning coats and top hats of Washington's elite.

He stood to the side with Starbuck and a few others as waiters made their way through the crowd with punch and champagne. "I don't see the President. Do you think he will make an appearance, Darius?"

"I've heard he is distraught about the whole affair," Starbuck replied. "You know this British dandy is considerably older than Grant's daughter. Could be he just can't face the music, especially knowing they will be moving to London. Odd, isn't it? Grant can't refuse his only daughter a whit, but Lincoln's General of the Army could send a whole corps to its destruction at Cold Harbor."

"Well, I do believe daughters are a father's weakness," Harper said, smiling. "I know that now my little El is five years old. Harper's mind wandered as he thought about the future of his only daughter. Would she make her own way in this strict patriarchal world? Would she find love? Happiness?"

Starbuck returned the smile and rolled his eyes in mock exasperation. "Well, Harp, let's just hope when she's of marrying age, you don't have to make this kind of investment to send her off into wedded bliss," he laughed while surveying the reception with a sweep of his arm.

Ellen Grant, "Nellie" to all, stood with her new husband, Algernon Sartoris, under the garland-strung cherry tree. At eighteen, Nellie was fair and quite pretty, if not a striking beauty. Everyone that really knew the President knew that she was his favorite. A large group of young gentlemen and ladies surrounded the couple, and easy laughter floated across the grounds. Toasts were made, followed by more toasts and salutations. The mood was light and merry even with the conspicuous absence of the father of the bride.

Nearby, the First Lady, Julia Grant, entertained a group of other guests. She appeared perfectly at ease while enjoying the congratulations and attention. Harper recognized Secretary of State Hamilton Fish in the party around the First Lady. Fish, a former governor and senator from New York had a reputation as a savvy politician and negotiator. He had quickly become Grant's loyal confidant and defender in Washington and abroad. Also in the crowd, Harper spied Attorney General George Williams, who was among the group Harper and the other agents were scheduled to meet with the next day. Williams was a radical reformer and had continued the prosecutions in southern states that effectively shut down the Ku Klux Klan.

He thought about the next day's planned meeting with the President, Williams, and other members of his cabinet and Congress. Being in Washington, he was inspired by the gravitas of the surroundings, its pace of political and business activity. While the relative quiet of Winston seemed to inhibit the push for progress, the capitol city's energy alone was a stimulant for

Harp to imagine the future. He actually was quite optimistic about the prospects of advancing the cause of the freed black citizens in North Carolina and the South.

Harper was taken by surprise as a loud, sarcastic voice intruded on the light mood. "Ah, here are our rebel friends just up from the unreconstructed provinces." A uniformed army major approached Harper and the group, followed by a small band of men in both military and civilian dress. Harper could smell the whiskey on the major's breath. He was a middle-aged, portly man with only one arm, the empty sleeve of his dress uniform pinned to his breast.

"No rebellion in this group, friend," Harper said, smiling while taking a step back from the whiskey stench. "We are all proud Americans to a man and honored to be here on this day of celebration."

"I bet you are honored, indeed… lucky, more like to be here," the major blustered, his large mustache dripping wet. "By my way of thinking, General Grant let you rebels off too easy. A lot of us see you southerners as traitors. Hell, what price has been paid for your rebellion?" His band of associates murmured their agreement. He then pulled a small flask from his waistband and with one hand nimbly uncorked it and took a strong gulp.

Starbuck interceded, trying to defuse the growing incident. "Sir, those were indeed dark times, but we are all trying to mend the wounds and move forward to a better place… both North and South."

"What do you know about wounds, sir?" the officer essentially spat the words. "You see this sleeve here?" he cried while offering the pinned vestment toward Starbuck. "This sleeve used to contain a damn good arm until it was blasted away at that God-forsaken ground called Petersburg." Other guests within hearing began to look and move in their direction.

Noticing the gathering crowd, Harper also attempted to mitigate the growing confrontation. "Sir, we are here at the behest of the President and are working to continue the task of solidifying the new freedoms of the former slaves; those freedoms won by the blood and lives of so many like yourself. We should make your sacrifice and that of the thousands of others count for something. Don't you agree?"

"I really don't give a damn about the freedom of a bunch of darkies," the drunken officer blurted out loudly. "I didn't fight for any of them, and they can go to Hell, as far as I'm concerned. And, I only see traitors in front of me...traitors that should have been hanged. Lee and all his officers should've been strung up right there on the spot where they surrendered. Hell, Grant didn't have the guts to do it, just like now he doesn't have the guts to put you boys in your place down South." With that and conscious of the several policemen moving in their direction, several of the man's company began to pull him away from the encounter. "Traitors! The whole lot of you," the inebriated office shouted as he was led away.

Harper looked at Starbuck and the others and slowly shook his head. This was a painful reminder that the war continued for many, both in their heads and ill-considered actions. He also thought about how multi-layered and complex the attitudes were about the war and its aftermath. The path to healing and redemption would continue to be long and difficult. His recent feelings of optimism were tempered.

Upon arriving at the White House the next day, Harper and the others were met by the President's private secretary, Orville Babcock. An aide on Grant's staff during the war, Babcock was one of the President's most trusted confidants. "The meeting will be held in The Treaty Room," Babcock announced warmly while leading them up the front stairs to the second floor. "It is where the President typically conducts cabinet meetings and other business. You might be interested to know that it was in this room where President Monroe signed his famous doctrine. Please make yourselves comfortable. The President and others will join you momentarily."

Harper and the other bureau agents, along with Starbuck and Superintendent Marshall, looked around the large room with its enormous gilded mirror positioned over the room's fireplace. Harper surveyed the massive rectangular table in the center of the room and wondered what consequential debates and decisions had been made around that table. Before he had much time to ponder those, Grant and the others entered the room. Approaching the group, the President called out genially, "Starbuck, my friend, how are you? Are you keeping the peace for us down there in Carolina?" He stuck his hand out and, in the other, held a half-consumed cigar.

"I'm fine, Mr. President, just fine, thank you," Starbuck replied. "Let me introduce you to my southern companions. Of course, you know John Marshall and the hard work he's done with the Bureau," he said while gesturing to the older man. Marshall smiled and shook Grant's hand. "And, here are our front line troops, if you will; three outstanding Bureau agents that have accomplished a lot of good works and have ideas for building on that even in the face of Congress' defunding," Starbuck said quickly, cutting a glance toward Grant's entourage.

Harper shook Grant's hand and felt a strange sense of déjà vu. He thought of that day a full nine years prior when he witnessed General Grant arriving to accept the Army of Northern Virginia's surrender in the little burg of Appomattox Court House. Mustering courage he disclosed, "Mr. President, you paroled me at Appomattox upon my oath never again to raise arms against the United States. I'll have you know that I have that parole pass tucked into my family bible as a tribute to your kindness that day."

Grant looked at him with gentle eyes. "I've taken a lot of criticism for my leniency over the years, but I've never second-guessed that action. Both President Lincoln and I were in perfect agreement that we must bind the wounds of both North and South and rebuild the Union as one people. That continues to be the overarching task of this administration. And that, sir, is a wonderful segue into our matter at hand." Grant then proceeded to introduce Attorney General George Williams and New York Senator Charles Sumner, a notable and radical republican consumed with the successful integration of the former slaves into society. Additionally, there were several other congressmen as well as aides for each of Williams and Sumner in attendance.

The meeting lasted well over an hour, with the President engaged and finishing yet another cigar. A number of worthy ideas were discussed, but it was painfully clear that money from Congress would be hard to come by. In truth, many in the country were weary of Reconstruction and wanted to move on to other priorities. This fact, coupled with the increasing deterioration of progress for the rights of black citizens in the South, made the future ominous. New Black Codes and other actions inhibiting property, workers, and voting rights threatened to erase the gains that Harper and others at the Freedmen's Bureau had worked so hard to achieve. Attorney General Williams was empathetic and promised continued prosecution of the Klan and other civil rights abusers but admitted that the federal government was limited in its ability to deal with local criminals and their offenses.

"I feel as if we are on our own," Harper said to Marshall and Starbuck as they boarded the train at Union Station for the long trip back to North Carolina. "The President commiserates with us, but his hands are tied. It's clear to me that Sumner and the Republicans don't have the sway in Congress to reinitiate funds for the Bureau."

Marshall looked on as Darius Starbuck replied, "It seems bleak. I am less encouraged about assistance from Washington than I was prior to this trip. It's a shame, but we in North Carolina have to do what we can to shape the outcome and impede those in Raleigh that want to take us back to the old days."

"Yes, that is unacceptable to me," Harper replied with a passion he truly felt. "I say we convene the former agents to put a plan together from this point forward. We can't go back. We can't. I keep thinking about that Major yesterday. Drunk as he was, I'm sure he reflects the opinion of many who say, "leave the Southerners to their fate…it's not our worry." Well, I, for one, need to see something better come out of the madness of the war and the chaos of the years since. If not us, then who?" Harper felt a keen emotional defiance, but to what exactly - the majority of opinion or simply the way of the world in 1874?

"Well said, Clayton," Marshall drawled. "We make the difference we can make."

"I'm sorry, sir, but that is not enough in my mind," Harper replied softly with resignation.

***

The morning heat was stifling. Jacob could feel the warmth through the thick drapes covering the window. His head was thick and ached from the glasses of champagne the night before. Squinting, he saw the little table clock read 11:15. He then remembered his lunch date with Anika and sprang from the bed to quickly bathe, shave and dress. The bath was a refreshing tonic, and coming down the stairs to the morning dining room he whistled Mozart's Eine Kleine Nachtmusik, the tune stuck in his head from the string quartet's performance the night before.

Entering the room, he saw Silas and Rob, both hunched over their coffee mugs and looking somewhat worse for wear. "Brothers, you look as if you are in a recovery of some sort," he teased brightly. "Please don't tell me that life in my little burg is too much for a couple of hardy men of New York."

"Lower your voice, for God's sake," Silas muttered. "Champagne is champagne. I don't care where it's served, and last night I was over-served."

"Well said, Gabriel," Rob rejoined. "My plan is to finish this coffee and retire again to my room. Perhaps when I wake again, my head will not have this current spike being driven through it."

"Well, I'm glad you both enjoyed the evening. I'm sure there will be more than one local lady inquiring about each of you," he replied with a laugh. "Have either of you seen Anika this fine Sunday morning?"

Both shook their heads just as Mrs. Vogler came into the room with a tray of breads and lavender honey along with a pot of coffee. "Ah, there you are Mr. Clayton," the innkeeper affirmed. "Miss Anika has left for the station… taking the noon train to Greensboro, I do believe. I asked if I should wake you, but she said no. She did ask me to give you this letter," she continued while pulling a small envelope from her apron.

Jacob was bewildered as he took the envelope. He opened it as he walked to the door leading to the front porch of the boardinghouse. There he began to read.

"Dearest Jacob,

When I was a little girl in Holland, my family had a wonderful flower farm along the dikes and canals just outside the town of Leiden. There were many hectares of tulips growing across the fertile fields, beautiful reds and yellows, purples and whites. I remember exploring the fields with my sisters and wondering if that was what heaven was like…a rich, fragrant sea of color.

With the blessing of my ouders (parents), I left for university in America but promised myself that I would come back to this heaven on earth. I did after several years and the homecoming was ever so sweet. I tell you this only to say that, just as my heart brought me back to those tulips, I hope to reunite with you someday.

Alas, not now. There are too many bridges yet for you and me to cross. You are on your way to great things. Go. Accomplish them. I, too, have dreams to design great towers and other marvels, things only men have designed before. And, if it's meant to be, we will find each other again in the moonlight. Our love will endure.

In my heart,

Anika

Jacob slowly folded the letter and placed it back into its envelope. From the Vogler porch, he looked out onto Main Street, unfocused and stunned. In the distance, the Home Moravian Church bells called the faithful to worship. After a prolonged moment, he remembered to breathe.

CHAPTER 13: EARLY AUTUMN 1901

Christian Harmon was well respected with a reputation as a savvy lawyer and honest broker. After he, Harper, and the others collected the evidence against the Flemings, a petition was brought before Winston's district attorney, Walter Hedrich, to bring assault charges. Christian made his case, and Hedrich agreed to issue an arrest warrant for the brothers. Sherriff Bolton had served the warrant, and the two brothers were willingly brought in front of the magistrate. Each was given bail in the paltry amount of $90, which was promptly paid with their immediate release. With a detestable arrogance, Seth Fleming declared to the local newspapermen gathered outside the jail that he and his brother were wholly innocent of the charges. He declared Harper Clayton was only trying to malign his good name. He admonished that he and Mathias would prove these claims to be false and malicious in court. Moreover, he threatened to sue Clayton in turn for egregious libel.

Harper and Christian knew their case was frustratingly weak. Kiger was nowhere to be found. Tom's account of his conversation with the Flemings would not be compelling since there were no witnesses. And then, there were Lans' efforts to draw Mathias out. Mathias' words at the card game, while suggesting guilt, were circumstantial at best. These realities notwithstanding, they decided to push forward to bring justice to the two brothers.

"I don't know why this isn't enough to put these bastards away," Eli railed while pacing the law office. "We know they did it, Kiger said they did it, and Mathias, as much as admitted to Tom, they did it. Why won't all this convict those two crooks? I don't understand the law. Why make it so hard to convict somebody that is obviously guilty?"

Eli had not sat down since the group gathered in the Clayton-Harmon offices on an unseasonably cool morning. In addition to Harper, Christian, and Eli, there were Jacob, Tom, Lans, and Silver to establish the strategy for the trial scheduled to begin September 1.

"Our American justice system is by design hard to achieve a conviction, and rightly so," Harper responded. "Imagine what could happen if one could be tried and convicted on hearsay and unsubstantiated claims. People would have little to no confidence in justice. Chaos would ensue. There's no doubt. So, as frustrating as our situation is now, the rule of law has to hold."

"They can't get away with it. They're not going to get away with it!" Tom declared with obvious despair. "Where is Kiger? His confession is clear enough to me to take them down with his first-hand account. He has to be found!" The young man was agitated as well. The group knew that Tom's own desire for revenge against the rogue brothers was driving his emotions. If the Flemings could be convicted and jailed, then perhaps the damage he had caused Harper and the family could be rectified, at least partially.

Harper could see the pain and desperation in Tom. He felt his own sense of sadness for what his son-in-law had endured. "Tom, as you know, we have had men trying to locate Levi for the better part of the summer. He has disappeared. I don't hold out much hope of running him down at this point."

Lans jumped in. "My guess is that Levi Kiger has been dealt with one way or another, and they've made damn sure he can't testify. I wouldn't put a killin' past them. I agree with Harp. We won't have Kiger here to make the case."

Christian then stood and summarized, "So, that leaves us with Kiger's statement, which he didn't write himself. And we have Tom's testimony with no corroborating witnesses. Then, there are the other disclosures by Mathias in front of witnesses with only general allusions that really aren't incriminating." He smiled ruefully at Harper and added, "Not the best ammunition to go to war with, eh partner?" He shook his head slowly and continued, "We don't like to go to trial with such a thin case. Remember the Crater affair? We knew that land swindle could not be proven, so we got what we could with a settlement of parties out of court. But, I'm guessing you aren't looking for any settlement here," he added with a bemused look.

Harper inhaled deeply and looked around the room. "Jacob, Silver, you've both been quiet. What do you think we should do? Should we plow ahead?" Silver immediately replied as if he was a spring waiting to uncoil. "Harp, we have to try our best to convince that jury. I wrote down, word for word, what Levi said. I looked in those miserable eyes and saw that his confession was true and the Fleming bastards telling him to do it was true. I'll get up in that court and tell them that. It's the truth...they have to believe, don't they?"

"Well, I, for one, believe you, Silver," Jacob claimed good-naturedly. "And, you know what? I agree with you wholeheartedly that we've got to try to get justice for Papa. I know we don't have the strongest case, but I think we have one that can convince a jury. Hell, everyone knows the Flemings and their ways. Our evidence reinforces those perceptions in my mind. I say let's proceed. Mr. Harmon is the best, right?"

"Damn right, he's the best, brother," Eli grinned while looking at Christian. "We'll get these thugs, alright."

Harper and Christian looked at each other and nodded. "Yes, we'll go to trial with what we have," Harper said evenly. "Christian, if you will inform Walt of our decision and prep him with the case strategy, witnesses, and so on, I'd appreciate it. Facing those bastards in court will be some justice in itself."

Harper rose slowly and steadied himself with his stronger arm on the heavy oak table. The rest stood in acknowledgment and began to leave the office, each absorbed in thought.

***

"*Not guilty*," called the foreman of the jury in response to the judge's inquiry. After a four-day trial, the jury had taken the better part of a day to reach their verdict. Standing at the defense table, Seth and Mathias Fleming broke into broad grins at the pronouncement. Exuberant backslapping and congratulations ensued with their attorneys and supporters in the courtroom.

The Flemings Go Free

Harper, Christian, and the others sat stone-faced at the result. It was not a surprise. As they had feared, without Kiger as a key witness, the defense attorneys effectively made the case that it was Harper's word against the Flemings. The district attorney had called Eli, Lans, and Silver to provide testimony about the signed confession, and each had told a truthful account. Yet the defense made the case that the written confession, even if it was, in fact, from Kiger, could have and probably was made under duress. Tom was called and gave a passionate account of his encounter with the Flemings and Mathias' allusions to the assault, but the defense easily discounted it as purely circumstantial. In the end, there was enough doubt created in the case that the jury could not help but find the Flemings not guilty.

Seth Fleming looked around and located Harper. "Next time, you had better think twice about trying to bring down two innocent men," he said loudly for all to hear. "I'm seriously considering suing you for malicious libel just to let you know you can't get away with this kind of deceit."

"Shut your foul mouth, you son-of-a-bitch," Eli shouted while moving toward the lankly older man. Jacob and Silver quickly grabbed Eli, holding him back.

Tom jumped in and bawled, "You had Kiger do it, you bastards. You know it, and we know it. You just watch your back, you crooks."

"Best keep your boys in line, Harper. I may just bring charges against them as well. That will be another black eye for you, Claytons, and your precious reputation." He turned to his brother, and both laughed harshly.

By this time, the courtroom bailiffs interceded and steered Eli, Tom, and the others toward the door. Harper and Christian had remained silent during the whole altercation. Hedrich offered his apologies. "Harp, Christian, I'm awful sorry about the outcome. Justice is hard sometimes, and I know you both know that."

"No apologies needed, Walt," Harper consoled. "You put on the best prosecution we could muster. We knew it was going to be tough without direct testimony and impartial witnesses. They won the case, but I got to confront them in a court of law. They know that I know they're guilty, and that's something."

The early September sun was low in the sky as they left the courthouse. Susan, Eleanor, and Kat had sat through the trial and now descended the steps with Harper. Susan put her arm into her husband's. "Love, you have suffered through this dreadfulness for the better part of a year, and I think it's time we put it all behind us and look to the future. God will judge those two ultimately."

"I believe you're right. I do. Now, please tell that to them," he said quietly, pointing to Eli, Jacob, Tom, Lans, and Silver, who continued to be engaged in heated dialogue down the sidewalk on Main Street.

***

The trial was the talk of the town for days but then died down when replaced by other momentous news, the assassination of President William McKinley. McKinley, while attending a public event in Buffalo, New York, on September 6, had been shot by a violent anarchist. He died eight days later on September 14, at which time Vice-President Theodore Roosevelt assumed the Presidency.

The family had gathered after church at Harper and Susan's. All were there with the exception of Jacob, who was in Raleigh discussing some new assignment that he said had to remain a secret for now. Blanche, with help from Susan and Nell, had prepared a special Sunday spread of fried chicken, fresh green beans and tomatoes from the garden, mashed potatoes with gravy and biscuits, and cucumber and onions marinated in vinegar.

"Being President has become quite dangerous," Eli quipped off-handedly while biting into a fat chicken breast. "Three assassinations in about the last thirty-five years; that's quite a record."

"I would appreciate it if you were not so flippant about such tragedy, son," Susan said with more than a little feeling as Kat kicked her husband under the table. "The President didn't deserve this awful fate, and oh, the poor man's family will not see a moment's peace from the newspapers, I'm sure."

"They say that some sort of presidential guard is now being formed to better protect the President," Harper asserted, "something called the Secret Service."

"Well, our new President Roosevelt will be the beneficiary," Eli continued. "However, assuming it's true that he likes to portray that brazen manliness that we all hear about, he may just refuse the new protections. I bet our Philli would have been the first to volunteer for his former fearless leader. I remember little brother telling us of the man's exploits out West and, of course, against the Spanish. Philli loved the man."

There was a distinct pause as thoughts of Phillip were surely evident around the table. "I do hope Roosevelt is the man for the job," Susan added with a serious tone. "God knows we need a strong leader in this new century."

Tom sat silently throughout the exchange, head down, focused on his plate. That was not unusual these days; he had become increasingly morose since the trial. Eleanor had tried to cheer him to no avail. Even though he had said little over the past several weeks, she knew Tom was consumed with hate for the Flemings. She was afraid he would act on his hatred and do something foolish. She intended to engage her father for guidance as soon as she could get him alone.

After lunch, the family moved to the porch to enjoy the pleasant early autumn weather while James and Noah, Tee, and the other youngsters diverted to the yard and chased each other in a lively game of tag. Harper leaned on the porch railing and smiled at the merriment from the lawn below. Inhaling deeply, he felt grateful for these simple blessings yet continued to harbor a dark discontentment. He had been wrong. Confronting the Flemings in court was not enough. The disgusting image of Seth Fleming's exultation in that courtroom had continued to haunt his private thoughts. There had to be a better justice.

"Oh, for the carefree exuberance of children," Eleanor exclaimed as she approached and took her father's arm. "Was I ever that happy-go-lucky, Papa?"

"Of course you were, most certainly. You were so breezy at that age," Harper replied while observing the noisy competition going on below. "I remember you chasing after Eli and his friends all around Bethania, determined to be part of his gang of chums." He smiled at the memory. "And all the good-natured kidding you gave to Jacob and Philli was as entertaining to your Mother and me as it was to you. It's the pull of responsibility and setbacks that can weigh us, adults, down. If only we could maintain that fine simplicity of a child as we take on the cares of the world." Harper looked across the yard, not at his daughter.

"Well, that's the perfect lead into something I need to talk to you about," Eleanor confided as she glanced behind to ensure the others were out of earshot. "I'm worried about Tom. I'm worried about what he might do to get back at the Flemings. Between what they did to you and how they cheated him, I'm just afraid that he is going to do something foolish to seek vengeance. Now that they have gotten off scot-free well, I'm so fearful that will be the trigger for Tom. He won't talk to me. I don't know what to do, Papa."

Harper looked at his daughter and saw her obvious distress. "I can talk to him," Harper said slowly. "I have noticed his gloom. Perhaps if he knew that I, too, am struggling with this sorry mess and want a more fitting reckoning. I know he holds the Flemings to account for corruption beyond what they did to me, but we can't have him turn vigilante and risk being hurt or worse."

Eleanor reached up and touched her father's cheek. "Thank you, Papa. I love you so."

Harper smiled and nodded. From the yard, a high-pitched squeal went up as one of the young girls was tagged and sent laughing and rolling on the grass.

***

The Danville Road was dusty and dry as he hid behind a laurel thicket along a desolate stretch of the old plank turnpike just north of Winston. Tom had been shadowing the Flemings for several days. From his surveillance, he knew they would be headed home late Sunday afternoon after the Apple Fest. He scoffed as he imagined the two crooks strutting around the festival as judges while feigning the role of reputable civic luminaries. How they could continue to command respect among legitimate town leaders was impossible for him to grasp.

For a year, he had struggled with going to the sheriff or police chief to expose the corruption from the bribery of town officials. To indict the brothers, Tom would have to reveal his own complicity in the sorry affair. Finding the resolve eluded him, however, as he could not face Eleanor, Harper, and the rest. Tom knew he lacked the moral courage to divulge his guilt, which only deepened his remorse. It was this utter sense of shame that had brought him to this lonely place along the plank road.

Tom shook his head at the thought of how his own road had taken such a crooked and desperate course. How had the promise of a grand future with El and Tee faded so completely? God must surely choose favorites to flourish in life here on earth, he mused. How else to explain the prejudice of it all? Perhaps it's simply the luck of the draw that explains why cheats like Seth and Mathias Fleming can win again and again at the expense of other poor fools. Fools such as himself, he thought.

The young man shivered involuntarily as he looked down at the revolver in his hand. A thin baleful smile emerged as he thought about how his father had given him the Colt double-action revolver. He had just turned eighteen and recently engaged to be married. It was the only gift he could remember his father had ever given him. He recalled the pride in his father's voice that day as he confided, "Every man needs a sidearm to demonstrate the strength and will to protect his family."

The nickel-plated revolver had a six-round capacity. Its double-action feature was notoriously vulnerable to misfires owing to a flawed design in self-cocking the hammer. Tom had experienced this flaw at times during his infrequent practice shooting over the years. He had learned to pull the hammer back when this happened to create a single-action fire with the trigger, although it inevitably created a surprise and delay in the firing.

It was near seven o'clock, and Tom began to think the Flemings were not coming after all. He had considered wearing a hood to prevent the Flemings from identifying him but then realized that would defeat his purpose. He wanted them both to know who it was exacting revenge. He thought of leaving and stood to retrieve his horse when he heard the faint sound of carriage wheels on the road headed in his direction. He ducked back down behind some laurel bushes, his pulse quickening. Bowing his head, Tom thought briefly of Eleanor and Tee and how this act of revenge would be some redemption for him in their eyes.

Within moments the carriage was near. Tom rose and walked deliberately onto the road with gun raised. Mathias held the reins with a young, rough-looking woman adjacent to him on the seat, nuzzling his neck. Tom was surprised to see that Seth Fleming was not in the carriage. Noticing the carriage slowing, the woman raised her head and followed Fleming's eyes to Tom. She then let out a small shriek and tried to move behind her companion.

After the briefest of pauses, Mathias let forth a repugnant snort and called, "Moser, put that gun down before I run you over where you stand."

Tom stood expressionless and kept the revolver raised at the older man. He sensed he was in a lingering dream that was now reaching its long-anticipated, ugly conclusion.

Mathias continued derisively, "You don't have the backbone. You…."

At that moment, Tom pulled the trigger expecting the recoil. Nothing happened, and Tom knew the firing mechanism had failed. Mathias laughed evilly and opened his wide mouth to castigate the young man again. Suddenly, the gun fired, sending a .38 caliber bullet into Mathias. Tom had instinctively remembered to drag the hammer back after the misfire and pulled the trigger a second time. Both Mathias and the woman screamed, he from pain, she from fright. This caused the horse to lurch forward on the run. Before he could fire a second round, Tom dove off the road to avoid being trampled. From his side, he watched the carriage careening down the turnpike, raising a cloud of fine red dust.

***

After sending Tee off to the West Winston Graded School the next morning, both Tom and Eleanor expected Sheriff Bolton and several of his deputies to knock on their door at any time. Tom had divulged the prior day's episode to his wife, and Eleanor was beside herself with anxiety and fear. Tom was somewhat bewildered that he felt none of his wife's apprehension – none of her dread. He wondered why this was so but then surmised it must be due to the fact that a reckoning on some level had been achieved. In any event, he was surprisingly calm.

"It will be ok, sweetheart," he reassured her. "Don't be frightened. Once the sheriff arrives, I'll go with him to the magistrate and post a bond for release. Then I should be home before Tee gets home from school. It will work out; you'll see."

Eleanor responded with alarm, "No, I don't see. You'll be charged with attempted murder, Tom. Don't you understand? Will they even let you post a bond? I'm afraid, Tom."

At this, she began to cry, unnerving him. It always tore at his heart when he thought he had hurt his wife. "Pl…please don't cry, El. I will find a way to fix this. I will."

By noon the sheriff had not called on the Glade Street house, and Tom began to wonder what the delay could be. Surely Seth and Mathias would not let this go unanswered. They would solicit their pals at the sheriff's office to immediately draw up the warrant for his arrest. Wouldn't they? His mind began to race, exploring other scenarios. What if Mathias never made it home and wrecked the carriage down the road? But Seth or someone else traveling the road would have discovered the wreckage, right? What if Mathias was dead; what if the wound had been fatal? The woman with Mathias witnessed everything and would have told Seth, giving a description of Tom to the older Fleming. Thus, it still must be just a matter of time before the sheriff and deputies come for him.

Eleanor had retired upstairs to lie down and try to calm herself. As the hours crawled by, Tom began to feel the strain as well. He tried to relax by working in his darkroom on some of his recent photography work of the new streetcars put into service earlier that year along the Fourth and Main Street tramways. The box and open passenger cars were equipped for electric power and had become quite popular over the past decade. Tom had been hired by the Fries Manufacturing & Power Company, owner of the local streetcar system, to produce photography of their latest trolley car acquisitions. The company intended to use the photos in newspaper ads across the area.

After a half hour or so, he gave up the effort, unable to concentrate on processing the negatives. Coming up from the basement, Tom felt a headache swiftly coming on. At the top of the stairs, he closed his eyes while pressing his temples. He thought briefly of going to Eli to divulge what he had done and ask his advice. Tom was wrestling with whether to act on this notion when he heard a knock at the door. He froze momentarily. His mind racing, Tom walked slowly to the front door but couldn't see anyone through the leaded glass panes. He opened the door and was surprised to see a small boy, no more than nine or ten years old, holding an envelope.

"Uh, excuse me, sir. The man told me to give this to you," the youngster said, holding the envelope out to Tom.

"What man?" Tom replied rapidly while looking up and down Glade Street.

"I don't know, sir. He just said to run to this house, knock on the door and give this here letter to whoever comes to the door. He gave me this quarter to do it, so I said I would sure do it."

Tom took the envelope, and the boy then scampered down the steps and ran toward Fourth Street without looking back. Tom made another inspection of the area and then moved to the front porch glider. He saw that his name was typed on the outside of the envelope. He slowly tore it open to find a simple one sheet with the typewritten words… "*You're a dead man.*"

It all became clear in an instant. The Flemings would enact their own justice. They were clever enough to realize that a trial would bring them nothing but harmful exposure; the briberies of city officials, the questionable shortcuts on the reservoir construction, even the retelling of their orchestrated attack on Harper Clayton. Tom knew it all and having that testified to in court would not go well for the Flemings. The brothers would take care of the matter in their own malicious way.

***

The next several weeks were anxiety-ridden for Tom and Eleanor for different reasons. Eleanor still feared Tom's arrest no matter how he tried to reassure her. He had not shared with her his revelation of why he would not be arrested, although he knew it was only a matter of time before she arrived at the same conclusion. He, in fact, feared for his life and began carrying the Colt revolver with him outside the house. While outside, he was careful to avoid going anywhere without a number of witnesses about.

The evening and morning air began to cool as the autumn of 1901 presented a lovely Indian summer. The yellow, red, orange, and gold foliage on the hardwoods presented a striking palette and inspired local painters to capture the display on canvas. The evening light was sweet and the air mild, encouraging many West End residents to stroll the rolling sidewalks and renew local acquaintances.

At Eleanor's urging, Tom agreed to meet her parents and Nell at Grace Park Friday evening for a small picnic. Maria and little Susannah would also be there. "We have to continue to live our normal lives, Tom," she encouraged. "Who knows what will happen, but let's not shut out the family. They are a source of strength and love. Besides, we need a diversion to get our minds off this stressful business."

Gathering Tee and the basket Eleanor had prepared, they began the brief walk to the little park at the top of Glade Street. Tom was careful to conceal the gun inside his coat. He was glad to notice several other neighbors out and about. As they reached the base of the hill below the West End Hotel, Tom turned to see two men swiftly descending the granite stairwell from Primrose Alley. The heavily shaded alley behind the new hotel had recently been finished as a pedestrian footpath that connected Glade and Fourth streets. The men began walking briskly in the same direction, about fifty yards distant.

Quickening his pace, Tom discretely looked back to see the two strangers still following. "Slow down, Tom," Eleanor laughed. "You know, Tee and I can't match your long-legged strides."

Hiding his concern, Tom responded in a light manner he did not feel. "Nothing like some good fast-paced exercise to get our hearts pumping. Tee, let's see if you can keep up."

"I can do better than that, Papa," the boy replied. "I'll just beat you and Mama to the park." Tee took off running. Tom could hear his son laughing, invigorated by the fun and games. They began to round the final uphill grade to Grace Park. With a final nervous look over his shoulder, Tom saw the two men pick up the pace and begin to close the gap. He then grabbed Eleanor's hand and exclaimed, "We can't let our boy beat us, can we, sweetheart?" Grabbing the basket from her, he began to run, pulling his startled wife behind him.

"Whoa, Tom! You're going to pull me down," she protested while at the same time laughing.

Tom glanced behind once more and observed that the two men had stopped their pursuit, obviously perplexed at what to do next. By then, Tom and Eleanor were cresting the hill with the park just ahead. Tee had already arrived and was sharing his victory with Nell and the others. One last time he looked behind. The two men were gone.

***

CHAPTER 14: LATE AUTUMN 1901

The city streets were dark at 5:20 a.m. on the morning of November 2. A mist hung close to the ground around the reservoir. The air was still, and the early morning quiet. Suddenly, a low groan emanated from the north wall of the water works. The vibration quickly transformed into a great smashing din as the wall collapsed upon itself, emptying about one million gallons into Eight and Trade streets. A wall of water and detritus of brick, concrete, splintered wood, and mud rushed down the steep hill demolishing houses, businesses, and other structures in its path.

Reservoir Disaster

When the fire alarm rang from Town Hall at about 6:00 a.m., hundreds rushed to the reservoir to assist the injured and help locate the missing. One witness said that the mighty crash sounded like an earthquake, and he looked out his window to see a huge river rushing down the street carrying parts of houses and all sorts of debris. One man escaped injury by clinging to a fence while another couple rode out the flood on their mattress, landing safely about five hundred yards from their home. Others were not so lucky. Several people had been crushed under the rubble of bricks and stones, while even more were swept away by the powerful force. By midmorning, a crowd of several thousand had gathered at the scene of the disaster. The reservoir was destroyed. By the final tally, when all had been accounted for, nine people had been killed and dozens injured.

Mayor Eaton called an emergency meeting of the Board of Alderman for 12:00 p.m. to discuss the catastrophe and take the necessary immediate action to alleviate the suffering of the victims. The Board quickly detailed police officers and other city employees with instructions to begin supplying all aid and assistance. Anticipating numerous claims for loss of life, personal injury, and significant property damage, a committee of aldermen Norfleet, Lüpfert, and Brown was appointed to facilitate the speedy repair of such claims. In addition, the Board enlisted Horace Efird, the town attorney, to begin the work of safeguarding the town's interest in the face of such a disaster. By unanimous vote, the Board also agreed to appoint a committee, with Lansford Hall as chairman, to investigate the cause of the disaster.

Lans immediately summoned Captain Henry, Supervisor of the Water Works, and Mr. Burgher, Pumping Station

Manager, to give an account of all pumping station and reservoir systems leading up to the break. Henry stated that the reservoir was in use, as usual, the night before, but no water gauges had yet been installed from the new pumping station at the Belo pond. Consequently, he had been sending a watchman at night to the reservoir to report back to Burgher on the water levels. The previous night, the watchman had reported that the water in the reservoir was within two feet of the overflow pipe. Burgher confirmed that he had then instructed the fireman on duty to slow the pumps and continue reducing the speed throughout the night in order to not exceed the usual nightly town consumption of 150,000 gallons. Burgher also added that he believed the fireman followed these orders as he was thoroughly reliable.

Satisfied that all the proper procedures were followed in the pumping station and reservoir operations, Lans then recalled Jacob Clayton mentioning concern over the speed and processes for building the reservoir and, of course, the Flemings' company managing the construction. Lans suggested to the committee that the Flemings, as well as the engineering firm hired to design the reservoir, be called to give an account of the design and building process. In addition, they decided to summon Randal Shelton, Captain Henry's predecessor, as Chief Superintendent of Water Works, who had retired immediately after the reservoir completion. Shelton would have been in charge of approving the design as well as authorizing the key permitting milestones along the way of the build.

Attempts to telephone the Flemings were unsuccessful throughout the day. (The rumor was that Seth Fleming had supposedly bribed the local telephone company several years prior to run a new line from town north along the Danville Road. Poles were erected, and lines were strung the five-mile distance to connect only one customer, Seth Fleming.) After repeated attempts to reach the Flemings, Captain Henry dispensed a messenger to the house. The young messenger returned after sunset, saying Fleming was not there and a work crew was swiftly clearing belongings from the house.

"What the hell? This looks mighty suspicious. The reservoir fails, and the Flemings vanish. We need to get the sheriff and chief in on this," Lans declared to Henry and the others gathered in the town hall. His mind quickly put together a deadly scenario, with his instincts screaming that the Flemings had compromised the safety of the reservoir in order to further line their pockets.

"Sheriff Bolton and Chief Smalls should still be at the reservoir. Let's get them in here to bring them up to speed," he announced. "Henry, where is Shelton? We need to get the full background from him…all the approvals, inspections, and the complete record of sign-offs. And let's get whatever paperwork there is in your office."

"Strange, now that I think of it, I haven't seen Randal all day," Superintendent Henry answered. "Surely, he would have been there today to survey the damage. I'll go call and get him here as soon as possible. Oh, and I'll retrieve those permits and other documents from the past eighteen months."

Harper, Eli, and Jacob had come earlier to offer their assistance. Lans thanked them for coming and asked them to wait until the committee broke up. As they adjourned, Lans walked outside and saw the three coming down Main Street. Grim-faced, they apparently were returning from the site.

"What an awful tragedy, Lans," Harper lamented. "There's nothing left of the two houses that were close to the north wall…just gone except for the meager foundations. Hundreds of people are still there helping clear the damage and support the families," he added.

"The town is gonna do right by the victims," Lans responded. "Eaton got the alderman together earlier, and several actions are already taken to assist the victims. Harp, did you see Chief Smalls there? We got problems."

All three searched Lans with puzzled looks and waited for him to continue. After a deliberate pause, Lans told them about the Flemings' disappearance and his suspicions of their culpability.

It was Jacob that reacted first. "I knew there was something off about the whole deal…especially how quickly they put the walls up on top of the recently poured foundation. I meant to go back for a closer inspection but got swallowed up with the new hotel. I feel awful for not following up."

"Don't beat yourself up, brother," Eli asserted. "This is the Flemings' doings. Are any of us one bit surprised? I bet those two swindlers are halfway to California by now. Now they've got murder on their miserable hands. Bolton and Smalls need to get on this pronto. Lans, we did see Smalls at the reservoir directing a group of his men there. He might be back at the station by now."

Jacob added, "I also think we need to find out what, if anything, Tom knows about the proceedings, especially who signed off on the work and did the permitting. Tom may have seen or heard something that can point to any shenanigans on the part of the Flemings or the foreman being in cahoots with the city."

Lans jumped in, "I agree with you, Jacob. In fact, I sent Superintendent Henry earlier to find Randal Shelton and get him in here to go over the inspections paperwork."

It was late when Henry and Burgher finally located Shelton after an extensive search. His wife had told them that Randal was in a foul mood and had left the house several hours earlier, saying he needed a drink. The former water works superintendent was found at the Green Street Saloon, a rather seedy drink house, and was well into what looked like his second bottle of whiskey. Shelton was not known as a "drinker." This didn't look good.

Shelton was a beefy man with a thick neck and forearms. Like most other local men over the age of fifty, he had fought with the Confederacy. In fact, he donated his left hand early in the war at one of the battles around Richmond. Mustered out in the invalid corps, he was long commended for continuing his service in the quartermaster ranks. He developed a reputation for procuring supplies with extraordinary imagination and resolve. This credit helped him secure a position with the town after the war, where he stayed for the next thirty-five years.

The two saw the older man alone and seemingly unaware of the few others in the saloon. The lone bartender eyed the two new arrivals with suspicion. Ignoring his stare, they approached the table where Shelton sat, shoulders hunched and staring at the empty glass on the scarred table in front of him. Henry reached down and touched the inebriated man's shoulder, causing him to jump. His head swiveled around and, with bloodshot eyes, considered the two. Shelton was slow to recognize either man; however, when he did, he then returned his gaze to the table and remained silent.

"Randal," Henry said clearly. "There's been an awful calamity up Trade Street at the reservoir. The north wall failed early this morning. There are quite a few casualties, I'm afraid, and there is considerable property damage."

Shelton didn't react to the news. Instead, without acknowledging Henry and Burger, he deliberately poured the remaining whiskey from the bottle into his glass. The two looked at each other with queried expressions but then with recognition. Randal Shelton clearly knew something.

"People are dead, Randal!" Burgher exclaimed with eyes wide "Do you realize what has happened? This is a disaster most grave, arguably the biggest catastrophe to ever befall Winston. And, as the water works supervisors, we have to figure out what happened…what caused this tragedy!"

"What caused it?" Shelton responded without pause. "No mystery there, boys. What caused this fiasco, this misery? You're lookin' at it. Right here. Randal Wallace Shelton…the man that let himself be bought, pure and simple. For a few hundred dollars, the man signed them foundation inspection permits, knowing full damn well it was not fully cured. Hell, I never, in my wildest dream, thought anything like this would happen. Flemings have pushed me before to cut a few corners to their advantage. They wanted that bonus for finishing ahead of the timetable, and he said he'd be cuttin' me in on it. Never did, though. Don't matter none now, does it?" Shelton looked at the two men, totally distraught. Tears rolled down his puffed cheeks. He then stood up rather quickly, knocking an empty bottle to the floor and breaking it. "Now it's time to pay the piper, right? If you boys would bear me to Chief Smalls' office, I would appreciate it. I'll tell him the full story. Nothing to hide now, is there?"

With resignation and even sadness, they accompanied the tormented man to the police station at town hall. A cold November wind had picked up, causing the men to pull their coats up tight around their necks. It was well past eleven o'clock by the time they arrived.

The town's investigation, led by city attorney Efird, quickly implicated Shelton. Documents showed he had signed off on the foundation permit and forged his assistant's signature for the corroborating stamp as was required by North Carolina law. Independent engineers inspected the foundation ruins and determined that the concrete had, in fact, not fully cured before the north wall was constructed.

These findings also clearly indicted the town, and Mayor Eaton swiftly brought in outside attorneys to manage the liability cases that were sure to come. Harper, at Lans' urging, was one of the attorneys asked to assist in the process. Harper agreed to help; however, it soon became apparent that he would have a conflict of interest in doing so. While Shelton's testimony confirmed the bribery from Mathias and Seth Fleming, it also brought Tom Moser into the spotlight. Shelton revealed that Mathias Fleming offered the bribe, but Tom was present with Fleming that day. Harper was distressed but not shocked at this revelation. He knew Tom had temporarily lost his way in his misguided will to stand tall. This new evidence of Tom's knowledge of Flemings' bribe of a public official, while not technically a crime, would compromise Harper's credibility in the investigation. So, his son-in-law's involvement in the matter was a non-starter for him.

Chief Smalls stood in front of his old wooden desk in the rather spacious office. He had summoned the full force of thirteen men to the office and provided clear instructions. The chief was clearly agitated. His distinctive square head was sweating even as the day remained cold.

"The Flemings' corruption and criminal acts are now clear," he proclaimed as Sargent Rankin and several other patrolmen cut nervous glances between each other. "I want those two found and held to account. Until such time, everyone is on duty. Rankin, take your squad out to the Flemings' place and go over the house and grounds with a fine-tooth comb. There's gotta be some clue as to where they were headed. Smithson, get your boys to all the railroad stations in the area and find out who has seen anything. Men, nine people are dead, over thirty injured and much property destroyed. Justice must be dealt. Now, go do your duty and bring those crooks to me."

As no statewide law enforcement agency existed at the time, separate police departments in Raleigh, Charlotte, and across the state were notified of the case and enlisted in the manhunt. Beyond the state, the call went out to cities and towns, especially those along the key railroad routes, to help locate and apprehend the fugitives. The publisher of the local Union-Republic newspaper assisted in providing North Carolina newspapers with information about the manhunt and the $5,000 reward offered by the town.

Harper returned home looking for Susan and called for her. It was cold for early November, and he stoked the parlor room fire and added a few pieces of hardwood from the box, rekindling the flames. The revelation that Tom had abetted Fleming's bribery was yet another distressing example of how he had taken such a wayward path. Why in the world could Tom let himself get so entwined with those two? Tom's reputation in the community was now ruined. There was no question about that. Such poor judgment by his son-in-law would feasibly rub off on him, but that did not bother him. But he worried for Tom and Eleanor. How would this shape their relationships in the community and future prospects?

"You look so weary, dear," Susan said softly, entering the room. "Please sit down and rest. I've boiled coffee and cream. Let me get a cup for you." Returning with the two cups of coffee, she declared tearfully, "Oh, those poor people! What an awful, awful thing. What will happen to the families, Harp? I hope you can help them get some relief from this misery."

Harp replied, "I will do what I can, but what I can't do is engage with the town on this." He saw Susan's quizzical look and continued, "More bad news, I'm afraid. For now, let's just enjoy the coffee." They sat together on the couch, facing the revitalized fire radiating comforting warmth. After a moment, Harp laid his head on Susan's shoulder and slowly drifted into a shadowy daydream.

Seeing the collapsed reservoir had brought back a deep-seated distant memory for Harper. The reservoir collapse conjured up the sudden disintegration of the Confederate lines at Petersburg, setting into motion the war's end game and the South's surrender.

In February 1865, the siege was in its eighth month. Petersburg was the major rail nexus in Virginia, providing the flow of arms, food, and other essential supplies to the beleaguered Confederate army. Early in the siege, repeated Union assaults on the entrenched rebel lines had failed to capture the vital supply center. However, the battle settled into an uneasy stalemate through the fall and winter. The two armies faced each other across the ragged battle lines east and south of Petersburg with little fighting except the occasional action along various supply routes. While the Union army was continually resupplied overland and via the James River, the Southern supply lines were increasingly closed off, straining General Lee's ill-equipped, starving soldiers in the trenches.

The 1st NC Battalion had returned to Lee's army at Petersburg in December via the Weldon Railway, the only remaining rail line still under Confederate control. While the men were relieved to end the provost duty, they were shocked at what they saw in the defense line around Petersburg. In their four-month absence, conditions in the trenches had deteriorated significantly. Food was in such short supply, with rations meager and inconsistent that trench rats had become a much sought-after bounty. It was not unusual to see a rodent dressed and speared over a paltry fire. Most uniforms were ragged, with few winter coats, and shoes were in short supply. Many had resorted to tying rags around their feet in an attempt to prevent frostbite and gangrene. It was a miserable existence as the 1ˢᵗ Battalion had taken their place on the southwestern edge of the U-shaped line as part of General Robert Johnston's brigade. Morale was low.

In the six weeks since being deployed in the trench lines, both battalion companies had suffered greatly from exposure, lack of food, and the unbearable boredom of inactivity. Harper had tried his best to boost morale with words of encouragement. He was determined to remain visible to and engaged with the company. Nevertheless, it was a desperate time. Private Welsh had recently died, and his remains were buried in the ever-expanding 2ⁿᵈ Corps cemetery along the Boydton Plank Road. The surgeon said it was sickness and malnourishment, but Harper was sure that lost hope played a role.

"Sergeant, prepare the men to move," Harper instructed Sergeant Nissen early February 5ᵗʰ. "There is a supply train of wagons coming up from the Stony Creek railhead, and the regiment's orders are to guard it from Gregg's cavalry while leading it into the western line." Union Brig. General David Gregg's cavalry division had been active in the area since the battalion had arrived, raiding supply trains and rear-guard troops. Weary as the men were, the order to march was a welcome respite from the dreadful sickness and tedium in the trenches.

"Yes sir, Captain," the sergeant replied and began to work his way among the troops just now stirring around small fires. Harper was impressed with George Nissen's fortitude. Even with such misery, Nissen remained attentive and vigilant to orders and the company. A native of Winston, his father, Charles, had built a successful wagon works over the preceding three decades. Before the war, Nissen wagons could be found across central and western North Carolina carrying tobacco, other crops, and goods to market.

Harper fed his bony mount a handful of rather moldy oats and then saddled the poor beast. From the saddle, he observed the two companies shuffling into formation. Lans walked his horse to where Harper was positioned.

"Lans, you are in no shape to ride, let alone engage the enemy. You need to stay in camp and have the doc see to you."

Lans had been down with an intermittent fever for the past week, unable to walk the line and engage the company. He had been in and out of the surgeon's tent and was too weak to stand two days prior when Harper had last seen him.

"I'm fit to ride, and I'll damn well do my duty," he retorted with a hacking cough. "Let's see that these supplies get here. Maybe the battalion will get a share of 'em." Lans turned his mount toward the men and away from his friend. Harper knew Lans' fierce pride would not let him show any weakness, and at that moment, he felt an acute sadness for the younger man.

They both knew that the men needed rations desperately. Ensuring this alleged supply train got through was most critical, although they had no idea what, if any, foodstuffs were in the wagons. Regardless, it was an assignment the battalion would carry out just as the numerous others over the previous three and a half years.

"Forward," Harper commanded as Company B led the regiment from the entrenchments to the Boydton Plank Road a few miles west of their position and one of the only roads remaining clear into the Petersburg lines. Arriving at the designated location just after eight o'clock, Harper and A Company's Lieutenant Woodruff deployed the men on the plank roadside of Hatcher's Run while the three other regimental companies moved forward adjacent to the road.

Hatcher's Run was a large stream running east to the Appomattox River and provided a shield from any attack coming from the north. The men were ordered to throw up what meager breastworks they could using the downed limbs from a sparse line of trees along the river.

The rumble of the half-mile-long train could be heard before it came into view. The grinding wagons along with the shouts of the drovers encouraging the mules and horses forward, were heard from down the slight grade of the road. Within minutes, they saw the lead supply teams moving toward them at a slow pace.

"God, I pray there's food in those wagons," declared a private behind Harper and Nissen. Harper turned to reply that was his wish too. He noticed all the men and boys around him with eyes eagerly fixed on the arriving train. Everything now, except survival, is blurred, he thought. When men are pared to their primal selves, life becomes quite clear. Food was the object; not home… not friends…not even love. The thought of rations coming sustained them yet also made them intensely feel the holes in their stomachs.

The troops guarding the potential treasure began to dismount, and others jumped off several of the wagons behind as the train reached the battalion. "Hey, whatcha haulin', boys?" asked the same private. "Something to eat, I hope."

Before any of the escorts could answer, a fusillade of rifle fire came from the tree line southeast of the road. An advance regiment from Gregg's division had arrived on the scene and had dismounted without being discovered. Several guards fell instantly.

Harper immediately took command of the men around him, shouting, "form ranks! Prepare to fire!" The train had shielded them from the volley, but they could see the Yankee regiment emerge from the tree line and begin to move forward, firing without stopping to reload. "Of course," he thought. "Gregg's men would surely be carrying Spenser repeating rifles." He had seen this marvel from a few captured in the Shenandoah Valley fighting last fall. With its automatic loading innovation by pulling the trigger guard lever, a rate of fire unheard of with the standard muzzle-loaders could be achieved. Harper wondered how many of Gregg's troopers carried the Spenser.

The main body of Gregg's troopers abruptly wheeled left to focus on the last piece of the wagon train that had become mired on the wet plank road and separated from the bulk of the train. The thought struck Harper that this is what a predator would do in the face of weaker, wounded prey.

General Johnston ordered the regiment to maneuver below the train to set up a blocking defense of the wagons that had just reached them. Dark storm clouds were forming in the west, and the wind picked up as he deployed his men on either side of the road. There was little cover, but the battalion formed ranks creating two lines of fire on the left side of the wagons. Harper then sent his company runner to the regimental command to confirm the battalion was in position.

Harper was relieved to see the other companies taking up supporting positions on his left flank and along Hatcher's Run. Across the field, in the trees, Gregg's remaining regiment held their position without advancing, and Harper surmised these men would remain in reserve until more Union troops arrived on the field. Sure enough, within minutes, the signs of a large Union infantry force, at least two divisions with skirmishers out front, were spotted on the march.

"Move! Defend the train," a voice thundered. Harper was surprised to see Brig. Gen. Johnston on a large grey horse just behind him beside the nearest wagon. The general had brought the whole brigade to the plank road to ensure the supplies made it into the lines. Johnston continued, "Officers, organize your men for a fighting withdrawal. We will not give up these wagons, gentlemen!"

Chaos ensued. Wagons lumbered forward with wagon masters whipping mules as companies attempted to maintain a coherent order while facing the pressing enemy. Lans and Harper ensured the battalion stayed in contact with the train and, at the same time, sent ragged volleys into the approaching infantry.

By now, Harper was sure that a whole corps of Yankee infantry was in pursuit of the prize. He saw the battle flags of Union Major General Warren's 5th Corps and quickly estimated at least five thousand troops closing on their retreat. He was struck at the stark visual comparison between these well-outfitted men and his own ragged command, some even without shoes. Unless reinforcements arrived soon, the brigade's meager force would surely be overwhelmed before making the three miles to Petersburg.

"Reform your lines," Lans yelled. "Stay on the move! Reload and fire!" Emaciated from his recent sickness and with all color drained from his face, the small officer looked like a wraith in the flat morning light. He raised his sword signaling the company to rally on him. They formed a line and sent a sheet of fire into the oncoming front line of the enemy, momentarily slowing their progress.

This act repeated itself until ammunition ran low. Union fire became devastating. The private who so wanted the food stuffs was shot dead, a minie ball through his heart. A short distance behind, a colonel's horse was shot out from under him. When the officer stood, he, too, was killed. It was a desperate fight with some engaged hand to hand with the enemy. Several more wagons were captured, but as they neared the defensive lines of Petersburg, Warren called off the attack.

In all, sixty-four of the original ninety wagons made it to safety. The 1st Battalion lost fourteen men, three killed and eleven wounded. The supplies did indeed include a satisfying amount of food rations: salted meat including cured pork, tins of beans, peaches and other dried fruit, good flour, sugar, and molasses. It was a godsend to the starving troops. Once the wounded were cared for, and the companies regrouped, Harper and Lans ensured each man received a proper ration on the spot. The regimental quartermaster secured a satisfactory supply of rations for their return to the lines.

The next six weeks were a return to misery in the trenches. Grants forces did not initiate any new assaults either directly against the line or efforts to turn the Confederate flanks. However, the rebel army was melting away through disease, hunger, and exposure. Cold rains and sleet storms only compounded the agony. Harper and Lans both knew the command was incapable of fending off another major assault which they knew would be forthcoming when the weather cleared.

"There's talk of hooking up with Joe Johnston's army in the Carolinas," Lans asserted as he and Harper sat beside the evening cook fire. He had regained most of his strength in the past weeks, and Harper was glad of it.

"Maybe. But the word is that Sherman's got him bottled up south of Raleigh," Harper replied without emotion. Leaning close to his friend, Harper intoned, "I just want it to be over. I want to see my Sudie again. And it's almost planting time. I wonder what's left of the fields now with so few to work them."

Lans stared at Harper and slowly nodded. "It seems like a million lives ago, Harp. Even if we ultimately survive this war, what's to become of us? How do we even think to put our lives back together?"

Harper didn't respond to the questions he had no answers for. He recalled the last letter he had received from Susan and shook from the worry and yearning. The tone in her letter was strange. For the first time, there was a direct appeal to come home. While she provided little specifics, there was fear and apprehension in her words. He could only guess at the troubles that existed back home. The concern about the unknown and the helplessness of not being there weighed heavily on him.

He stared into the small campfire, stoking it with a blackened cooking iron.

The second day of April dawned with a bright sun rising behind the hundred thousand-plus Union army. The last several days had seen the renewed thrusts of Grant's forces in piecemeal attempts to extend the line west and get behind the defenders. The critical Boydton Plank Road supply line was finally captured, and a crushing assault at the Five Forks crossroads overwhelmed the Confederate left flank with many prisoners taken.

A terrible foreboding of impending defeat filled the ranks as the day broke with the battalion awaiting orders from the brigade staff. Within the hour, an all-out Union assault up and down the entire siege line was launched. The battalion's two companies were swiftly overpowered by the thousands of Yankees storming the breastworks, sending them scrambling to the rear for escape. It was an immediate and total collapse of the line. A wild and disorganized retreat commenced westward across the Appomattox River.

It was a fight for survival. The cacophony of cannon and rifle fire and shouts and screams of men in flight and pursuit filled the morning air. Whole regiments melted away in the face of the Yankee tidal wave, with hundreds killed, thousands wounded, and tens of thousands captured. Excess equipment, including rifles, was discarded in mass to facilitate the flight.

Harper knew this was the beginning of the final act. His thoughts now were on preserving as many of his men as possible. Along with the rest of the brigade, he and Lans kept driving the company westward just out of reach of the overwhelming Union force.

The rout continued through the night and next several days. "How long can we keep this running up?" Lans asked plaintively, pulling up aside Harper. "We'll soon be out of ammunition, eliminating any hope for a firing line. I don't know how long we can hold out, especially with no rations to speak of."

"Johnston says we're to turn and offer resistance up ahead at a place called Sailor's Creek," Harper replied hastily, knowing such efforts were futile at this stage. Men and boys were falling out, essentially giving up all along the retreat. He looked and grimaced at the staggering oncoming host of blue spread across the east and south of their position.

***

CHAPTER 15: CHRISTMAS 1901

The search for the Flemings continued, now into a second month. Police Chief Small's men had fanned out, chasing down leads from New Bern to Asheville and into the surrounding states.

With the crime widely exposed, several citizens came forward to divulge conversations they had either had or heard, citing the corruption and transgressions of one or both of the brothers.

Tanner Bost, the bartender at the Fourth Street Tavern, revealed that Mathias, when into his cups, was prone to brag about all manner of malefactions, illicit or otherwise. He specifically recalled Mathias crowing about blackmailing Davis and Williams into selling their Salem water plants at a lowball price. Bost recollected the villain sounding off, "Hell, these people are easy marks. All it takes is the suggestion of threats against them and their business, and they fold up shop in nothing flat."

Charlie Boyles, from Arista Mills, had also come to Small's office early one morning to share an encounter he had with Mathias. "I'm sorry, chief. I shoulda come to you sooner. I know that now. Last winter... I guess it was about early February... I was with Mathias one night at Rooster's place, and he got to bragging about "working the system," Boyles said sheepishly as he held index and middle fingers up in the air on each hand to signify the quotation. "He says all it took was a little palm greasing to get those boys in the town engineering office to play ball. I really didn't know what he was all about. I swear it, chief! Well, I guess I do now. And I'm just broken about it… those poor folks around that water building. They didn't deserve any of that."

Smalls had one of his men, Angus Shelton, travel to Atlanta to track down John Robeson, the firm hired by Fleming to draw production plans for the reservoir. Robeson's firm had been involved in other projects, mainly around Atlanta, where other scandals arose. None of this was brought to light with the Winston reservoir project, however, due to Mathias' efforts in suppressing the due diligence work of the town.

After taking the early train from Greensboro, Shelton arrived at Robeson's office late afternoon as a weak sun was setting behind the row of soot-covered two and three story brick buildings. Not surprisingly, he was nowhere to be found. The Robeson & Associates offices were locked and dark. Other business owners in the neighborhood were canvassed, yet no one knew anything about the whereabouts of the curious little man.

In Winston, the Flemings' house and grounds were searched and searched again. It was clear that the brothers left in a hurry, as some furniture and other belongings were left behind. Food even remained in the pantry and smokehouse. On a second search, a sheriff deputy dug around in the burn pit and discovered the charred remains, just bones really, of Levi Kiger. Of course, the remains were not identified initially. With subsequent forensics ordered by the court, the remains were thought to be Kiger based on evidence of the broken right femur he was known to have suffered in the past.

***

"He came at her with a big ol' hunting knife, and she shot him dead on the spot," the Charleston constable drawled in a matter-of-fact fashion as they surveyed the corpse on the morgue slab. "Miss Lavenia said he called himself Jones from up Raleigh way…been frequenting the place for the last few weeks, causing some kind of drunken mischief just about every night. Thursday last was the worst. Drunk and raging, he near tore up the place and then went after Prissy. Chased her up the stairs and into her room. She said he was wild-eyed and screaming some woman's name, Reva or something like that. Thank the Lord she had her little Colt on the side table…took it out and shot him in the mouth… as you can see. He went face down pronto. His papers say his name is Fleming, Mathias Fleming from Winston. That's why I called you boys to come down and take a look. We have no plans to charge the girl; it's a pretty clear case of self-defense. Hell, he was still gripping that big knife hard in his hand."

Angus Shelton, who had taken the train from Atlanta, replied evenly, "Well, thanks for bringing it to our attention. This is, in fact, Mathias Fleming. He'd been on the run for over a month for multiple crimes up our way." Looking down at the cold cadaver, he continued, "Looks like he suffered another recent wound. See that hole in his right shoulder? Appears to be a fairly recent bullet wound. What do you think, Tom?"

"Uh, uh, well yeah. Looks like a bullet wound to me," Tom said hesitantly, recalling the story behind the injury. Tom had all but insisted to Chief Smalls on traveling down to Charleston to meet up with Shelton in order to confirm Mathias' death. He pleaded that he needed to atone in some small part for his past sins with the Flemings. And now, looking at the lifeless body, Tom felt a renewed sense of remorse for his unholy alliance with such rotten characters. Changing the subject, he inquired of the constable, "Do you have any information about the brother, Seth Fleming? Is he in Charleston? Any word about his whereabouts?"

"No, Nothing. There's been no mention of him. He certainly has not been seen with his brother at Miss Lavenia's," the constable asserted. "I hope we see neither hide nor hair of the man if he is anything like his brother. Say, is there any other kin in Winston or, are you boys gonna claim the body to take back to Winston?"

"Hell no!" Tom blurted instinctively while Shelton flinched at the bitter response. "There're no other kin we know of. You can just plant him in your potter's field down here in Charleston. That's where you bury paupers and criminals, ain't it?"

***

"Shot dead in a Charleston brothel. Is that not a fitting end for that lowlife? I couldn't imagine a more perfect exit. Hell, I'm sure it was him that also did in Levi. For that heinous act as well as all the others in his filthy history, I say he got his just deserts." Eli, as usual, was the most vocal about anything to do with the Flemings. He was up and orchestrating the current situation. "So, the slow-witted, vicious brother has been dealt with in a not-so-surprising manner. Now we just need to locate his no-good older brother. He's not stupid like the recently departed. Seth's a conniver and sly bastard and gonna be harder to find. We know he was the mastermind behind the reservoir corruption and Kiger's attack on Harp. This isn't over until Seth is held fully to account…either in front of the judge or winding up like his brother. Really, I don't care which."

Harper, along with Silver and Lans, listened as they had gathered in Harper's study on a cold and windy day in December. Silver rose to stoke the dry split oak burning brightly in the small fireplace.

"Either way is fine by me," Silver responded while poking the burning red embers. "I guess the chief and the sheriff have struck out in tryin' to track him down. I just wonder how long they'll be lookin'? And, I swear, even with all his evil-doins' all these years, I don't believe ol' Levi deserved to wind up that way…killed and burnt up in an old sorry trash pit."

"I agree with you, Silver," Harper said solemnly. "Levi caused all kinds of devilry over these many years, but it was usually at the bidding of rogues like Seth Fleming. God will bring His own justice down on Seth even if we don't bring it in this lifetime. I do pray for those souls lost at the reservoir, all due to Seth and Mathias' greed and corruption. One way or another, there will be a reckoning… for all of it."

Harper looked weary. These last weeks had weighed heavily on his heart. Increasingly, he looked back across his sixty years; the war, the trials of Reconstruction, and the endeavor to provide a solid foundation and future for his family. He felt tired but not defeated. As Eli and the others fed the conversation about settling scores with Fleming, Harper leaned back in his chair, closed his eyes and drifted to another time long ago. He was weary then, too…oh so weary. As now, he knew then it was time to turn the page in his life.

***

It had been a few months shy of four full years. The realization of it all gave him a start. Indeed, it seemed much longer since he had marched off to war full of vigor and determination. The strong, confident youth of twenty was returning a worn, unsettled twenty-four-year-old man. Yesterday's hopes of glory, of triumph, were now today's troubling realism of defeat and uncertainty.

The Great Wagon Road, that well-traveled migration route from Pennsylvania to the Carolinas for over one hundred years, was muddy from the April rains. Harper and Lans had been walking for just over a week now, headed home to Bethania. Their uniforms and shoes showed the hardship of the past months of no resupply. They had parted company with the other parolees periodically along the way on their trek south. Now, it was just the two of them.

The battalion had been paroled at Appomattox along with the other remnants of the Army of Northern Virginia after Lee's signing of the surrender. They had heard that, in all, over twenty-eight thousand defeated confederate soldiers were pardoned during the second week of April and allowed to take their long guns with them for hunting when they returned home. Officers were even allowed to keep their side arms. They each carried a signed prisoner parole pass that provided the bearer *"permission to go to his home and there remain undisturbed."*

Pulling the pass from his coat pocket, Harper read it again and lamented bitterly, "*Remain undisturbed,*" it says. Lans, I'm not sure if I will ever again be "*undisturbed.*" I feel old and weak, and I sure as hell feel disturbed."

Lans looked at the budding dogwoods and poplars along the road and countered, "Yes, these past four years have been a horrible trial; an ordeal that we endured and managed, by God's grace, to come through. Losing Jacob so early was a bitter blow. I know it changed something inside me. But we have come through it. We are here now, going home, while a good many friends are left in the ground in Virginia, Pennsylvania, and the Carolina coast. I long for Bethania, its fresh springtime air and crops newly planted," the solemn young man offered with his familiar measured smile.

"Of course, you are right, friend. As the Gospels say, we are called to walk in the light, not in darkness. There's been so much darkness. How do we ever escape it?" he asked rhetorically. "I've got such a mix of feelings running through my brain. I still feel pride for the stand we took to protect our homeland, yet I'm torn with guilt. When Lincoln emancipated the slaves, it seems that the fight changed to one over slavery, not sovereignty. I damn sure know that neither one of us signed up for that. I feel like we were betrayed and used up in the cause of slaveholders. The nobler justice of states' rights just seems to have disappeared." He continued, "I'll be honest with you, I don't know what we'll face at home, but I know with God's grace, we will rebuild a life. We will work together to survive… but what about the black man? I wonder about the black folks. It's a scary, unsettling future they face. They're free, but how do they survive? How do they build a life with little to nothing to start with?"

The two walked on in silence for a while, each in their own thoughts. After a bit, Harp brightened and exclaimed, "I too long for home, Lans. And I pray Sudie is there waiting for me. I remember her sweet smell even to this day. I'm going to ask

Clay Bostic for her hand, and then I'll go straight and ask her to marry me. Now that's the promise of a life redeemed," he announced. "And, we gotta find you a sweetheart, some girl that's pretty and sweet, someone to share your biggest dreams with. What do you think?"

Harper grinned as he saw his friend redden. Lans Hall was easily embarrassed when the talk turned personal and the focus on him.

"I'm not sure if I can find a girl that will have me," he rejoined. Harper could not tell if he was serious or not. Lans continued, "I'll be happy to get back home and help with the rest of the spring planting, work the horses, and… just be. The thought of riding the hills around Bethania without orders, without the oily smoke of a hundred campfires, and without men everywhere I look is a very pleasing one, I must say. It frees my mind."

The late April sun was sinking behind the budding green on the trees as they spied a small wooden signpost just ahead. It read, "North Carolina-Virginia State Line." Harp and Lans looked at each other and smiled. At that moment, a musket fired with a bullet whistling between their heads, sending both men to the ground.

"Where's it from?" Harper asked Lans as they both scrambled for cover.

"Sounded like from up ahead, but I didn't see any flash," Lans responded. "Hell, I just realized I don't have any caps. You?"

"Yeah, I've got a few in the box. Here's a couple," he said, handing the felt-lined cap box over to Lans. They each proceeded to muzzle load their Enfield rifles and placed a percussion cap on the pulled-back hammer while peering through the brush down the road. The light was quickly fading, with long shadows overlaying the muddy road.

"What do you think? More than one out there?" Lans inquired. Without waiting for a response, he continued, "I'll move around to the right and try to see what we're dealing with."

"Hold on. Let me see what this is," Harper replied and then called out, "The war is over, friends. We're just two soldiers trying to make our way back to Carolina. We mean no trouble for you." He waited for an answer but was only met with silence. Lans began to maneuver to his right through the undergrowth along the road. Harper waited, wondering what to do next. Idly, he thought of the absurdity of all he had suffered, only to be killed *after* the war and on his journey home. He started to repeat his message of peace when he heard a commotion down at the curve of the road.

"Let me go. Let me go, I tell ya." Harper was surprised to hear the tinny voice of a young boy.

"Harp, come on over here. I've discovered our opposing force," Lans proclaimed with obvious enjoyment in his voice. Harper stood and walked to where Lans held a boy by the collar no older than ten or eleven. Beside him stood an even younger lad of about seven with his mouth open in astonishment.

"Now, now, son. We mean you no harm," Harper confided. "But why did you fire on us?"

"I thought you was some more of those Yankee raiders comin' through to take the rest of our food and stock. Stoneman's men they said they was when they came through here yesterday. You better leave my ma alone. I'll kill any man that hurts her again." The boy's eyes burned with hatred.

On the road, Harp and Lans had heard about General Stoneman's raid that commenced in the eastern Tennessee mountains and was working its way through central North Carolina, firing bridges and barns and creating panic among the home guard and civilian population.

Within a few moments, Harper and Lans had convinced the boys that they were friends and followed them along a path through the woods to a small, dark cabin. They announced their arrival to soothe any fears of those inside. Upon entering the little shanty, they discovered a young woman no more than twenty-five with a toddler at her feet.

"Your boys should make you proud. They are defending you and the babe," Harper said carefully.

"I *am* proud of 'em," the woman replied in a steady voice. "They've protected this place these past hard years. Our name is Rudolph. My husband was with the 33rd Virginia calvary, Elisha White's Commanches bunch. He got killed up yonder at Brandy Station a couple of years back."

Harper looked at the severe young woman in front of him and instantly thought of the thousands of like cases across the

South and North, for that matter. The country had paid an enormous price and would continue to pay. "Well, Mrs. Rudolph, my name is Harper Clayton, and my friend here is Lans Hall. We are on the road home. Have you heard about the surrender? The war is over here in Virginia."

"The war may be done with, but the suffering will continue, I assure you, Mr. Clayton. What is to become of poor wretches like us with no man to provide?" Harper felt pity for the woman and her young family. "I'm afraid you are right. There will be struggle. But, let me offer this. In exchange for a place to sleep tonight, Mr. Hall and I will work to get plenty of wood cut and stacked for your stove and some game for your larder."

They wound up staying two days and nights. During that time, Lans shot and dressed a deer as well as several rabbits. Harper chopped at least half a cord of wood and even repaired several holes in the cabin roof. On the third morning and with mixed emotions, they bid goodbye to the forlorn group knowing the trials they would certainly face in the future.

Yet, they yearned for their own homes and family. With only a few short respites, they made over twenty miles that day, coming ever closer to Bethania. Just after sunset, they spread their thin blanket rolls well off the road under a canopy of longleaf pines where the fallen needles were thick and made for a rather soft bed. At dawn, the two travelers were on the road. They were shocked to see the surroundings as they made their way into the Piedmont. Little spring planting had been done with most fields untended. Houses, some in disrepair, were dark and quiet. Most folks they did see carried looks of suspicion. Even the children in the yards appeared dispirited.

This sad state of affairs only made the journeymen that more eager to reach home.

"Washington Town should be over the next rise if my memory holds," Lans said anxiously. The crossroads was a free black settlement established several decades before on the wagon road just east of Bethania. The folks there typically worked the local farms as hirelings for the white Moravian and Lutheran landowners.

"You're right. Then, on to our home sweet home. I wonder if folks will remember us," Harper said mostly in jest and with a grim smile. "It's been almost three years since our only home leave, yet it seems like a longer shadowy dream."

Washington Town was, in fact, over the next hill, and what they saw disturbed them greatly. Where once stood small cabins and tents was now a smoldering wreck. The few inhabitants in sight were silently going about the work of clearing debris and trying to rebuild a few shelters. Leaving the road, Harper and Lans walked to the nearest group. "What happened here? Yankee raiders?" Harper asked plaintively.

"Oh, no, sir. No, sir," a man named Samuel looked up and answered quickly. He looked to be about forty, with very broad shoulders, and was sweating in the mid-morning sunshine. "That Yankee troupe came through here sure enough, 'bouts a week ago. Right up the wagon road, they came, swords and bayonets shining in the sun. They left every one of us be...just like over in Bethania. No, they just wanted a guide to the shallow ford across the Yadkin. Old Jameson said he'd do it, and he did. That's him over yonder by those smokin' logs. He just got back a few days back and saw the sorry destruction.

306

No, this here devilry was done by a home guard, that no good Fleming and his crowd. They came on us a few days back and tore up the place...says we were aidin' the Yankees. I thinks they was lookin' to do meanness, that's all; just like always over these past few years."

Lans and Harper had heard stories about the home guard, their depredations, and lawlessness, all in the name of protecting the local population. They were made up principally of shirkers and other no-goods who had escaped military duty for one corrupt reason or another. Sure, there were some legitimate members, wounded veterans unfit for active service. Mostly, the guard was a gang of ruffians out to gain at the expense of a vulnerable population without prime-age men to defend the homesteads. Eli Augustus, Harp's father, had told him in a prior letter that Seth Fleming specifically had weaseled an exemption from the governor under the pretenses of supplying leather goods to the army.

"Well, the war is over now, friend. Have you heard? They'll be others like us comin' home to start over. And I tell you, we're all in for some hard times, but the home guard won't be runnin' people down anymore. It's time to help each other get back to something that seems regular-like."

"We're on to Bethania," Lans joined in with a serious tone. "But I'm tellin' you, this lawlessness won't stand. You have my word that we'll be back with others to help you, folks."

Harp surveyed his earnest, cold sober friend with the steel-blue eyes and nodded deliberately.

The bright sun was high overhead when Harp and Lans first saw the small village marker on the road. "Welcome to Bethania, NC est. 1759" --no sign had ever looked so splendid. They first noted that the little burg looked essentially intact, unlike some other small communities up the road. That was reassuring as the two parted ways, each headed for their respective family homes.

Harp wasn't sure what he would find at home, but he quickened his pace, nonetheless. The Clayton farm was about a mile southwest of the town, and he came upon the familiar whitewashed gate in short order. He stopped momentarily to take in the scene. The west field was plowed with tobacco seedlings, already planted, poking their green tips above the rich piedmont soil.

Not seeing anyone around, he made his way toward the timbered farmhouse with the stone foundation. A rush of childhood memories flooded his brain; a warm wood stove on chilly mornings, hiding from brother Jacob in the root cellar with its unforgettable pungent, earthy smell and playing king of the mountain in the cavernous hay barn. As Harp approached the house, the front screen door swung open, revealing his mother with eyes wide and hands pressed to her face.

"Harp, my boy! My God Almighty, you've come home!" she exclaimed, tears welling up in her soft brown eyes. Harp quickly climbed the steps and embraced her as she began to sob.

Homecoming

"Yes, I'm home, mama, and I ain't leaving," Harper responded, surprised at his own emotions. Rebecca Clayton held on tight to her oldest son, but after a moment, she stepped back and declared, "Let me see you. My, oh my, you're a scarecrow, Harp! You're just a shadow of when you left us last. No matter. We'll get you fattened up in short order. It's a dream come true to have you home."

Harper looked at his mother and saw the trials of the last years on her lined face. The letters he received from his mother over the last two years spoke only of the positive happenings on the farm and Bethania, but he knew the times had been hard with a moribund economy and bullies and thugs roaming the land.

"Where's papa?" he asked hesitantly, looking beyond her into the house. He was somewhat ambivalent about seeing his father, Eli Augustus. They had not parted on the best of terms, as Eli had not wanted his boys to enlist in what he saw as a rich man's war. Harper recalled his words, "This is the way it's been down through the ages. The powerful start the war, and the common man dies for it. What good comes of all the suffering?" Eli did not see his boys off when they left the farm to enlist in the Confederate army. After Jacob's death in the Richmond battles in June 1862, Harper could feel the animus from his father in the few letters he received from home. He wondered if his father still carried the pain.

"He's taken Flossie and Gabriel down to Miesner's to be re-shod," his mother replied. "You remember ol' Flossie and Gabriel...they're the only horses now. Oh, when Eli sees you, his heart will burst. We've been wonderin' when you'd make it back. We just heard about the surrender a few days back. It's an awful thing, but I can't say I'm sorry it is over."

With the mention of the war, Harper immediately returned to the desperate events of the last few months--the starvation in the Petersburg trenches, the fight for survival during the panicked retreat, and the hopeless end at Appomattox. "Lans and I walked home from a place called Appomattox Court House. That's where the surrender happened."

"Let's not think about any of that now, Harp. Come 'round the back, and let's burn those rags you're wearing and the lice they're carrying," she said emphatically. "Then I'll serve up something good to start putting some weight back on you.

First, I'll heat up water on the stove, and you can have a real bath for the first time in ages, I imagine."

As he covered himself with the large cotton towel his mother brought him, he took the lye soap offered. She then said, "get to it," with a broad smile, and went to work in the kitchen. It was pure heaven as he lowered himself into the large zinc tub lined with a white cotton sheet. Harper vigorously rubbed the soap on his hands and splashed the warm water on his face and hair. Had anything ever felt so good? He tried to recall the "last real bath" he had enjoyed. He vaguely remembered the Winchester hotel he, Lans, and a few other officers had visited while on a two-day leave last September. There, they each paid a confederate dollar to get their own hot bath and towel. But this was better. This was home.

Afterward, Rebecca pulled some of his old clothes out of the cedar chest, but they were clearly too big and hung loosely on him. Harper figured he had lost forty to fifty pounds since leaving home four years ago. She then raised her finger, having an idea, and returned carrying trousers and shirt.

"You might recognize these as your brother's," she said with a touch of sadness. They should fit you some better." They were indeed an improved fit since Jacob had always been considerably smaller than his older brother.

Inhaling deeply, he followed his mother into the kitchen with all its familiar smells that carried him back to better times. Even though fresh summer vegetables were several months away, Harper hadn't seen such a meal since going off to war. He ate all that his mother put in front of him-- cured ham, fried chicken, candied yams, pickled beets and beans, and a small loaf of yeast bread. To top it off, she brought an apple pie warm from the oven, made with last year's crop from the little orchard behind the barn. Afterward, he suffered the pains of overeating with a stomach sorely diminished from the months of limited rations. But it was worth it. He was home.

His father returned home later that evening and was surprised to see his son. With tears in his eyes, Eli cried out, "Harp, you've made it home. I knew you would. I knew it! This is a day!" The three embraced, heads touching. Harper felt a deep sense of relief at his father's reaction.

They all had a cry about brother Jacob, and Harper gave a sobering account of the last disastrous months of the war. It all felt so strange even now. It felt as if he were outside, peering into a dark inside of monstrous shapes and hideous groans. As they continued talking about the war as well as the state of things back home, mother noticed his agitation and suggested he sleep for a bit. Harper felt as if he could surely sleep for a week, but there was something he had to do.

"How's my Sudie?" he asked tentatively. "Is she well? Does she know the war is over?" He had a thousand questions he wanted to ask Susan Bostic.

His mother first looked at her husband nervously and then said in an uncertain tone, "uh…she's fine and well, best we know," mother replied. "You go see for yourself. I just know she will be strengthened to know you are home. She's been lookin' up the road most days, I hear," she added assuredly.

He was surprised at how nervous he felt. The three miles to the Bostic farm on the north side of town seemed longer than he remembered. Harper had known Susan since they were young, playing with other children in the meadows, woods, and creeks around Bethania. As adolescents, they professed their love for one another. Then war intervened. Would they still have that unspoken connection? Would she look at him in the same way that made his heart leap? The one thing he was sure of was that the thought of her easy smile and kind spirit had sustained him throughout these past four years. He knew he wanted to spend the rest of his life, in peace, with this loving creature. He recalled the urgency in her last letter, beseeching him to return home. Was this a natural yearning to be together, or was it something more?

The sun was setting as he walked Flossie down the lane to the tidy little farmhouse. Summoning a determination, Harper walked up the steps and knocked on the whitewashed door. Within moments the door opened, and Clay Bostic stood there appraising the visitor with a puzzled look on his weathered face. "Hello, Mr. Bostic…it's me, Harper Clayton."

The older man paused for a moment, and then a look of recognition crossed his face. "Harper Clayton! I didn't realize it was you…you're so darn skinny. We heard about that surrender up there in Virginia but didn't know where all you boys were. Come on in, come on in." Then over his shoulder, he shouted, "Lizze, come look who is paying us a visit."

Harper stepped inside the door and removed the felt hat his mother had given him. Several oil lamps burned in the open front room producing a hazy golden candescence.

In response to Bostic's announcement, his wife, Elizabeth, and Clay Jr. appeared from the back part of the house.

"Hello, Mrs. Bostic", he said shyly. "It sure is good to see you. And, Junior, you have grown a foot since I saw you last."

"Oh, Harper. It is a blessing to see you again. Sudie's gone for water at the well, but I expect she'll be back soon." Elizabeth reassured him.

"Thank you, Mrs. Bostic. If it's ok, maybe I can meet her out back and help carry," Harper said earnestly.

Before she could respond, Clay Jr. blurted, "We heard you was dead."

"Hush that talk now, Junior," she declared swiftly. "We didn't believe any of that loose talk."

Turning to Harper, Elizabeth smiled with a pained look and replied, "Of course, Harper. I'm sure she'd like that very much. You are a welcome sight."

Harper nodded. Feeling both a twinge of embarrassment and excitement, he headed out the back door into the fading evening light. Walking out to the top of the back porch stairs, he stopped abruptly. Coming up the path was Eliza Susan Bostic, head down, carrying full buckets and humming a melancholy tune. She had not noticed Harper on the porch.

"Sudie," he said softly.

She looked up and saw him above her. Dropping the buckets, her mouth formed a perfect "O," yet no sound emerged. He met her striking grey hazel eyes and made his way down the stairs two at a time. They embraced, neither speaking. After a long moment, Harper pulled back yet still holding her hands tight. Tears flowed down her delicate porcelain cheeks. He felt like Odysseus returning home to Penelope.

"Don't cry, Sudie. I'm here. I made it," Harper said reassuringly.

"I haven't heard a word from you in so long. They said you wouldn't be coming back. They said you were dead and buried in Virginia," she sobbed.

Harper held her close again and felt her body shake. "Who said this?" he appealed.

"Seth Fleming has been the most sure of it. But others like Sam Belton and Ham Dilworth have added to the story. They're a constant presence wooing me, and I've been so distraught and confused these days."

Harper let her words sink in for a moment. His instincts howled an alarm, and he knew then that a reckoning would be forthcoming.

***

The small group of men gathered in the early light by the little creek that flowed through the southern edge of town. Seth Fleming had called the impromptu meeting of the Bethania Home Guard. Besides Fleming, the guard consisted of Eury Meyers, a small farmer that was critical of the war;

Antin Dilworth, a stout, pug-nosed young man that had been wounded at Winchester and declared unfit for active service; Sam Belton, a young man who, like Fleming had maneuvered an exemption from service due to his family's dealings with an English arms dealer; and, Reuben Hauser, the middle-aged village blacksmith with a well-known reputation as a bully. Between the five, they had meted out justice as they saw fit, with most of the young male population being gone. They had few supporters in the village and surrounding area. The guard was notorious for stealing and taking advantage in a variety of ways.

"Fellas, we now know that our war for independence is over," Fleming blustered. "The cause is lost. The boys we sent to fight for it have fallen short and give up. I might even say they have betrayed us all that solemnly protected the sacred homeland these past four years."

The other four men looked at each other, not sure what to say. Finally, Eury Meyers, a grizzled man of about fifty, replied, "Seth, I don't like that word, "betrayed." My boy, Lucius, was kilt up there at Gettysburg with his face toward the enemy. He died a hero, not some traitor. You know that. This war has been a harsh bloodletting, and most of all, our families have felt the jolt. You need to respect that, son."

"Yes, of course, you are right, Eury. Oh, to the gallant warriors that fell for the cause. Yet, there are others not so noble; the shirkers, the cowards, and even those now coming back in defeat. I expect they'll be wantin' everything to be just fine and dandy. I say no, sir. We're the ones that protected their homes and families these last years. They'll be wantin' to go back to the ways things were…like nothin's changed. We will sure let them know it's a new world they're comin' back to… a town with rules to keep the peace, and us, Home Guard will do just that."

Young Fleming was getting quite worked up, Sam Belton thought with a chuckle. He knew why. "This wouldn't have anything to do with Harper Clayton and Lans Hall's homecoming, would it?" Belton inquired with feigned innocence.

The others joined in with nervous laughter. While they acknowledged Belton's jape, no one wanted to mock Seth Fleming openly. The tall, easy-talking young man was known to carry a grudge and not hesitate to bring ruin on one he considered an enemy. They all knew that Harper and Seth had words when Harper enlisted, words about Fleming's equivocation to join the fight. They also knew that Susan Kiger was Harper's sweetheart before the war and that Seth had been set on changing that.

"Hell no, Belton!" Fleming shouted, now red-faced. "It's about letting all these so-called veterans know who is in charge now. We've had to take some harsh measures to see things right, but the Home Guard has kept Bethania from ruination. And I, for one, don't want to see our hard work gutted."

"So, what are we doin' here, Seth?" Antin Dilworth inquired. "Get on with it. What are you sayin' we do about all this?"

Seth Fleming looked at Dilworth and then the others. "We need to do what's necessary to keep matters as they are. And yes, Sam, knowin' Clayton and Hall, I expect those two to be the ringleaders in tryin' to disrupt things to their advantage. Stay vigilant, all of you."

The next day Harper rode to the Bostic farm and asked Clay Bostic's permission for Susan's hand in marriage. He shared his feelings for his fine daughter and a vision for a proper life together. Harper said that he knew the future was uncertain but promised to support and love her without fail. To his surprise, Bostic gave his blessing on the spot. The father had seen how several local young men, especially Seth Fleming, had increasingly pressured his daughter and her recent nervous state. He wanted to end that strain, and he believed the young man before him to be sincere and hardworking. With this blessing, Harper immediately rode to the village where Bostic said Susan was with other ladies making salves and liniments for Doc Maynard, Bethania's only physician.

He made his way into the town proper, the first planned Moravian village in North Carolina. Just over one hundred years old, Bethania was the only Germanic-styled agricultural village in the South. Its linear lots and roads were laid out in a cohesive protective design surrounded by orchards fields and bottomlands. The main street intersected the north-south Great Wagon Road.

Harper approached the gathering of ladies as they went about mashing and mixing the herbal concoctions. He could see a mix of girls, young and older women. Heads down, they created a soft murmur that Harper found a bit odd. From his horse, he looked for Susan among the group. Not seeing her, he called out, "Good morning, ladies. Is Susan Bostic about?" Heads came up nervously, looking both at him and then down the street a short distance.

Harper then heard Susan's voice a short distance away. "Seth, I did no such thing! I appreciate your words, but I never promised to be your wife," Susan declared plaintively. "I said I would consider your proposal and let you know by the end of summer. You had told me for weeks that Harp was killed at Petersburg. You lied to me." The two were facing off under a small maple tree set between the village dry goods merchant and tobacconist. Several other men stood apart from the two but were obviously amused at the interchange.

Harper was off the horse in an instant. So consumed was Fleming in his confrontation with Susan that he didn't see Harper approach. The young man reached out to take Susan's arm and pronounced, "You will be my…"

Before he could finish, Harper grabbed Fleming's shoulder, spinning him around. "Let her be, Seth," Harper said with growing indignation. "You heard her plain as day. I know I did. She's not promised you anything. There's surely no honor in bullying her. You go on now and leave her alone."

Recovering from the initial shock of Harper's appearance, Seth gathered his angular frame and spat, "Why, it's Clayton, home… home from being whipped by those Yankees?" The other men moved in closer, grinning. Fleming, sensing the support, continued with confidence. "You don't know the way of things around here, Clayton. You've been gone way too long. My boys and me, well, we're the ones that have kept things right. And we intend to keep it right."

"By right, you mean seizing crops and livestock from old men and women and lining your own pockets? … Or wreaking havoc on poor black souls just trying to scratch out a living?

I've seen the evidence," Harper replied. "And, by right, you mean selling the army low-quality leather bridles and straps and such? I've seen for myself the inferior Fleming quality in the field; bridles tearing loose after a time, cartridge boxes falling apart. Quartermasters from New Bern to Winchester have cursed your second-rate goods, Fleming."

"Why, you miserable bastard. I'll kill you for such slander." Seth looked quickly toward his posse to ensure they were primed. The other men moved in, and Seth then approached Harper with both fists clenched. Harper, adrenaline flowing, surprised the taller man with two lightning quick, successive blows sending him to the ground. Harper then put Susan behind him and prepared to take on Fleming's bullyboys. Curiously, he noticed them hesitate and move away as they looked over Harper's shoulder. Harper turned and was relieved to see Lans and six other men coming up the street carrying sticks and clubs.

Lans announced, "I just happened to be in town and heard that Fleming was, uh, let's just say, he was being ungentlemanly towards Miss Susan. Me and the boys here thought she could use some support, but it looks like you have things in hand nicely, Harp," he said with that familiar weak smile.

"No, you were just in time, as a matter of fact. I thank all you boys," Harper confided.

"Yes, thank you ever so much, Lans," Susan said earnestly and gave the embarrassed man a peck on the cheek.

By that time, Fleming's band had gotten their woeful chief back on his feet and were leading him away. He suddenly wrenched free of their supporting hands and turned to face Harper again, shouting, "This is not the end of us, Clayton. No, sir. You and I will have a rendezvous." With that, he turned away again and stumbled down Main Street to where the horses were hitched. Harper watched until Fleming and company had disappeared from town.

Turning to Susan, he asked, "Sudie, are you okay? Did he hurt you?"

"I'm just fine," she replied, "but I must admit Seth Fleming scared me. I'm not sure what he would have done if you hadn't intervened. I thank you for that but promise me you'll stay clear of him…you don't know what he is capable of."

Harp just smiled and nodded.

A small crowd had gathered in response to the commotion, and Harper felt somewhat ashamed of the scene he had just been a part of. To his surprise, the crowd shouted their approval.

Susan reassured him, saying, "Nobody's stood up to Seth since he and his band took over. People are sick and tired of being intimidated and victimized. So, this is a bit of recompense for everyone, I would say." She now smiled and pulled his arm to her.

"There's something I want to ask you, Sudie," he said gently. "But let's first go to our special place. You remember, don't you? I expect the early wildflowers are putting forth in the meadow."

They walked the horses west from the village while a bright red cardinal offered its three-part whistle, a resonating trill of *cheer, cheer, cheer.*

***

Since returning from Charleston, his obsession with finding the other Fleming had only grown. The fate that Mathias had met didn't bother Tom in the least, but it also was not enough. He knew Mathias was only a stooge, albeit a violent one, in the Fleming affairs. Seth was the maestro conducting a corrupt orchestra of crooked players and nefarious schemes. And Tom burned with resolve to hold him to account.

Eleanor continued to worry about her afflicted husband. She felt his distraught spirit, which left her at a loss as to how to comfort him. They had certainly drifted apart these past few months. The intimacy had waned in their relationship. Tom had abandoned his photography work that had previously energized him. In his compulsion to locate Fleming, he even had taken less of an interest in Tee, which was noticed by his wife and other family members.

"There is a sheriff over there in Chattanooga that says he's seen Fleming," Tom exclaimed as he came into the parlor waving a telegram. "He says a dapper man fitting Fleming's description is new to town and spreading money around. Smalls says he can't send anyone there until the New Year, so

I'm going to catch the train to Columbia and then over to Chattanooga to verify and get him arrested."

Eleanor saw the spark in her husband's eyes and felt his agitated manner. "Why you? Why should you go when this is an obvious police matter? I'm worried for you. You know what Seth Fleming is capable of."

"I have to go if we're ever to see justice…ever to see peace. You see, El?" Tom implored. "This is the only way to make things square. If I bring this swindler to account, then we can move toward a future that is worth something. Besides, by the time Smalls sends somebody there, Seth might be long gone in the wind."

She knew better than to argue with him at this point. She knew better than to say what she felt-- that they had a deserving future regardless of Seth Fleming. But she also knew that he was now closed to any other path. Tom Moser was wholly consumed with revenge on Fleming; in his mind, he would have it.

He took the early morning train from Winston to Greensboro. From there, he connected to Columbia and finally on to Chattanooga, arriving late at night. Before leaving, he promised Eleanor and Tee to be home in time for Christmas.

***

This was to be a different sort of Clayton Christmas. In early December, Susan had an idea. The reservoir calamity had left families without loved ones and homes either gone or uninhabitable. Susan approached Harper with the notion of the Claytons hosting those families with a Christmas Eve supper and remembrance. Harper recalled with affection how her sublime eyes had shone as she innocently asked for his approval...as if she required it.

Plans had proceeded swiftly, with Eleanor, Kat, and Nell taking active roles. Lucia Hall and Sadie both wanted to assist and were welcomed gladly in the planning and preparations. There was much to do, the first being to get the word out. Susan sent Jacob to the mayor's office to enlist his help in reaching out to the families in the reservoir district. She also dispatched Eli and Lucas Hall to the upper end of 8th Street, where the most severe damage and majority of fatalities occurred. She sent instructions with the two to encourage those folks to join in on Christmas Eve. With Susan's wholehearted blessing, Silver and Sadie made their way to the Belo Pond neighborhood at the bottom of 8th Street, where many black folks had lost their homes, to convey the invite.

The initial tally from both parties was well above one hundred. Moreover, Jacob had brought back the request from Mayor Eaton to attend with the whole town council and their families, of course. When Susan heard this, she inhaled deeply, closing her eyes to consider the ramifications of hosting such a crowd at the 5th Street house.

"We'll just have to let the issue flow throughout the house and across the lawn," she declared to the ladies gathered in the parlor. "We will have the men secure and erect a canvas pavilion to provide shelter from any precipitous weather, God forbid. And I'm sure the young boys will jump at the chance to tend the bonfires in the yard."

Kat added, "It's sure gonna take a lot of planning and fixing to gather up enough food for this kind of horde. I know Eli will happily take charge of slow roasting a pig, but it's gonna take all of us."

"Lord, don't you know that Blanche will faint dead away when she hears?" Nell quipped as the thought of the trusty cook contemplating the mountain of foodstuffs to be made ready provoked laughter around the room.

Sadie then spoke up tentatively. "If you ladies see it right, I know my girls down around Holly Avenue will jump at the chance to help out, especially knowin' those poor souls are sufferin' so. Jesus says we're to help out the neighbor that's low."

"That's a fine notion, Sadie," Susan declared. "If they can cook like you, I know we'll have some extra specials for these folks."

"Yes, mam, Miss Susan. Lordy, the things those Holly girls can do with a yam are just out of this world," Sadie whispered and then broke down laughing while convulsing forward in her chair. The other ladies looked at each other for a moment and then cracked-up as well.

Eli broke the news to the twins that the annual deer hunt was off. "Nana's big supper is taking priority this year," he told them. The boys, now twelve and confident of their skills with the rifle, had joined Eli several times that autumn in the woods hunting rabbits.

"I wanted to show Grandpa and Jacob how I can shoot," James grumbled. "They don't need to load for me anymore."

"I was planning on getting my first buck this year, Papa," Noah followed up plaintively.

"Boys, now you know how important this occasion is to your Ma and Nana Sudie. Folks are hurting, and we're gonna do just a bit to help them forget the hurt, if only for a while. Besides, Grandpa and me have already talked about taking you out to the Yadkin to get your deer on the New Year. Oh, and I almost forgot, we've got a special job for you boys and Tee for the big supper... firekeepers. You three will take charge of the bonfires in the yard, setting 'em up and keeping 'em going."

At that news, both boys were pulled out of their forlorn moods. Indeed, they brightened considerably.

Preparations for the big event proceeded apace with the town's holiday festivities. Word had spread of the Claytons' benevolent gesture, and volunteers to assist with food and supplies came from a host of sources. Cecil Vernon, a proprietor of Liberty Street Grocery, offered to provide fifty canned peaches and other treats. Charlie Linville, who entertained various civic groups with outdoor barbeques, volunteered his chuck wagon to supplement the cooking. Lena Schaus, owner of the beloved German bakery in Winston, got every mouth watering with her offer to bake a large batch of streuselkuchen, her delicious Bavarian cake covered with sweet crumbles and berries. In her good-natured way, Susan also secured a promise from Lena to bake her seasonal gingerbread men for the many children that would surely be there.

Harper called on Will Reynolds for the loan of a large canvas tent that the Reynolds family used when hosting friends and employees. Harper and Susan had been to several of these splendid outdoor affairs and knew the tent would fit their needs nicely. He also asked Silver if the Dixies would play for the crowd, and Silver said they would be honored to do so.

It was the week of Christmas, and all in all, Susan was pleased with where things stood. Eleanor had compiled a list of the expected guests, as well as could be ascertained. They were saddened and a bit angry, but nevertheless unsurprised, to hear that some twenty or so white families had refused to attend when they heard that black folks were coming. Some of these refusals even came from council members. Susan told Harper, "If something like the reservoir tragedy can't pull the town together, I don't know if anything ever will." He replied that she shouldn't let this weigh her down and reassured her they were doing the right thing.

Kat recorded, in what Eli called her fancy green silk book, the array of foods that were to be cooked at the house as well as those promised by the volunteers. It was an impressive list that was shared with the other Clayton women. Well over one hundred and fifty people were expected to be on hand, which didn't include the sizable Clayton clan. Susan and Kat figured enough food would be on hand but not by much.

Christmas Eve arrived with a cold and blustery wind sweeping down 5th Street. All had been working well into the previous evening with the cooking, wood gathering, and other preparations, so there was little activity around the house as the sun broke. Jacob arrived early for two reasons. One, he wanted to be available in case he was needed with last-minute tasks, and two, he had news.

Entering the quiet house, he proceeded to the warm kitchen in the back of the house to find Blanche busy filling a large pot with water. Even this early in the day, bright beads of sweat gathered on her aged ebony face. He smiled as she hummed merrily to herself, unaware of her recent visitor.

"Good morning, Blanche, and Merry Christmas to you," he announced brightly while snatching a hot biscuit apparently just out of the modern electric oven.

The old cook jumped. "Lord, Mr. Jacob. Don't you snook up on me. Why, you gave me the scare. I was in my own world fixin' up these stews for this evenin'."

"Well, it sure does smell good, Blanche. I hear you've been workin' hard these past days to get all this food ready. What would Mama do without you?" he teased cheerfully, all the while knowing she always adored such praise.

"Aw, pshaw, Mr. Jacob. Ain't you so sweet," the woman purred, eyes lighting up. "Now, you get on out of here. I got heaps more to do," she continued while wiping ancient hands on a faded checkered apron.

Retreating from the kitchen, he found his mother up, beginning to place a considerable collection of red poinsettias clustered on the parlor floor. She beamed at his appearance. "Merry Christmas!" she proclaimed while looking up. "How about helping your old mama place these Christmas flowers around the rooms and along the porch? Mr. Simmons brought these by for this evening. Wasn't that kind of him?"

"Uh huh," Jacob mumbled absentmindedly. He was thinking of how his mother had recently begun to show her age. Her beautiful black hair was now almost entirely silver, and her soft skin now showed small wrinkles around the eyes and mouth. Why this dismayed him, he wasn't quite sure. Was it that he longed for those simpler times when sheltered by this warm and loving mother? He thought not. Perhaps it was merely the thought of her mortality and the inevitability of it.

He took several flowers, placing them adjacent to one another on the front steps. Over his shoulder, he called, "Where is Papa?"

"He and Silver had a devil of a time with those canvases yesterday," she replied while coming out on the porch and pointing to the large tent spread over the front lawn. "You know, the wind? It took them into the dark to get them set and tied down securely. I could tell he was exhausted when he came to bed. He was still asleep when I got up, and I left him to it."

"Well, I've got something to tell you both, and I can hardly wait," Jacob enthused.

Susan looked at her son inquisitively and then replied. "I know he will want to hear it when I do. You know your father," she said with a wink. "I'll go roust him up."

Jacob paced the floor while waiting for his mother and father to come down.

"I thought I heard a beggar at the door," a familiar voice asserted.

Turning around, Jacob saw Nell coming down the staircase. Dressed in a rich blue velour robe, his sister's hair was a mess, but her eyes were alight. As with his mother, he thought of how Nell, now sixteen, was changing. The innocent girl of yesterday was becoming a handsome young woman. For the first time, he saw Eleanor's beauty in his younger sister.

"Getting your beauty sleep, sister?" he joked. "It's time to get a move on, don't you think? Lots to do, lots to do."

"Oh, I have a long list drawn up just for you, dearest brother," she countered with a laugh. "By the time you're finished, you'll be wanting another bath, no doubt."

Before he could volley a clever riposte, mother and father came down the stairs.

"Well, if it isn't our very own Christopher Wren," Harper smiled while stifling a yawn. "Mother tells me you have important news that can't wait for me to rise. I was having the most pleasant dream about our courting days in Bethania. I do hope this news justifies the interruption," he said in jest.

"Pray to tell, brother," Nell opined playfully. "Have you been chosen to rework Wren's St Paul's in London? Or has Anika Van Dijk convinced you to try your hand in Holland?"

At first, Jacob was taken aback by his sister's awareness of the highly esteemed but long-gone, English architect. Recovering his composure, he said evenly, "Everyone, please sit. And yes, dear sis, you are too shrewd to divine that Miss

Van Dijk figures into this. You all may recall that I have spent several occasions in Raleigh and New York over these past few months. I am sorry to have kept it all a mystery, but I was sworn to secrecy. But I can now say that Winston's own Simeon-Stone firm has been selected, along with my friends at McKim in New York, to oversee the first-ever major renovation of the White House." Jacob paused for effect, enjoying the astonished looks before him. "Yes, *that* White House. President Roosevelt and the first lady have the vision to modernize the White House, or "the People's House," as the President calls it. Now it's a patchwork quilt of various odd alterations that have been done over the last century. We have been asked to restore the old girl with a modern and coherent design to make all Americans proud."

For a moment, there was stunned silence, and no one spoke. Then Nell exclaimed, "But how? Why you?"

"Now that's a good story, sis. A couple of months back, Governor Aycock just happened to have business at the White House the same day McKim was there to confer with the President on a potential restoration. When the Governor was made privy to the project, he made a strong case to involve a Southern firm as well. He then, of course, brought up our firm and his most favorable impression of the West End. The Governor kindly added my name to the conversation, and McKim recognized it from my time with his company. Roosevelt thought Aycock's idea to have North and South involved was splendid, and McKim agreed on the spot."

"I can't believe it!" his mother cried. "What a great honor for you, son!"

"I would say the Governor had more than just a "favorable impression" of you, son," Harper added with a chuckle. "I, for one, couldn't be more proud of you."

"I have to hand it to you, brother," Nell confided. "You've left us all behind here in little ol' Winston. But what about Anika? Where does she figure into this?"

"Oh yes, Anika. Not surprisingly, McKim has chosen her to be the firm's chief designer on the project. Seems like she and I will be seeing quite a bit of one another," Jacob said with a mischievous look.

The day had turned cloudy, yet fortunately, the wind subsided, making the near-freezing temperatures bearable. Harper and Susan gathered family and friends on the porch mid-afternoon before the guests began to arrive. "We just want to thank everyone for all their hard work pulling this endeavor off," Susan said with conviction. "You have made this possible, and I pray that we can bring just a little hope into the lives of those hurt by the disaster. So, Harp and I thank you from the bottom of our hearts. Now, let's get ready for this invasion of hungry patrons!" she proclaimed with arms raised as the group shouted in unison, "Hurrah!"

Eli's wood-fired smoker and Charlie Linville's chuck wagon filled the air with a sublime smoky atmosphere. The twins had enthusiastically built two bonfires of dry-cut hardwood, each in the front and back yards, adding to the kindled ambiance. Tables and chairs, secured from Augsburg church, were spread across the lawns and under the tents. Several food tables were positioned inside and out to facilitate the serving.

Harper looked up at the sky and said to no one in particular, "Feels like some moisture is coming our way." He then spied Eleanor rearranging a serving table and clearly saw she was distressed. Walking to her, he reassured her, "Don't worry. He'll be back soon enough."

"Oh, Papa. I haven't heard a word since he got to Chattanooga over a week ago. Tom said he would be home by now. I'm so worried that something has happened. Why hasn't he sent word?" She started to cry.

Putting his arm around her, Harper said firmly, "I'll talk to Chief Smalls when he arrives and have him get ahold of his contacts out there. I'm sure all is well," he said, trying to convince both his distraught daughter and himself. In fact, he was worried, too. He chided himself for not intervening more, and truth be told, there was a guilty part of him that saw Tom's trip to Chatanooga as justice on several fronts.

The guests began to arrive in twos and small groups late in the afternoon. They came by foot, horse, wagon, and carriage. By five o'clock, a sizable crowd had gathered, with more making their way down 5th and Broad streets. Harper had enlisted Silver, Jeff, and some friends to organize a temporary livery stable in the nearby field adjacent to 6th Street.

Susan asked Harper to welcome the growing crowd and officially initiate the proceedings. She was keen on putting everyone at ease, especially the black citizens, who she noticed were apprehensive within the large group. Her heart went out to all the survivors, both black and white, as she noticed their attempts to present as well as they could. Even so, their impoverished state was evident.

"Welcome, welcome!" Harper called out in his strongest voice. "And Merry Christmas to you all! My family and friends are so glad you're here. We've got all kinds of tasty food here, so don't be shy about filling your plates. May God bless you all as we celebrate Christmas and remember and pray for all those souls that tragically perished last month. Now, I'm going to ask my good friend, Thomas Silver and the Dixies, to liven things up a bit with their special brand of music," he said while pointing to Silver and the band that had set up on the corner of the porch. "Ok, eat up everyone and enjoy!"

Kat, Eleanor, and the others guided the guests through the food lines, and the scene swiftly evolved into a busy mix of hungry, eager participants. The servers stayed on the go bringing savory dishes out and taking empty ones back in. Jacob, standing back, smiled as he acknowledged the buzz of a hundred happy voices. At least thirty or so young folks danced to a lively holiday tune. He noticed Nell twirling along with a fresh-faced boy; eyes fixed on her partner. He chuckled as he thought again of his duckling-to-swan baby sister.

As the light faded, older folks sat and talked, full and satisfied. They listened to the Dixies perform a range of familiar Christmas hymns and holiday carols. A swarm of boys and girls ran laughing through the yard, some devouring gingerbread men as they went. Their work done, Harper and Susan stood on the porch overlooking the satisfying scene.

Harper surveyed the happy throng and said, "This is a healing affair for the town. You've done a good thing here, Sudie Clayton."

"Susan leaned back to look up at her husband. "You mean, *we've* done a good thing here. And maybe, just maybe, this will help some to turn the page." She searched Harp's eyes as he stared keenly across the lively yard below.

It had begun to snow with large, delicate flakes descending slowly from a starless sky.

EPILOGUE

Christmas Eve 1901: Strange, the snow didn't feel cold, he thought. Indeed, it felt rather comfortable, and he wanted to lay there in peace.

Tom then remembered venturing to the Walnut Street Bridge in Chattanooga that spanned the Tennessee River. Since arriving in town, he had made inquiries in at least two dozen places regarding his quarry. Based on information he had gotten from a local hotel manager named Sullivan, a man fitting Seth Fleming's description had been seen and heard around the affluent Fort Wood neighborhood on the south side of the bridge. Notably, Sullivan had informed him that the man was said to be seeking investors in a range of public works projects. Hearing that, Tom was convinced he had discovered his foe's whereabouts and immediately set out in the twilight to confront him. The streets were mostly deserted as the late-day snow had taken families and celebrations indoors. It was Christmas Eve.

The cold began to penetrate his coat, trousers, even his whole body. He began to shiver as he felt the wound in his stomach. He pondered the incongruity of the warmth of the blood and the intensity of the growing cold. He held his hand up to consider the tepid, bright red blood. The recollection of the single assailant, without a word, firing his pistol from only a few feet away made him involuntarily shiver again. It had all happened so fast.

He felt totally alone on the bridge. While he was not afraid, he longed to see Eleanor and Tee again and fulfill his promise of being home for Christmas. Tears ran down both sides of his face as he looked up into the falling snow. Idly, he wondered what goings-on would ensue at the family Christmas gathering. Would they remember and speak fondly of him? Would they ever know his fate?

Once again, a feeling of warmth came over him. He blinked snowflakes off his eyelashes and marveled at the absolute stillness of the night.

***

February 1902: The night train from Raleigh pulled into the Baltimore & Potomac station in the nation's capital, with an extended blast of smoke and steam. The engineer activated the brake blocks creating a loud, high-pitched racket. Jacob noticed the station's gaudy Gothic architectural style and recalled the recent movement in Congress to have it torn down and removed from the national mall. In the two decades since President Garfield had been shot at the station, a dark shadow seemed to have lingered over the terminal.

It was late, and the January night was icy cold as he stepped down to the platform with his bag in hand. Other passengers disembarked and drifted out to their final destinations. He was glad his own journey's end, the St James Hotel, was just adjacent to the station. While not one of Washington's fancier hotels, the St James, was nonetheless popular due to its convenient location at 6th and Pennsylvania avenues.

Jacob walked past several carriages being loaded with bags and clientele and even saw a motorcar with its operator fussing over the front crank. Spying the hotel entrance just ahead, his pace quickened. He wondered if she would be waiting for him at this hour.

Jacob had not seen Anika since the West End gala and, of course, her flight back to New York. He recalled her letter with its foreshadowing of hope, *"And if it's meant to be, we will find each other again in the moonlight."* They had corresponded over the past several months about the thrilling White House renovation culminating in this rendezvous. They were to convene with the First Lady and other White House officials to hear the Roosevelts' vision for the renewal as well as to offer their own initial thoughts.

As he entered the large revolving brass door, he saw Anika across the lobby, head down and obviously immersed in the pile of papers in front of her on a low table. Other than a sleepy front desk clerk, no one else was in the lobby at this late hour.

"Anika," he said softly.

Looking up, the young woman instantly broke into a radiant smile. "Jacob! You made it! I've been waiting for you. And besides, I couldn't sleep. Can you believe our good fortune? The White House!"

Jacob's first instinct was to tell her how beautiful she was, even more exquisite than the last time they were together. However, with some effort, the love-struck young admirer provided a more detached response. "Yes! Can you believe the Roosevelts' luck…landing the two of us to realize their dream?" he announced with mock bravado.

Her ice-blue eyes danced at the light-hearted banter. Reaching for his hand, Anika invited Jacob to join her on the divan. They shared ideas for the grand renewal late into the night.

***

April 1902: The first sixty-mile segment of the Roanoke & Southern Railway, from Winston to Martinsville, Virginia, was complete and ahead of schedule. The second sixty-mile segment to Roanoke was underway, but the challenging Blue Ridge mountain terrain made the work considerably more difficult with blasting required through the ancient rock. Even so, the line completion was now expected to be in late summer.

Most members of the Winston Roanoke Railway committee had traveled to Martinsville for the ceremony. All agreed that the project was one of the most efficient the town had embarked upon, and enthusiasm was high given the progress made. Harper was humbled the committee insisted that he hammer the ceremonial spike.

He picked up the heavy sledgehammer with both hands. Looking around at the small crowd gathered. Harper smiled. "I hope I can handle this," he said. Slowly raising it above his head, he then brought it squarely down on the silver rail spike creating a distinct metallic knell. He repeated the action and then turned to Francis Fries handing him the maul. "Colonel, finish if you will." With three more strikes, the ceremonial spike was secure in the base plate, bringing hearty applause from the group of civic leaders and investors.

"One down. One to go!" Fries pronounced, his face flushed from the endeavor. "This is progress, ladies and gentlemen. Later this year, we'll have Winston and Salem's goods traveling this line to reach new markets across Virginia, Maryland, and beyond. And, of course, we'll have the pleasure of new goods coming our way for the first time...fish from the Chesapeake, modern machine tools in Philadelphia, and much more. This new century is full of promise, and our dear towns are right in the middle of it."

"Colonel, you are right!" Will Reynolds added with a grin. Then, with an exaggerated wink to the crowd, he continued, "You are so right, but let's save some of your renowned speech-making for when the line is actually finished."

Fries laughed along with the crowd. In his usual good-natured manner, he replied, "Will, I can always count on you to hold me in check. But I tell you this. I will start on my big finale speech post-haste."

Harper had been buoyed by the crowd's energy and the reward of the past sixteen-month efforts. Returning to Winston with Silver, he was quiet. His mind returned to the recent years, chapters of both trial and blessing. *I expect it's the intended human condition*, he reflected... *pain from loss, pleasure from gain, but to keep going in the face of the changes that are surely coming. Lord knows I've tried my best to heed the apostle's counsel to forget what is behind and press on to what is ahead.*

He leaned back into the carriage seat and closed his eyes. Silver gently flicked the whip, keeping Jenny at an even trot down the Danville Road.

The End